ISLAM

BETWEEN GLOBALIZATION

& COUNTER-TERRORISM

Ali A. Mazrui

ISLAM
BETWEEN GLOBALIZATION
& COUNTER-TERRORISM

edited by
Shalahudin Kafrawi
Alamin M. Mazrui
Ruzima Sebuharara

Africa World Press, Inc.

P.O. Box 1892  P.O. Box 48
Trenton, NJ 08607 Asmara, ERITREA

Africa World Press, Inc.

P.O. Box 1892
Trenton, NJ 08607

P.O. Box 48
Asmara, ERITREA

Book Design: Shalahudin Kafrawi
Cover Design: Ashraful Haque

Library of Congress Cataloging-in-Publication Data

Mazrui, Ali Al'Amin.
   Islam : between globalization & counter-terrorism / Ali A. Mazrui ; edited by Shalahudin Kafrawi, Alamin M. Mazrui, Ruzima Sebuharara.
      p. cm.
   Includes bibliographical references and index.
   ISBN 1-59221-325-1 (hardcover) -- ISBN 1-59221-326-X (pbk.)
1. Globalization--Religious aspects--Islam. 2. Islam and world politics. 3. Terrorism--Religious aspects--Islam. 4. Islamic renewal. 5. Terrorism--Islamic countries--Prevention. 6. Islamic countries--Politics and government. I. Kafrawi, Shalahudin, 1969- II. Mazrui, Alamin M. III. Sebuharara, Ruzima. IV. Title.

   BP163.M387 2004
   297.2'7—dc22

                                      2004024911

Published in England by:

James Currey Ltd.,
73 Botley Road
Oxford OX2 0BS

CONTENTS

❊❊

SECTION ONE
NORTH-SOUTH: THE POLITICAL DIVIDE

❊❊

❊❊

SECTION TWO
OCCIDENT-ORIENT: THE CULTURAL DIVIDE

❊❊

CONTENTS

�֍✖✖✖✖✖✖✖✖✖✖✖✖✖✖✖✖✖✖✖✖✖✖✖✖✖✖✖✖✖✖✖✖✖✖✖✖

SECTION THREE
DOMESTIC-INTERNATIONAL: THE "GLOBAL" DIVIDE

✖✖✖✖✖✖✖✖✖✖✖✖✖✖✖✖✖✖✖✖✖✖✖✖✖✖✖✖✖✖✖✖✖✖✖✖✖✖✖

❌❌❌❌❌❌❌❌❌❌❌❌❌❌❌❌❌❌❌❌❌❌❌❌❌❌❌❌❌❌❌❌❌❌❌

SECTION FOUR
TOWARDS A MARRIAGE OF CIVILIZATIONS

❌❌❌❌❌❌❌❌❌❌❌❌❌❌❌❌❌❌❌❌❌❌❌❌❌❌❌❌❌❌❌❌❌❌❌

EDITORS' INTRODUCTION

THE GLOBALIZATION
OF AN AFRICAN MUSLIM

Ali A. Mazrui became politically conscious in the shadow of a liberation war. He was in his late teens when the Mau Mau War exploded in the British colony of Kenya. It was the first armed struggle against colonization in Africa in the second half of the twentieth century. The British regarded Mau Mau as "terrorists." Jomo Kenyatta was tried by colonial judges on charges of being a founder of Mau Mau. He was found guilty and sentenced to imprisonment. The real Mau Mau leader in the forests, Dedan Kimathi, was subsequently sentenced to death by the British and executed.

It was against this background that Ali Mazrui was introduced to the vocabulary of "terrorism" and "counter-terrorism." He was learning about the problem of deciding when a liberation war became a terrorist movement.

BETWEEN AFRICA AND THE WEST

The Mau Mau War was a confrontation between indigenous African rights and Western power. The British imported an army to fight the war, and dropped bombs from their planes on alleged Mau Mau hide-outs in the forests. Indigenous African rights were up against Western military might. The British won the military battles, but lost the political war. British colonialism in Kenya and East Africa as a whole came to an end.

Half a century later, the issue of indigenous rights against Western might had become globalized. The vocabulary of "terrorism" and "counter-terrorism" was now international. Kenya was still a battleground but this time for other people's wars. In order to kill twelve Americans, Middle Eastern terrorists killed over two hundred Kenyans outside the United States' Embassy in August 1998. In November 2002, a suicide bomber in Mombasa hit the Israeli-owned and Israeli-patronized Paradise Hotel. Three times as many Kenyans as Israelis were killed. In between those two Kenyan events was epoch-making suicide smashing of the Pentagon and the World Trade Center on September 11, 2001. Instead of British planes dropping bombs on Mau Mau in the 1950s, the world witnessed hijacked American planes used as missiles against American targets.

In the Mau Mau War, there had been no Islamic factor. The duel was between African aspirations and British imperialism. In the phenomenon of intercontinental terrorism, the duel is between Muslim grievances and American might. Ali Mazrui has been in the shadow of these clashes of civilizations from the Mau Mau days of Dedan Kimathi and Jomo Kenyatta to the Al-Qaeda days of Usama bin Laden and the Taliban.

As a matter of fact, Ali A. Mazrui regards himself as a product of three civilizations—Africanity, Islam and Western culture. However, his more than twenty books have been mainly about two of those legacies—Africa's relationship with the Western world. The

Islamic component was underrepresented before his 1986 television series, *The Africans: A Triple Heritage* (BBC and PBS, 1986), in spite of his highly religious Islamic background. [His father was the Chief Kadhi (supreme Islamic Jurist) of Kenya in the 1940s]. The Mau Mau War had triggered his sympathies for the oppressed Blacks, but his political Islam was dormant.

Although as an individual Ali Mazrui has always been immersed in Islam as a sacred culture, there was a political "disconnect" in his concerns as a scholar. The question now arises: What were the stages in the academic Islamization of Ali Mazrui? Was this also a process of his own globalization as a scholar?

BETWEEN AFRICANITY AND ARABISM

Ali Mazrui's British education in the 1950s and 1960s did indeed deepen his westernization, but paradoxically it also reactivated his interest in Arab culture (as distinct from Islam). Both at the Huddersfield Technical College when he completed his secondary education, and at the University of Manchester where he was an undergraduate, Ali Mazrui studied for examination in the Arabic language and passed with Distinction. He seemed more fascinated by Arab history than by Islam.

Although as an undergraduate at Manchester he was more active in African affairs than in Middle Eastern (even becoming President of the African Students' Association), Ali Mazrui did have for the first time Arab friends who had no connection with Africa, such as Iraqis and Syrians. In his student apartment in Manchester he entertained both African and Middle Eastern students from time to time.

The 1956 Suez War occurred within Mazrui's first year as a student in England. The invasion of Egypt by Britain, France and Israel propelled young Ali Marui into the students' debates of the day. He was passionately against the tripartite invasion of Egypt. The Suez War helped to deepen Marui's political interest in the Arab world, as distinct from his more passive cultural interest in Islam.

Unlike the Mau Mau War, which was still raging in 1956, the

Suez War was not seen as "terrorist" in any sense. In Africa and Asia, however, Egypt's resistance in 1956 was widely applauded as a war of liberation. As in the case of the Mau Mau War, Western imperialism won the military battles at Suez and Sinai, but the West and Israel lost the broader political war. Gamel Abdel Nasser, although defeated militarily, emerged triumphant as a political hero.

As a doctoral student at Oxford University, Ali Mazrui maintained an interest in the Arabs and the Middle East as a "minor" (secondary to his interest in Africa). He even wrote an article for the British journal, *African Affairs,* about Gamal Abdel Nasser's policy towards Africa.

His subsequent ten years as a professor at Makerere University in Uganda deepened his interest in African concerns without excluding an interest in the Arab world. He became even more sensitive to Middle Eastern politics as he observed the increasing influence of Israel in Uganda and Kenya. In the first postcolonial decades in Kenya, it was clear that the regimes discriminated against Arab countries in favor of Israel. In Uganda, the Zionists even helped Idi Amin to overthrow the government of Milton Obote in January 1971. For at least a year after that, Israel was overtly triumphant in Idi Amin's Uganda. Ali Mazrui became increasingly immersed in Middle Eastern debates from an African perspective.

The Israelis later ran afoul with Idi Amin and were expelled from Uganda. But the Israelis led their revenge with the Entebbe raid of 1975. An air commando shot their way into Entebbe airport, rescued Jewish hostages, and killed many Ugandans at the airport in the process. The Arabization of Mazrui's professional concerns deepened.

BETWEEN ISLAM AND GLOBALIZATION

The real political Islamization of Ali Mazrui had to wait until he was resident in the United States. His sympathy for Palestinians under Israeli occupation deepened when he was in Uganda. His broader sympathies for the Muslim world against the new Pax Americana began to flourish in the face of the new American Empire.

His role as a scholar was globalized and Islamized from the 1970s onwards. When the British Broadcasting Corporation (BBC) invited him to give the 1979 World Service radio lectures, he still saw Africa primarily in terms of confrontation between indigenous rights and Western might. His six lectures were entitled *The African Condition* and were heard by an estimated eighty million people worldwide. Islam was almost totally absent from the lectures.

However, when in the 1980s the BBC invited him to do a nine-part television series about Africa, his vision of Africa had encompassed Islam more decisively. Mazrui's TV series was subsequently entitled *The Africans: A Triple Heritage*. It was about the convergence of three legacies in modern Africa—Africanity, the West, and the impact of Islam. The television series and subsequent videos were an important next stage in both his globalization as a scholar and his Islamization as a political analyst. Both his BBC Radio Lectures of 1979 and his BBC/PBS Television Series of 1986 included issues of conflict, war and the ethics of armed struggle.

A third major project that propelled Mazrui towards globalized scholarship was his involvement in the World Order Models Project, an international movement committed to generating ideas about world reform. The project had participants from Western Europe, Asia, Latin America, North America, the Middle East and Africa. The project was partly activist on global change and partly academic in publishing studies on new policies for world order. From the late 1960s to the 1980s, the group met in locations as diverse as Poona, Munich, Kampala, Villa Serbelloni, New York, Oxford, and New Delhi.

Several major books on world order emerged out of this project over the years. Mazrui's own book in this project was his most ambitious in world affairs—*A World Federation of Cultures: An African Perspective* (New York: Free Press, 1976). Again, the volume did include issues of liberation and the ethics of political violence. There was less about Islam in this volume than there would have been had Mazrui written it ten years later. His pace of scholarly globalization was faster than his pace of academic Islamization.

A CONCLUSION

There is little doubt that Mazrui's television series on Africa's triple heritage opened up a whole new chapter in his involvement in Islamic studies. Many people discovered for the first time that Ali Mazrui was an emerging Islamicist and not merely an Africanist. Before long he was receiving invitations to lecture about Islam as well as about African affairs. He also attracted attention as a possible Muslim leader in the United States. Since then he has served on Boards of Directors of such organizations as the American Muslim Council, the American Muslim Alliance, the Center for the Study of Islam and Democracy, the Center for Muslim Christian Understanding at Georgetown University, the Crescent University Foundation, the Graduate School of Islamic and Social Sciences and the Oxford Centre for Islamic Studies, England.

The aftermath of September 11, 2001 has generated new levels of scholarly activism and academic output by Ali Mazrui on issues of globalization and Islam's relationship with the Western world. He has recently lectured about such issues in cities, which have ranged from Berlin to Durban, from Oslo to Dar es Salam, from Kuwait city to Chicago, from Cyprus to Cape Town, from Kuala Lumpur to Kampala.

This book represents a sample of the work of Ali Mazrui as a child of Africa's triple heritage who has now gone truly global. His Islamic side is now better represented in both his professional concerns and his commitment to global reform.

He has paid a price for some of the positions he has taken. Right wing white racists in the United States have been known to distribute abusive leaflets denouncing him as an "over-paid nigger." Zionist extremists have demonstrated outside his office, denouncing him as a "cancer on the body politic of the university." Juvenile liars have accused him of being a fundraiser for Saddam Hussein. His home in America has been pelted with raw eggs. In the days of the Cold War, the left wing accused him of being a CIA agent and the right wing accused him of being a KGB agent. More recently, at an American airport he was interrogated for many hours about whether he be-lieved in *jihād* and what Muslim organizations he belonged to. The interrogators at Miami airport in 2003 included agents of the Joint Anti-Terrorism Task Force and the Department of Homeland Secu-rity. That particular interrogation at Miami airport ended amicably. Ali Mazrui was released. However, uncertainties of the future persist in Mazrui's life as a global scholar and in his activism for a more just world order. In his political life, the fire started with Mau Mau, but the struggle continues.

This volume is dedicated to the pursuit of such a just world.

Author's Introduction

ISLAM BETWEEN GLOBALIZATION AND PAX-AMERICANA
A Toynbean Analysis

This volume examines Islam in the context of two worldwide forces—the historic force of globalization and the more recent campaign against terrorism. In its most comprehensive sense, globalization consists of all the forces that are helping to turn the world into a global village. In this broad historic sense, globalization is the villagization of the world.

The newness of the word "globalization" disguises how ancient the process actually has been. Globalization has been going on for centuries—fostered by the four engines of empire, economy, technology and religion. Christianity and Islam have themselves been globalizing forces—creating a convergence of values across vast distances.

Capitalism, imperialism, and the industrial revolution have thus been central to the process of villagizing the world. All these three latter forces of capitalism, empire and technology have converged on a single global pinnacle—the United States of America. Never in history has one single power been so far ahead of its nearest rivals. In military might, the United States is ahead of the next ten countries added together. Economically, the United States is central to the economy of the whole world. In science and technology American researchers continue to win a disproportionate share of the relevant Nobel prizes almost every year. America continues to invent and innovate.

If the four engines of globalization are empire, economy, technology and religion, and the United States leads the way in the first three, where does the engine of religion fit in? This is where Islam looms into relevance.

The great British historian, Arnold J. Toynbee (1889-1975), argued that civilizations rise and fall in proportion to how successfully they respond to new challenges. One interpretation of Toynbee's account of the Roman Empire is that it declined when it was unable to respond creatively to the challenges of the new religion of Christianity. Constantine the Great (280-337 A.D.) was the first Roman Emperor to be converted to Christianity. But he was ambivalent enough to let himself continue to be worshipped in his empire as God.

Christianity gradually eroded Rome's imperial will to govern and its will to grandeur. The new great religion of Christ softened the old great empire of Caesar. Although Christians continued to be persecuted and fed to the lions a little while longer, their faith eventually eroded the might of Rome.[1]

It is too early to be sure whether what Christianity did to the Roman Empire Islam will do to the American Empire. If Rome failed the challenge of Christianity and began to decline, will the United States as a hegemone fail to respond creatively to the challenge of Islam—and similarly begin to decline?

According to Arnold Toynbee, there had been a conflict for two centuries between Caesar-worship and God-worship, and the worship of God finally prevailed, at least for a while. Are we now witnessing the worship of America in conflict with the worship of God—and wondering who is likely to win?

If America is a civilization in the Toynbean sense, we know that it did successfully face and transcend the challenge of communism. But American civilization is now facing a different kind of challenge—the challenge of Islam, perhaps comparable to the Christian challenge faced by the Roman Empire two thousand years earlier.

The challenge of Christianity to Rome was basically doctrinal. The legacy of Jesus was challenging the values of the Roman Empire. On the other hand, the challenge of Islam to the American empire is a challenge to the power of the United States rather than to its values. Islamists do not seem to be challenging the religious values of the United States. The terrorists of September 11, 2001, targeted the World Trade Center as a symbol of American economic power. They targeted the Pentagon as a symbol of American military power. The fourth plane which was brought down in Pennsylvania was probably intended to target a symbol of American political power—either Congress or the White House. But there seemed to be no effort by the terrorists to target an American cathedral or any other symbol of America's religious heritage.

The worst of the Muslim militants are extremists out to kill their perceived adversaries. But the most rational of the Islamists do believe that the world system has lost the restraints of checks and balances, that the United States has become too powerful, and that Islam must introduce a countervailing force to the American empire.

If the United States meets this Islamic challenge as successfully as it met the challenge of communism in the twentieth century, America as a Toynbean civilization could triumphantly proceed to the next stage of its destiny. But if the United States fails to find creative ways of meeting the Islamic challenge, and descends to the equivalent of feeding Muslims to the lions, then the American Empire may experience as decisive a decline as the Roman Empire once sustained.

EMPIRE BETWEEN GIBBON AND DARWIN

More directly focused on the decline of the Roman Empire was Edward Gibbon, the English rationalist historian (1737-1794). By a curious irony of history, Gibbon published his first volume of *The History of the Decline and Fall of the Roman Empire* in 1776—the year when destiny witnessed the birth of a future equivalent of the Roman Empire.[2] 1776 was of course the year of America's unilateral declaration of independence from British rule. The seed of a future "Rome" germinated in the very year in which Edward Gibbon began publishing the story of the death of the original Roman Empire.

Gibbon believed that Christianity helped to erode the original spirit of freedom, which had once characterized the classical civilization of Rome. The last two chapters of his first volume caused a literary and theological scandal because of Gibbon's unfavorable account of the rise of Christianity at the expense of Roman culture.

But there was another paradox. While Gibbon regarded Christianity as a major cause of the decline of the Western half of the Roman Empire with its headquarters in Rome, he regarded Islam as the final *coup de grace,* which killed the Eastern half of the Roman Empire, based in Constantinople. Gibbon's history of Roman civilization ends with the siege of Constantinople by Muslim forces, and the final collapse of Byzantium in 1453. In other words, Christianity had, according to Gibbon, undermined the strength of the Roman Empire internally, while Islam eventually dealt the final blow to the eastern empire externally.

Arnold Toynbee in the twentieth century, studied past civilizations in terms of challenge and response, but Edward Gibbon in the eighteenth century had studied the Roman Empire in terms of intrinsic and extrinsic forces. Both macro-historians saw the collapse of ancient Rome partly as a result of unfolding religious energies in history.

Arnold Toynbee's thesis about challenge and response had strong Darwinian echoes. Like biological species, civilizations are subject to comparable laws of "natural selection" and to laws of "the survival of the fittest." Charles Darwin articulated these concepts in his *On the Origin of Species* (1859).

If a civilization is challenged it may respond creatively and adapt to changing circumstances. Alternatively, it may lack the vision for adaptation and either slowly decay or become totally extinct. The Roman Empire decayed and finally became extinct. To paraphrase a poet:

> Art after art went out;
> Skill after skill died out;
> Morality, blushing, veiled her sacred fires,
> And almost unawares, a culture expired.[3]

This gradual extinction was the fate of the Roman Empire when it failed to respond constructively to the challenge of Christianity. Europe subsequently suffered the Dark Ages when neither the legacy of Rome nor the new heritage of Christ was serving the people well.

It is to be hoped that the challenge of Islam to Western civilization and the American Empire in this twenty-first century is not mishandled. Gross miscalculations on either side could indeed lead to a new Dark Age for the human race.

This book is an introduction to this historic drama of vast proportions. Three of the four engines of globalization (empire, economy and technology) have converged to make the United States the mightiest hegemone in history. The fourth engine of globalization is indeed religion. Will this fourth engine of globalization run counter to the other three? Is Islam already providing a countervailing force to the otherwise unchallenged might of the United States?

This book is an exploration of the forces at work. A future volume may attempt a more definitive conclusion. Amen.

NOTES

1. Arnold J. Toynbee, *A Study of History,* 12 volumes (Oxford: Oxford University Press, 1934-1961).

2. Volume I of Gibbon's masterpiece, *The History of the Decline and Fall of the Roman Empire* was published in 1776; Volumes 2 and 3 were published in 1781; while Volumes 4 to 6 emerged in 1788. There were numerous later editions of this monumental macro-history of an empire in decline.

3. These lines were partly inspired by the poetry of Alexander Pope (1688-1744).

SECTION ONE

NORTH-SOUTH:
THE POLITICAL DIVIDE

CHAPTER ONE

THE IMPERIAL CULTURE
OF NORTH-SOUTH RELATIONS
THE CASE OF ISLAM AND THE WEST[1]

PREAMBLE AND OVERVIEW

In much of the first half of the twentieth century, at least two thirds of the Muslim world was within the formal collective empire of the Western world. In much of the second half of the twentieth century, most of the Muslim world has been within the informal collective empire of the West. In the years of formal imperialism, and especially after the collapse of the Ottoman Empire, Muslim countries were colonies and dependencies of such countries as Britain, France, the Netherlands, and Italy. In a special sense, Russia was also a colonizer of Muslims. In the more recent years of informal imperialism the United States has assumed a more pre-eminent hegemonic position, supported by two or three of the major European powers.

During the years of formal Empire, the Muslim world underwent substantial cultural Westernization—in values, dress code, educational systems, lifestyle, and economically. In the more recent years of informal Empire, the West is beginning to undergo some demographic Islamization. Muslims are on their way towards outnumbering Jews in the United States, France and potentially all over Western Europe. However, although Muslims may outnumber Jews, yet will they really overshadow them in anything in less than a century?

If the twentieth century is the century of global war, it is also the century of global Empire. The British attempted to globalize formal empire—a territorial vastness over which the sun never set—from Karachi to Kingston, Jamaica; from Maiduguri in Nigeria to Melbourne in Australia; and from Quebec to Kuala Lumpur.

The British attempt at globalizing formal empire was impressive, but still fell far short of encompassing the world. It is the American informal empire that is much closer to a real global scale. But the United States is not acting alone. It is a global imperial power with sub-hegemonic lieutenants—with Britain and France in global political affairs; with Germany and Japan in global economic affairs.

This chapter is about the informal imperial relations between this Western hegemonic system and the Muslim world. During the Cold War the West had, *de facto*, divided the world into *Dār al-Ḥarb* (the Abode of War, i.e. the Communist World), *Dār al-Maghrib* or *Dār al-Gharb* (the Abode of the West) and *Dār al-Ṣulḥ* or *Dār al-'Ahd* (the Abode of Dependencies like Muslim countries and much of the rest of the Third World). The West used the United Nations as one of its instruments of manipulation. Informal Empire had indeed gone global.

In this century of Global Empire it is not just the periphery that is multinational. The imperial core is also multinational. Hence the hegemony of the multinational West over the multinational Islamic world as a special case of North-South relations.

In the second half of the twentieth century no discussion of the aftermath of Empires can be complete without a discussion of the role of the United Nations System. Applying for admission to the

4

UN is one of the first acts of post-colonial sovereignty. And yet the UN itself is part of the machinery of Pax Occidental—the Western imperial umbrella. This chapter is partly about the United Nations as a partial reconstitution of Western imperial power.

It is also worth distinguishing between imperial reconstitution and imperial re-incarnation. Imperial reconstitution involves a complete or partial resurrection of the same imperial power, recently dethroned. Imperial reincarnation, on the other hand, may mean a perceived transmigration of the soul of Empire from one center to another empathetic center, usually a relative.

During Harold Macmillan's premiership in Britain, Dean Acheson in the United States had made the following pronouncement: "Britain has lost an empire and has not found a role." In reply, a somewhat irritated Prime Minister Macmillan felt compelled to reassure the British people that Britain was great and would remain great.

But was Britain going to find a "role"? In fact Britain's new role was to piggy-back on the hegemonic power of the United States. Britain became a lieutenant to the informal imperialism of the United States. Harold Macmillan—a classicist by education—saw Britain "playing Greeks to American Romans." Britain was to play Greek sophistication to American cowboy power. Has this been a case of the transmigration of the soul of Anglo-imperialism from *Pax Britannica* to *Pax Americana?*

In the Suez crisis of 1956, Britain and the USA were on opposite sides politically. But that was before the premiership of Harold Macmillan. Since then Great Britain has, on the whole, decided to play largely a piggy-back role to the informal empire of the United States—an imperial re-incarnation.

The idea of a special relationship has been cultivated, especially by London. Although the British have not given up all diplomatic independence in their dealings with the Muslim world, it has been a cornerstone of British policy to try and be supportive of American goals as far as possible.

This included pro-Iraqi policies during the Iran-Iraq war; the

5

anti-Iraqi policies in the 1990s; British collaboration with U.S. military and political decisions about Libya; Britain's unwavering loyalty to the U.S. insistence on continuing sanctions against Iraq year after year, long after the end of Desert Storm. Both "Anglo-Saxon" powers have used the United Nations to lend legitimacy to this reincarnation from *Pax Britannica* to *Pax Americana*. Even in Muslim countries previously ruled by Britain—like Egypt, Sudan, Pakistan and elsewhere—London is content to play second fiddle to Washington. And when the United States terminated its membership of an apparently Muslim-dominated UNESCO, Britain meekly followed the US.

The globalization of Empire that the British attempted in the formal sense has been carried further by the Americans in an informal Empire—with sanctions against dissidents. The imperial soul has transmigrated. The century of global Empire uses the term "world community" or "international community" to mean the United States and its closest allies.

BETWEEN DISENGAGEMENT AND AUTOCOLONIZATION

While the British have linked themselves with *Pax Americana*, they have more completely attempted to disengage from formal *Pax Britannica*. They have attempted to be second in command to the American informal empire while more decisively dismantling their own formal empire.

As compared with the French, Britain had over-disengaged from its formal empire, accepting comparatively little responsibility for what happened in the former colonies after independence day. The Muslim world has been among those affected. There was a social revolution in Zanzibar in 1964 within a matter of days after independence. Britain did almost nothing to intervene apart from giving political asylum to the deposed Sultan. A civil war broke out in Sudan between Muslim north and non-Muslim south in 1955 as British rule was coming to an end—a civil war that lasted until 1972 when the Addis Ababa Accords were signed. This was the first Sudanese civil war. More vigorous British efforts could have ended the war much sooner. A civil war broke out in Nigeria six years after independence. More robust British political involvement in the events that led to the civil war might have averted it. The Nigerian civil war cost 750,000 lives. Former British colonies in Africa, which have experienced severe conflicts since independence, have also included Uganda, Sierra Leone, as well as the white settler dominated countries of South Africa and Rhodesia/Zimbabwe. In former British Africa since independence two to three million lives have perished in civil conflicts. In former French Africa the casualties are in hundreds of thousands, mainly in Chad.

Decolonization in the French empire was more clearly in stages. The first major stage was the granting of nominal political independence in the 1960s, without economic or monetary independence. Outside Guinea [Conakry] the French continued to dominate the economies of their former colonies, but also helped them with the backing of the French franc for their currencies, and with budget-subsidies where necessary. The French also had troops in Africa, and were not unduly inhibited either in instigating coups against rulers who were out of favor in Paris, or preventing coups against rulers who were in favor in Paris. The readiness of the French to intervene did have the beneficial effect of relatively stabilizing the former French colonies, at least as compared with their Anglophone counterparts. The former French colonies were not necessarily spared military coups, but they seemed less prone to outright civil wars.

In 1964 the British did respond to written requests from the governments of Uganda, Kenya, and Tanganyika to send in British troops to disarm mutinous African soldiers. The British troops accomplished the job without firing a single shot. But that British intervention at the request of the three East African governments of the day against mutineers [as distinct from coup-plotters] stands out as a glaring exception in British policy. Since then the British have maintained a studied policy of almost total military and political disengagement from their former colonies. In most cases it has been a policy of irresponsible over-disengagement from the consequences of their own previous colonization of those societies.

On the other hand, the British have climbed the bandwagon of *Pax Americana*—trying to play second-in-command in the informal global dominion of the United States. Were the ties linking Britain to the United States rooted in a shared culture and civilization?

Different questions arise with regard to the French model of post-coloniality. The former French colonies maintained dependency relationships on France even after they ostensibly became politically "independent." Has this been a kind of autocolonization?

The concept of autocolonization has been used to refer in the first instance to relationships involving a hegemonic power in the Northern hemisphere. The acceptance by a smaller country of the imperial hegemony of a mightier power is at the core of the concept. But the concept of autocolonization does need to be related to other concepts that are older and have logical connections with it.

One such older concept or sister is "empire by invitation." This has been used to refer to the American protecting military presence in Western Europe after World War II and to the American economic penetration of Europe. In the Arab world, it can also be used to refer to the role of Syria in Lebanon from a Muslim perspective—a kind of *Pax Syriana*.

Another older sister to autocolonization is the formal concept of "protectorate" in which a weaker state seeks or is forced to accept the "protective" umbrella of a particular hegemonic power. Sometimes this resulted in a change in hegemony. In the nineteenth century, Moldavia and Walachia were in revolt against the Ottoman Empire and became protectorates of the Russians in 1829. They fell under wider international protection in 1856, and were united to constitute the sovereign state of Romania in 1878.

In the first half of the twentieth century the British used the concept of protectorate to checkmate their European rivals. For example, they got the Kabaka of Buganda to seek British protection with the 1900 Uganda Agreement—thus effectively keeping out the French from much of Eastern Africa. In the Muslim world, the British also persuaded the Sultan of Zanzibar to seek British protection for the Sultanate proper and for the Sultan's coastal dominion in what is today Kenya. At least in theory, these were situations where weaker states sought the protection of stronger ones. The Sultanate of Oman was a more informal British protectorate.

The third sister of autocolonization is the phenomenon of "colonialism by consent." The most dramatic illustration was the 1958 referendum fostered by President Charles deGaulle in the French empire in Africa. In the referendum the colonies were given a choice to opt for sovereign independence or for continuing colonial association with France. All the colonies in sub-Saharan Africa except the more radical Muslim Guinea [Conakry] voted in favor of a continuing relationship with France. Only Guinea under Sékou Touré had the courage to vote for complete independence. Were the others voting for "autocolonization"? The vote elsewhere in Africa for continuing dependency had implications for France's relationship with Africa for the rest of the twentieth century—even when the former colonies became nominally "independent" from 1960 onward.

The fourth sister to "autocolonization" is my own concept of "self-colonization," which began to be discussed in 1993 and 1994 in both newspapers and journals.[2] Self-colonization in my sense is a South-South phenomenon—the periphery colonizing the periphery. In Muslim Asia, this could include Indonesia's annexation of East Timor. In Muslim Africa it could include not only Morocco's attempted annexation of Western Sahara but also the absorption of Zanzibar into the United Republic of Tanzania in 1964. To all intents and purposes, Zanzibar was annexed by Tanganyika to create Tanzania.

The fifth sister of "autocolonization" is the whole phenomenon of "voluntary economic dependency." Most governments of the Third World have voluntarily submitted to economically dependent relationships with the Northern hemisphere. Certainly most Muslim governments have acquiesced in economic imperialism. Is this a special case of economic autocolonization? There is certainly a whole flood of literature on economic dependency. Once again we have to ask: Is this economic autocolonization? Or a new form of participation in

9

the wider capitalist world? It may in fact be both. Metaphorically it is a Faustian compact with the Devil.

A TRIPARTITE POLITICAL WORLD

In the summer of 1993, Professor Samuel P. Huntington of Harvard University unleashed a debate about the nature of conflict in the post-Cold War era. In an article in the influential American policy journal *Foreign Affairs*, Huntington argued that now that the Cold War was over, future conflicts would not be primarily between states or ideological blocs, but rather they would be between civilizations and cultural coalitions.[3] To use Huntington's own words:

> The fault lines between civilizations will be the battle lines of the future. Conflict between civilizations will be the latest phase in the evolution of conflict in the modern world.[4]

Huntington was at his best when he discussed how the West masquerades as "the world community," and uses the United Nations to give universalist credentials to Western interests. In Huntington's words:

> Global political and security issues are effectively settled by a directorate of the United States, Britain and France, world economic issues by a directorate of the United States, Germany and Japan, all of which maintain extraordinarily close relations with each other, to the exclusion of lesser and largely non-Western countries. Decisions made at the U.N. Security Council or in the International Monetary Fund that reflects the interests of the West are presented to the world as the desires of the world community. The very phrase "the world community" has become the euphemistic collective noun (replacing "the Free World") to give global legitimacy to actions reflecting the interests of the United States and other Western powers.[5]

We have here a situation where the universalism of the United

Nations is far less than it seems. The United Nations has become the collective fig-leaf for rapacious Western interests and actions.

On becoming a member of the *ummah*, a Muslim must recite the *Shahādah*, saying that "There is no God but Allah." It seems that to remain a member of the United Nations in good standing, all countries must acknowledge that "There is no political God but the West." Only the West has the right to determine when and how force should be used in world politics.

Huntington goes on to show how the West had used the U.N. Security Council to impose sanctions against Muslim countries or invoke the use of force. After Iraq occupied Kuwait, the West was faced with a choice between saving time and saving lives. The West chose to save time. In Huntington's words:

> Western domination of the U.N. Security Council and its decisions, tempered only by occasional abstention by China, produced U.N. legitimation of the West's use of force to drive Iraq out of Kuwait and its elimination of Iraq's sophisticated weapons and capacity to produce such weapons. It also produced the quite unprecedented action by the United States, Britain and France in getting the Security Council to demand that Libya hand over the Pan Am 103 bombing suspects and then to impose sanctions when Libya refused.[6]

In spite of the conviction of one Libyan under Scottish law, the case against the Libyans for Lockerbie has never been conclusive.[7] However, international sanctions forced the Libyan authorities to pay reparations for Lockerbie, and to abandon their quest for weapons of mass destruction.

Our own thesis in this chapter concurs with Huntington that there is indeed a clash of civilizations, but disagrees with him about the nature of that clash and about how old it is. We believe that the clash of civilizations did not begin with the end of the Cold War but is much older. We also believe that the chief cultural transgressor has throughout been the Western world.

Following the formation of the United Nations in 1945, a strange thing happened. Quite unconsciously the West adopted an ancient and medieval Islamic view of the world. Not long after the creation of the United Nations the West appropriated for itself—almost unconsciously—the tripartite division of the world of ancient Islamic jurists.[8]

Ancient international Islamic law divided the world into *Dār al-Islām* (the Abode of Islam); *Dār al-Ḥarb* (the Abode of War); and *Dār al-ʿAhd or Dār al-Ṣulḥ* (the Abode of Peaceful Co-Existence or Contractual Peace). Within *Dār al-Islām*, amity and cooperation on Islamic principles were supposed to prevail. *Pax Islamica* was supposed to be triumphant. It included both Muslims and non-Muslims of the tolerated communities ("People of the Book" or Dhimmīs), who enjoyed state protection against internal insecurity and external aggression.[9] *Dār al-Ḥarb*, the Abode of War, was not necessarily an arena of direct military confrontation. These were the lands of non-Muslims, often hostile to Islam, constituting the sort of situation that Thomas Hobbes was to describe much later as a condition without a shared sovereign.[10] Centuries before Hobbes, Muslim jurists had evolved the concept of *Dār al-Ḥarb*, a state of war, for cognizance of authorities in countries which did not agree on the sovereignty of God. As Khadduri points out, this recognition was necessitated for the survival of mankind:

> Islam's cognizance of non-Islamic sovereignties merely meant that some form of authority was by nature necessary for the survival of mankind, even when men lived in territories in the state of nature, outside the pale of the Islamic public order.[11]

The third category of countries under ancient international Islamic law were the countries of *Dār al-ʿAhd* or *Dār al-Ṣulḥ* (the Abode of Contractual Peace or Peaceful Co-Existence). These were the non-Muslim countries that worked out a deal with the Muslim rulers for greater autonomy and peace in exchange for some kind of tribute or collective tax paid to the Muslim treasury. The last-mentioned area was not universally recognized by most jurists, as they felt that "if the inhabitants of the territory concluded a peace treaty and paid tribute, it became part of the *Dār al-Islām* and its people were entitled to the protection of Islam."[12]

Following the formation of the United Nations the West appropriated this tripartite view of the world of ancient Islamic international law and simply substituted itself for Islam. For much of the second half of the twentieth century, during the period of the Cold War, there were the following categories:

1. *Dār al-Maghrib* or *Dār al-Gharb* (the Abode of the West) instead of Dār al-Islām;
2. *Dār al-Ḥarb* (the Abode of War—which was essentially the communist world);
3. *Dār al-'Ahd*—or *Dār al-Ṣulḥ* (the Abode of Peaceful Co-Existence which was the Third World). The Third World paid tribute to the West in the form of the debt-burden and other forms of economic exploitation. It was no different from the tribute paid by *Dār al-Ṣulḥ* countries to medieval Muslim rulers.

One major proviso needs to be emphasized in the second half of the 20th century. While doctrinally the Abode of War for the West was supposed to be the communist world, in practice the actual military fighting by the West in the second half of the twentieth century has been almost entirely in the Third World, including the World of Islam.[13]

The Korean War was in the Third World but not the Muslim world. In the case of Korea and Vietnam it was not easy to draw a distinction between the communist world and the Third World. Several million people perished in the two American-led wars of Korea and Vietnam. Militarily no member of the Warsaw Pact was hurt directly. The Warsaw Pact and the North Atlantic Treaty Organization (NATO) were basically fighting each other through intermediaries. The doctrinal Abode of War was not necessarily the literal abode of war. The U.S. armed itself to the teeth to fight the communist Second World—and turned on the Third World instead. In Korea this Western onslaught appropriated the flag of the United Nations.[14]

While Korea and Vietnam might have been cases where it was difficult to determine where the communist Second World ended and the Third World began, the Muslim world poses no such ambivalence. Muslim states have not been communist.[15] And yet since 1980 at least 500,000 Muslims have been killed by Western armaments. These casualties have included Libyans, Iranians, Lebanese, Palestinians, and Iraqis. The West has been trigger-happy in responding to Muslim political challenges. In the Gulf War of 1991, the West used the flag of the United Nations to give its militarism a universalistic appeal and legitimacy.[16] The human toll in Iraq is still continuing as a result of the deprivations caused by the Anglo-American economic sanctions, given universalistic legitimacy by the UN Security Council.[17] The rate of infant mortality in Iraq doubled, even tripled, and death of ordinary people from preventable diseases escalated.[18] On the other hand, while Iraq itself may have been physically and militarily emasculated, Saddam Hussein's hold on power appeared to be unshakable until the Iraqi war of 2003.[19]

The ostensible reason was to make sure that Iraq did not rebuild weapons of mass destruction. And yet each of the permanent members of the Security Council is possessive about its own weapons of mass destruction. Unlike France, Iraq did not reach the arrogance of testing nuclear weapons thousands of miles away from its own core population—and endangering the population of other lands. Protests by the militarily-weak Pacific nations have been manifested in the form of street demonstrations, diplomatic downgrading of relations, and boycotts of French goods—like wine.[20] Nor did Iraq under Saddam Hussein have the equivalent of a permanent member of the Security Council to say to it "scratch my nuclear back—and I will scratch yours." John Major scratching Jacques Chirac's back.

The West's doctrine of *Dār al-Ḥarb*, the Abode of War, was supposed to be the Communist world. The West's operational *Dār al-*

Ḥarb has been the developing world and the islands of the seas. The United Nations has sometimes provided a universalist umbrella for the West's operations in the Third World.

More than ever since the end of the Cold War, West theories of international relations in recent times are still grappling with the following distinctions:

1. A bipolar world (like the one of the Cold War between the USA and the Soviet Union)
2. A unipolar world (like the world with one superpower like the United States)
3. Multipolar world (encompassing new centers like China and one day India, which will outnumber China in population in another thirty years).

Unfortunately none of those superpowers or poles are basically Muslim, although they do include Muslim populations. Is a world with only one superpower—a unipolar world—in reality *Dār al-Ḥarb* in entirety? Was the old bipolar world of the Cold War *Dār al-Ḥarb?* Is a global village under non-Muslim control *Dār al-Ḥarb?* In other words, if globalization is creating one-world, and that world is *not* under Muslim control, is the whole world temporarily *Dār al-Ḥarb?*

BETWEEN WESTERNIZING ISLAM AND ISLAMIZING THE WEST

With or without the United Nations, at some stage we have to switch our focus from the broad theme of "Islam and the West" to the more intimate exploration of "Islam in the West." There was a time in history when the Muslim presence in the Western world was in terms of Islam's intellectual and scientific influence. These were the days when Arabic words like *algebra* and *cipher* entered Western scientific lexicons.

One of the remarkable things about the twentieth century is that it has combined the cultural Westernization of the Muslim world, on the one hand, and the more recent demographic Islamization of the Western world, on the other. The foundations for the cultural Westernization of the Muslim world were laid mainly in the first half of the twentieth century. The foundations of the demographic Islamization of the Western world are being laid in the second half of the twentieth century. Let us take each of these two phases of Euro-Islamic interaction in turn.

In the first half of this century the West had indeed colonized more than two thirds of the Muslim world—from Kano to Karachi, from Cairo to Kuala Lumpur, from Dakar to Jakarta. The first half of the twentieth century also witnessed the collapse of the Ottoman Empire and the more complete de-Islamization of the European state-system.

The aftermath included the abolition of the Caliphate as the symbolic center of Islamic authority. The *ummah* became more fragmented than ever and became even more receptive to Western cultural penetration.

Other forces which facilitated the cultural Westernization of the Muslim world included the replacement of Islamic and Qur'ānic schools with Western style schools; the increasing use of European languages in major Muslim countries; the impact of the Western media upon distribution of news, information and entertainment, ranging from magazines to cinema, from television and video to the new universe of computers.

Finally, there has been the omnipresent Western technology—carrying with it not only new skills but also new values. The net result has indeed been a form of globalization of aspects of culture. However, this has been a Eurocentric and Americocentric brand of globalization. What starts off as a piece of Western culture is eventually embraced by other cultures—and masquerades as universal. A cultural informal empire is born.

Two pieces of Eurocentric world culture may tell the story of things to come. One piece of Western culture which has become almost universal is the Western Christian calendar, especially the Gregorian calendar. The other piece of globalized Western culture is the (dress code) for men worldwide.

Many countries in Africa and Asia have adopted wholesale the Western Christian calendar as their own. They celebrate their independence day according to the Christian calendar, and write the history of their past according to Gregorian years [before or after Christ]. Some Muslim countries even recognize Sunday as the day of rest instead of Friday. In some languages the entire Islamic historiography has been re-periodized according to the Christian calendar instead of the Hijrah. The Western calendar has indeed got substantially universalized.

That globalization could mean pure Westernization is even better illustrated by another facet of ordinary life—dress code and dress culture. There was a time in English history when Shakespeare's Polonious could persuasively argue that "the apparel proclaims the man." The nationality, wealth, class, taste and education of a person could be revealed by how the person dressed. This is really no longer so. What has happened is the globalization of the West's masculine attire with special reference to the universalization of the Western suit. By the last quarter of the twentieth century a man from any culture on earth could wear a Western suit without looking culturally incongruous.

On the other hand, no Japanese man could wear Arab dress without appearing culturally odd; nor can an African wear a Hindu *dhoti* without occasioning acute perplexity. Nor can a Chinese man turn up dressed like a Yoruba aristocrat without compounding all cultural expectations.

In other words, while males of all cultures can and do wear Western dress, no other two cultures are freely interchangeable without causing confusion. If the story ended there, it would be bad enough but bearable. But the Western standard is now regarded as so "normal" that any male who dresses in his own culture at an international meeting is deemed to be making a political statement. It is regarded as abnormal to be non-Western.

I have a nephew in Canada who is a devout Muslim, dresses in a Muslim way and keeps a neat beard. In 1995 he traveled in the

Middle East for the first time. From one airport to another in the Muslim world his impeccable Islamic dress turned out to be much more of a liability than an asset. He was often taken aside for further interrogation by Muslim airport officials. He looked too Muslim to Muslims! Had he been dressed in a Western suit he would have saved himself a lot of trouble at Muslim airports. The Western suit is now the norm. Islamic dress is "abnormal" and potentially "fundamentalist." The Western suit has, in other words, got truly globalized. The informal empire of dress. But at what cost?

What about the dress code for women? In different non-Western cultures it has not been as overwhelmed by the West as the dress code for men. Women in India are still disproportionately attired in the *sari* and its equivalents. And Muslim women continue to maintain strict rules of modesty in dress well beyond contemporary Western standards of modesty.

But there are other costs. After the terrorist atrocity in Oklahoma City in 1995, the first suspicion was that the atrocity had been perpetrated by "Muslim terrorists." There was a lot of outrage against Muslims among Americans in some sectors of opinion in the US. In relation to dress the most vulnerable Muslim group turned out to be the Muslim woman in the US. This was not because of any women suspects in the bombing, but because Muslim women do dress Islamic. They are more obviously Muslim because of their dress code than are most Muslim men.

What this whole subject of Muslim targets after Oklahoma City returns us to is the subject of the new demographic presence of Islam within the Western world. In the second half of the twentieth century, both Muslim migration to the West and conversions to Islam within the West are consolidating a new human Islamic presence. In Europe as a whole there are now 20 million Muslims, eight million of whom are in Western Europe. This is excluding the Muslims of the Republic of Turkey, who number some 50 million. There are new mosques from Munich to Marseilles.

Paradoxically, the previous cultural Westernization of the Muslim world is one of the causes behind the subsequent demographic

Islamization of the West. The cultural Westernization of Muslims contributed to the brain drain of Muslim professionals and experts from their homes in Muslim countries to jobs and educational institutions in North America and the European Union. The old Western formal empires have now unleashed demographic counter-penetration.

Some of the best-qualified Muslims in the world have been attracted to jobs and positions in Europe or North America. It is in that sense that the cultural Westernization of the Muslim world in the first half of the twentieth century was part of the preparation for the demographic Islamization of the West in the second half of the twentieth century. However, not all Muslim migrants to the West are highly qualified by any means. The legacy of Western colonialism as a whole facilitated the migration of less qualified Muslims from places like Bangladesh, India, Pakistan and Algeria into Britain and France respectively. Again what happens is post-colonial demographic counterpenetration.

There have also been occasions when Western needs for cheap labor resulted in deliberately encouraging immigration of less qualified Muslims—as in the case of the importation of Turkish workers into the Federal Republic of Germany in the 1960s and 1970s. Also as a manifestation of the demographic Islamization of the Western world there are now over a thousand mosques and Qur'ānic centers in the US alone. And the country has professional associations for Muslim engineers, Muslim social scientists and Muslim educators. There are some six million American Muslims—and the number is rising impressively.

Muslims will outnumber Jews in the US by the end of the twentieth century. Currently Islam is the fastest growing religion in North America. In France Islam is becoming the second most important religion numerically after Catholicism. In Britain some Muslims have been experimenting with an Islamic parliament of their own, and others are demanding state subsidies for Muslim denominational schools. In the Federal Republic of Germany it has been belatedly realized that the importation of Turkish workers in the 1970s was

19

also an invitation to the muezzin and the minaret to establish themselves in German cities. Australia has discovered that it is a neighbor
to the largest Muslim country in the world in population (Indonesia).
Australia has also discovered an Islamic presence in its own body-
politic.

Judaism, Christianity and Islam are the three Abrahamic creeds
of world history. In the twentieth century the western world has often been described as a "Judeo-Christian civilization," thus linking
the West to two of those Abrahamic faiths. But if in countries like
the US Muslims will soon outnumber Jews, is Islam becoming the
second most important Abrahamic religion after Christianity? Numerically Islam in time may overshadow Judaism in much of the
West, regardless of future immigration policies.

The question has therefore arisen about how Islam is to be treated
in Western classrooms, textbooks and media as Islam becomes a more
integral part of Western society. In the Muslim world education has
got substantially Westernized. Is it now the turn of education in the
West to become partially Islamized? The Euro-Islamic story of interpenetration continues to unfold. Is this a new threshold for globalization? Or is it just another manifestation of the postcolonial condition in world history? In fact, it may be both.

NOTES

1. This chapter was written with the fund from the Smith Richardson
    Foundation and Co-sponsored by the Institute on Global Con-
    flict and Cooperation at the University of California—San Di-
    ego and the Social Science Research Council. This chapter first
    appeared as "The Imperial Culture of North-South Relations:
    The Case of Islam and the West," in Karen Dawisha and Bruce
    Parrott (eds.), *The End of Empire?: The Transformation of the
    USSR in a Comparative Perspective* (New York: Armonk, 1996),
    pp. 218 - 240.
2. See for example Ali A. Mazrui "Decaying Parts of Africa Need
    Benign Colonization," *International Herald Tribune* (Paris) (Au-
    gust 4, 1994).

3. See Samuel P. Huntington, "The Clash of Civilizations?" *Foreign Affairs*, vol. 72 no. 3 (Summer 1993): pp. 22-49. Responses by Fouad Ajami, Kishore Mahbubani, Robert L. Bartley, Liu Binyan, and Jeane J. Kirkpatrick, among others, were published in the next issue of *Foreign Affairs*, volume 72, no. 4 (September/October 1993), pp. 2-22.

4. Huntington, "The Clash of Civilizations?," p. 22.

5. *Ibid*, p. 39.

6. *Ibid*, p. 40.

7. For one account of the Lockerbie investigation that casts a wider net of suspects than Libya alone, see David Leppard, *On The Trail of Terror: The Inside Story of the Lockerbie Investigation* (London: Jonathan Cape, 1991). While Leppard emphasizes the Libyan connection, he also points to Iranian and Syrian connections in his last chapter. On the sanctions, see footnote 15 in Vera Gowlland-Debbas, "The Relationship Between the International Court of Justice and the Security Council in the Light of the Lockerbie Case," *American Journal of International Law* Volume 88 (October 1994), p. 646; and *The New York Times*, (March 31, 1995), Section A, p. 3.

8. Our discussion here is based on Majid Khadduri's introduction to his translation of *The Islamic Law of Nations: Shaybani's Siyar* (Baltimore, MD: Johns Hopkins Press, 1966), pp. 11-13, although he tends to emphasize the dual division.

9. *Ibid*, pp. 11-12.

10. Hobbes describes this condition in his seminal *Leviathan*; for one recent edition, see Edwin Curley, (ed.), *Leviathan; with Selected Variants from the Latin Edition of 1668/Thomas Hobbes* (Indianapolis: Hackett Pub. Co., 1994).

11. Khadduri, *The Islamic Law of Nations*, p. 13.

12. As pointed out by Majid Khadduri, *Ibid*, p. 12-13. However, for our analysis, this distinction will prove useful.

13. Although international relations scholars concentrated on the US-Soviet connections, some have pointed out that the West, particularly the United States, has had its most problematic international relations headaches in practice in the Third World. See for example, Charles W. Maynes, "America's Third World Hang-Ups," *Foreign Policy*, no. 71 (Summer 1988), pp. 117-140,

and Steven R. David, "Why the Third World Matters," *International Security* vol. 14, no. 1 (Summer 1989), pp. 50-85.

14. On the UN role in the Korean conflict, consult, for instance, Leon Gordenker, *The United Nations and the Peaceful Unification of Korea: The Politics of Field Operations, 1947-1950* (The Hague: M. Nijhoff, 1959); and for a specific examination of the US moves in the UN regarding Korea, consult Leland M. Goodrich, *Korea: A Study of U. S. Policy in the United Nations* (New York: Council on Foreign Relations, 1956).

15. Albania is demographically an Islamic country, but the religion was ruthlessly suppressed by the communist authorities.

16. See, for example, Burns H. Weston, "Security Council Resolution 678 and Persian Gulf Decision Making: Precarious Legitimacy," *American Journal of International Law* Volume 85 (July 1991), pp. 516-35.

17. For one recent analysis of the American stand on sanctions, see Eric Rouleau, "America's Unyielding Policy Toward Iraq," *Foreign Affairs*, vol. 74 (Jan/Feb 1995), pp. 59-72.

18. In fact, according to one study, the infant mortality rate had increased fivefold since the end of the war in 1991, killing almost 576, 000 Iraqi children; see *The New York Times* (December 1, 1995) Section A, p. 9.

19. For critical reports on the sanctions, see the analysis by Haris Gazdar and Jean Dreze, "Hunger and Poverty in Iraq, 1991," *World Development*, vol. 20 (July 1992), pp. 921-45, and Eric Hoskins, "Killing is Killing—Not Kindness," *New Statesman & Society*, vol. 5 (January 17, 1992), pp. 12-13. In spite of internal unrest and prominent defections, Saddam Hussein was not hurt by the sanctions, as pointed out, for example by Steve Platt, "Sanctions Don't Harm Saddam," *New Statesman & Society*, vol. 7 (November 4, 1994), p. 10.

20. French Beaujolais wine, according to one report in *The New York Times*, has lost many markets in a boycott of French products to protest against French nuclear tests in the Pacific. Markets lost include not only the Pacific nations of Japan, Australia, and New Zealand, but also the Netherlands, Scandinavia, and Germany. See *The New York Times* (November 17, 1995) Section A, p. 10.

CHAPTER TWO

THE GLOBAL HOSTAGE CRISIS
THE SOUTH BETWEEN UNDERDEVELOPMENT AND COUNTER-TERRORISM

During the hostage crisis of American diplomats after the Islamic Revolution in Iran in 1979, I addressed in a plenary session a big conference of political scientists in Great Britain. I had been invited by the late Professor Hedley Bull of the University of Oxford, England.

That was the first time that I had used the metaphor of "hostage crisis" to apply to the condition of the Third World. I argued that while world headlines were daily dramatizing the condition of the American hostages in Teheran, few realized that millions of people in poor countries were held hostage by the policies of the United States and its allies every day.

The commodities produced by less developed countries were often undervalued, their infant industries were unprotected, their mineral resources were exploited, their poverty unnecessarily prolonged, with rates of infant mortality atrociously and recklessly high.

Has something fundamentally changed since 1979? It is, in fact, possible to tell the story of hostage experience from the Iranian Revolution of 1979 to September 11, 2001. The developing countries continue to be held hostage by wider international forces over which they have no control. The process of globalization has its winners and losers. Most African countries are among the losers.

However, has September 11, 2001, initiated a new lesson—the lesson of reciprocal vulnerability between North and South? Are we beginning to learn that global stability is indivisible? Is the global village beginning to discover shared pain?

Perhaps the economic underdevelopment of the South has more clearly unleashed forces that will result in the political underdevelopment of the North. We may be discovering the reality of a mutual hostage crisis. The South is still burdened by its perennial economic underdevelopment—the North is now threatened by forces that may politically push it backwards to its pre-democratic tendencies of the past.

It has long been widely recognized that poverty in the South often destabilized the South. What the aftermath of September 11, 2001 demonstrates more clearly is that poverty in the South may destabilize the North. Poverty stricken Afghanistan became the training ground of Al-Qaeda. Desperate Third World militants may find solace in political extremism. There is also concern about poverty and anarchy in Somalia becoming a breeding ground for Al-Qaeda militants.

September 11 has demonstrated that it is not just capitalism that can be globalized. Instability can also be globalized. We are in the era of the globalization of instability. In other words, is stability indivisible?

AMERICAN RELAPSE INTO UNDERDEVELOPMENT

But what is politicized development? Much of the political science literature from the 1950s onwards has defined political development as expanding capacity for democratic self-governance and popular participation. A society is perceived to be making progress towards political development if it is acquiring greater skills in self-sustaining democratic governance. But what if a society that has already acquired such democratic skills then seem to be loosing them? A relapse back to political underdevelopment is a kind of political decay. Is September 11 the first indication that lack of economic development in the South can result in political decay in the North?

Much of the world is held hostage to the consequences of American foreign policy. The rage against the United States is partly a consequence at the rage against Israel. Terrorism is not a child of evil. It is a child of rage, frustration and despair. Both the Middle East and Africa have been paying a price for the anti-American terrorism. The violent price that the Middle East is paying is obvious, especially in Palestine, Iraq and in neighboring Afghanistan. What is the price that Africa is paying for terrorism against the United States?

Firstly, there is the issue of being caught in the crossfire. Africa has been the victim of violent action intended by the terrorists for the United States; Africa has also been a victim of violent action taken by the United States and intended for the terrorists. In order to kill twelve Americans, Middle Eastern terrorists killed about two hundred Kenyans in the streets of Nairobi a few years ago. This was the attack on the US Embassy in Nairobi in August 1998. There were also the many innocent Tanzanian casualties when the US Embassy in Dar es Salaam was targeted at the same time.[1]

On the other hand, Sudan was caught in the crossfire soon after when President Bill Clinton ordered the bombing of an apparently harmless pharmaceutical company near Khartoum.[2] President Ronald Reagan before Clinton had ordered the bombing of Tripoli and Benghazi in Libya because Reagan thought the Libyans were responsible for a bomb in a German bar that had killed Americans.

Violence between Americans and Middle Easterners had been spilling over into Africa for decades—violence from both Middle Easterners and the Americans.

An unknown number of Africans were killed at the World Trade
Center, in New York on September 11, 2001—Senegalese hawkers,
Nigerian investors, Ethiopian or Eritrean drivers or professionals,
Ghanaian students, Egyptian and South African tourists and others.
Who knows for certain?

September 11, 2001, has had other consequences for Africa. The
Security Forces of Africa have opened their doors to the United States'
Federal Bureau of Investigation (the FBI) and the Central Intelligence Agency (the CIA). Africa has fewer secrets from the Americans than ever, if Africa ever had any. The FBI reportedly arrived in
Tanzania after September 11 with 60 Muslim names for interrogation and potential action. The Kenyan authorities have been so eager
to please the Americans that they are tempted to repatriate their own
Kenyan citizens to the United States on the slightest encouragement.
Fortunately the American Embassy in Nairobi is sometimes more
cautious.

There is some anxiety that September 11 and its aftermath may
exacerbate tensions not only been pro-Western and anti-Western
schools of thought in this continent, but also between Christians and
Muslims in Africa. A demonstration by Nigerian Muslims in Kano
against the American war in Afghanistan provoked stone throwing
by Nigerian Christians in Kano, which flared up into communal riots. Churches and mosques were soon being burnt and at least 200
people were killed.[3] President Olusegun Obasanjo had to rush to Kano
to contain the tensions before they spilled over into secretarian riots
all over Nigeria.

The United States efforts to unite African governments against
terrorism may be dividing African people among themselves—a coalition of elites resulting in a contestation at the grassroots. The pressure on many African governments to enact new legislation against
terrorism may pose newer threats to civil liberties in Africa just at
the time when democratization was gathering momentum in some

African states. Nor must we forget that if America's own democracy decays, it makes it easier for Africa's own dictators to justify their own tyranny.[4] Indeed, the aftermath of September 11 has already been compromising some civil liberties in the United States itself:

1. There are hundreds of people in detention without trial.
2. The great majority of those in detention are not publicly announced as being in detention.[5]
3. Out of the hundreds in detention, less than a dozen show any evidence of knowing any particular terrorist suspect or being associated with any movement or charity accused of terrorism.
4. Out of the millions of illegal immigrants in the United States, and those whose visas have expired, the people chosen for detention without trial are almost certainly those with Muslim names or who come from the Middle East.[6]
5. The United States is actually planning to have military tribunals and secret trials for those suspected of terrorism. Even the leaders of Nazi Germany were given a public trial at Nuremberg after World War II with access to counsel and proper representation. Some of those tried at Nuremberg had been responsible for the death of millions of people.[7]
6. Israel continues to look for old Nazi militants so that they can be tried today in a court of law in Israel. Yet Israel feels free to kill Palestinian militants instead of capturing them for trial. Israel tried Adolf Eichmann in 1961 and protected him at the trial with a bulletproof glass cage so that he would not be assassinated. Yet both the USA and Israel in 2001 openly talked about killing terrorist suspects instead of capturing them. And even when Israel has illegally captured Palestinian or Lebanese suspects from across its own borders, the purpose has almost never been to give them fair trial (Adolf Eichmann-style) but to detain those suspects indefinitely without trial.
7. U.S. Attorney General John Ashcroft is about to empower the FBI to spy on churches, mosques, and other sacred places to an extent not envisaged in the country for a long time. Places of

prayer were once protected from close police scrutiny. However, mosques especially may soon be fair game for police raids in American cities, while *Synagogues* may enjoy de facto protection even if there is militant Zionism or fundamentalist Judaism being preached inside.

8. Attorney-General Ashcroft wants to breach attorney-client confidentiality if the client is suspected of terrorism. The Attorney General and President Bush repeatedly talk as if those suspected of terrorism were already proven terrorists. What happened to the U.S. principle that a person was innocent until proven guilty?

9. The CNN and other major TV networks in the United States were summoned to the White House and warned against giving Usamah bin Laden propaganda advantage with his videos. Whatever happened to editorial independence and freedom of the Press? Self-censorship by the American media is still disconcertingly rampant.

10. The ANS has been singling out particular nationalities (mainly Muslim) in the United States for discriminatory treatment, illegal harassment and unconstitutional imprisonment.

Many Americans may have to brace themselves for a less free America than the one that closed the twentieth century, but an America more religion-conscious than the one that opened the third millennium. If the erosion of civil liberties is justified on the grounds of the war against terrorism, this is a war with no recognizable finality of either a peace treaty with the enemy, or a demand of unconditional surrender.

What would constitute the end of this war? Would we be able to have a victory parade, open bottles of *ḥalāl* champagne or hug each other with joy in the streets? After World War II, there was VE Day (Victory in Europe) and V-J Day (Victory in Japan). What would constitute such a finality in the war on terrorism? If the United States managed to kill Usamah bin Laden, that would not be the end of terrorism. There was international terrorism before Al-Qaeda and Usamah bin Laden. And there may continue to be such terrorism long after Usama if the causes of international terrorism are not addressed. If this is a war without end, are American civil liberties going to be curtailed indefinitely? Human rights are being denied to many detainees simply because they are not American yet there are even American citizens detained without access to lawyers.

There have also been American Muslim educational institutions raided and their equipment impounded without due process. For such "search and seizure" the probable cause is probably just being Muslim. In addition to those new FBI powers to survey mosques and other places of worship—a heavy intrusion of the state into religious sanctuaries—there is now a new development. FBI has access to libraries (Muslim and non-Muslim) under the Patriot Act to check what Americans read. Libraries are also forbidden to talk about any FBI searches of their borrowing patterns. The Orwellian nightmare "big brother is watching what you read" is beginning to come true.

All these factors add up to an American throwback to its predemocratic standards. The United States has undergone a sudden and disturbing spasm of underdevelopment. Its corporate corruption as revealed by Enron, Andersen and World Com deepen the atmosphere of a relapse into the ethics of underdevelopment, though the causes of corporate corruption may be different from those of the American standards.

As for the condition of the Southern hemisphere, much of its underdevelopment continues to be fundamentally economic. Let us look more closely at this condition of the South.

POVERTY VERSUS STABILITY

Economic problems of the South fall under three temporal categories. Perennial problems include poverty, inadequate skills, and unfair terms of trade. Problems of postcoloniality include the Debt crisis, the Brain Drain, large-scale corruption and large-scale political instability. Problems of the Third Millennium include globalization and new diseases such as HIV-AIDS.

Since September 11, 2001, all these three categories of economic

problems have been affected. According to Alan Gelb, Chief Economist for the African Region, and Ian Goldin, Director of Development Policy at the World Bank, sub-Saharan Africa was expected to
suffer the most as a result of the economic setbacks of September11.
Sub-Saharan Africa has weak or no safety nets and has households
with minimal savings. The World Bank has estimated that globally
up to 40,000 more children under five years old die from the immediate economic consequences of September 11, 2001. Half of those
additional deaths of children were expected to be in Africa.[8] Com-
modity prices also fell. Among the hardest hit in Africa were cotton
exporters like Mali and Burkina Faso and exporters of beverages like
Uganda, Kenya, Cote d'Ivoire, Ghana and Ethiopia.

Travel and tourism, which represent about ten per cent of Africa's
merchandise exports, have been hit unevenly. Countries like Tanzania have been less adversely affected than countries like Kenya. However, the general impact on air travel is putting a strain on tourism as
an industry worldwide.

There was a tripling of direct foreign investment in Africa in
the 1990s—much of the capital going into mining and oil, though
some was responding to the new wave of privatization of other economic ventures. Slowly global growth since September 11, 2001, has
also hit the investment flows to Africa, as well as remittances to
Africa from Africans in the Gulf States and in the West.[9] Northern
subsides to Northern farmers have been hurting Southern farmers for
decades, but the situation took a turn for the worse with $190 billion
which went before the U.S. Congress in 2002. The *Los Angles Times*
reported in May 2002 as follows:

> Government officials and independent economists say the
> big subsidies doled out to U.S. farmers will contribute glo-
> bal overproduction of wheat, cotton and other basic crops.
> And that, in turn, will drive down world commodity prices,
> making it more difficult for small, unsubsidized Third World
> farmers to compete. African nations will be particularly hard
> hit because agriculture plays such a big role in their econo-

mies—accounting for more than 50% of the gross domestic products of some.[10]

More perennial in character are Africa's health problems, compounded by the continent's week medical infrastructure and limited personnel and resources. The developed world has not shown adequate sensitivity and concern. In the words of Huang and Stremlau:

> Of the 300 or so candidates seeking doctorates in molecular biology at Harvard Medical School, only two are studying malaria, a disease that kills one African every 30 seconds ... Each year, only about 5% of the $60 billion spent worldwide on biomedical research targets the illnesses that most affect 95% of the world's poorest populations, according to Nature magazine.[11]

Although HIV-AIDS is not yet a bigger killer than malaria in Africa, AIDS threatens to be the supreme killer of all time. But what is being done? According to a UN-AIDS report published on July 2, 2002, only 30,000 people out almost 30 million now living with HIV-AIDS in sub Saharan Africa are being given the drugs that help to keep AIDS patients alive in the Northern hemisphere, in spite of promises of help from rich countries in the last two years.

In 2001, almost as many people died of AIDS in Africa as died at the World Trade Center in New York on September 11—well over two million. In rich countries, where anti-retroviral drugs are available, only 25, 000 people died. In Botswana almost 40% of adults are HIV positive. Among pregnant women HIV prevalence has increased from 38.5% in 1997 to 44.9% in 2001. Among 25 to 29 year old pregnant women the HIV rates is 55.6%. The UN-AIDS report also draws attention to a steep rise in infections in Asia. China and India cause particular concern. The court victory of the South African government over drug companies in the year 2000 has not made drugs cheap enough. It has made drugs accessible only to 22,000 more people out of millions.[12]

Human beings competing with animals for space is a familiar story in Africa. Humans need more land to cultivate; wild animals are threatened by a shrinking wilderness. But when human beings give greater priority to feeding animals than to feeding fellow humans, this may be an ominous new scale of values. There has been a transition in agriculture from food grain (for people) to feed grain (for livestock). In Rifkin's words:

> Today more than 70% of the grain produced in the United States is fed to livestock, much of it cattle ... In the U.S., 157 million metric tons of cereal, legumes and vegetable protein suitable for human use are fed to livestock to produce 28 million metric tons of animal protein that (richer) humans consume annually ... This is new agricultural phenomenon, one that began in the US at the start of the 20th century, and spread to other countries after World War II ... Tragically, 80% of the world's hungry children live in countries with food surpluses, much of which is in the form of feed fed to animals that will be eaten by well-to-do consumers.[13]

A problem of postcoloniality is the debt crisis. The Society for International Development has grappled with this problem in previous world congresses. Although the United States has now cancelled Tanzania's debt to her, Africa continues to owe something in the region of $400 billion to Western governments, agencies and corporations.[14] And Akomolafe's lament of the 1990s is still substantially true today:

> Year in year out, Africa is repatriating in excess of ten billion US dollars to Euro-American banks and government. That is interest payments alone on the debt ... Many African countries are using more than half of their entire budget for debt servicing.[15]

Whose fault is it that much of the debt was incurred for no tangible or enduring returns? When US Secretary of the Treasury Paul H. O'Neil visited Wakiso, outside Uganda's capital, Kampala, he paid special attention to a well which had been built for a mere $1,000 and provided clean water for more than four hundred people. Secretary O'Neil said that he and the Governor of the Bank of Uganda (central bank) had informally calculated the night before that wells capable of serving the entire nation with clean water could be built for about $25 million. He wanted to know why this could not be done. He later referred to a loan of $300 million that the World Bank had extended to Uganda in the year 2001. "What was so important that there wasn't $21 million to $30 million to give everyone in Uganda clean water? Where did the money go?"[16] We in turn could ask whether Africa went into debt for the wrong priorities. There is enough blame to go around between the motives of the lenders and the behavior of the borrowers.

As for patterns of migration since September 11, two regions of the world were immediately affected—the Middle East (other than Israel) and South Asia. Visas to Middle Easterners to visit the United States dropped by about 52% (from 107,184 to 51,529 temporary visas issued between September 12, 2001 and March 31, 2002) as compared with the same period the previous year. For South Asia (which includes Bangladesh, India, Nepal, Pakistan and Sri Lanka) the drop of number of visas between September 12, 2001 and March 31, 2002, was over 30% (from 207,936 to 144,661 temporary visas issued) as compared with the previous year. This was in spite of the fact that South Asia had previously been a preferential region for migration to the United States because of the high computer skills and mathematical proficiency in the South Asian brain drain.

There were twenty-five countries which were classified by the US State Department as operational fields for Al-Qaeda and potential breeding ground for terrorists. Was this caution or the sin of arrogance? Alphabetically these countries were Afghanistan, Algeria, Bahrain, Djibouti, Egypt, Eritrea, Indonesia, Iran, Iraq, Jordan, Kuwait, Lebanon, Libya,

Malaysia, Morocco, Oman, Pakistan, Qatar, Saudi Arabia, Somalia, Sudan, Syria, Tunisia, the United Arab Emirates and Yemen. This range included more African countries and twelve Middle Eastern. What is obvious is that the twenty-five nations were overwhelmingly Muslim. Visas to the United States, of these states, went down dramatically as compared with the same period the previous year.[17]

The European Union (EU) has been trying to cope with illegal immigration by a search for Europe wide policies. In the summer of 2002 the members of the Union split publicly over the issue of linking foreign aid to cooperation with the EU about tackling illegal migration. France, Sweden and Finland opposed plans to make the European Union's 9.3 billion euro (Singapore $15.7 billion) development aid budget for the South conditional on repatriation agreements. As the Swedes argued, the EU has never gone so far as to make aid conditional on performance on human rights or conditional or full involvement on the war on terrorism. So why should European aid be made conditional on repatriation agreements with developing countries? Those who favored linking aid to such repatriation agreements were Britain, Italy, the Netherlands, Spain as well as the Germans who had once taken the lead.[18]

This whole issue of migration from the South to the North is part of the proposition that global stability is indivisible. The Algerian War of independence (1954-1962) nearly destroyed democracy in France. In 1958 France hovered over the brink of a civil war. In the end the war in Algeria did not destroy democracy in France; it only destroyed the Fourth Republic. After independence Algerian instability put all sorts of stresses on French democracy—ranging from fear of terrorism to rise of fascist anti-immigration parties. Algeria's instability has been pushing the Fifth Republic of France further and further to the right. Other European countries have also experienced the strengthening of right wing extremism, partly because of immigration from the South. Once again global stability is becoming increasingly indivisible.

THE ANGUISH OF INTERDEPENDENCE

We need to understand once again how September 11, 2001, underdeveloped the United States politically and may help to deepen the economic underdevelopment of the Southern hemisphere. The shock of September 11 has pushed back the United States by the criteria of political maturity; while the same shock of September 11 threatens to push back the Third World by the criteria of economic advancement.

Until September 11, 2001, phenomena like detention without trial and secrecy about who has disappeared behind bars were characteristics of underdeveloped postcolonial societies. Lack of access to lawyers, inadequate information to families about the detainees, lack of information to the detainees about what they are being detained for—all these were pre-eminently tendencies of political underdevelopment. Members of my own family in Mombasa in the postcolonial Kenya have sometimes been held for prolonged periods without access to a lawyer and without clarification of the charges against them. Harsh custody conditions have sometimes been part of such detention without trial. Sweeps on non-nationals in East Africa—accusing them of crimes of violence or drug trafficking—and sometimes deporting them without due process. This too was, before September 11, often a periodic manifestation of underdevelopment.

Since September 11, 2001, such manifestations of political underdevelopment have also unfolded in the United States. In the two months following September 11, more than 1,200 people were taken into custody in the United States in nationwide sweeps for possible foreign suspects of terrorism. Amnesty International has also received reports of cruel treatment, including prolonged solitary confinement heavy shackling of detainees, (including use of chains and leg shackles) during visits or court appearances, and inadequate outdoor exercise. Amnesty has also received allegations of physical and verbal abuse.

Finally, there is the impact of counter-terrorism on South-South

35

conflicts. In December 2001, I had occasion to warn Ethiopians in Addis Ababa not to become the equivalent of Pakistan to Somalia's Afghanistan. Under General Musharaff Pakistan became the United States' Trojan horse of penetrating Afghanistan. I cautioned our brothers and sisters in Addis Ababa not to let Ethiopia become America's Trojan horse for penetrating and controlling Somalia. I could give the same caution to my compatriots in Kenya—not to become America's Trojan horse for invading Somalia.

A more serious conflict between neighbors is that between India and Pakistan. My interpretation of the problem of Kashmir may lose me all my Indian friends. My proposed solution for Kashmir may lose me all my Pakistani friends. Is Kashmir like Algeria before independence in 1962? An elaboration on this issue is discussed in our chapter entitled "Islam between Christian Allies and Western Adversaries."

CONCLUSION

September 11 has started a new chapter. The North cannot long neglect the anguish of the South lest mad men take over. A new reciprocity is emerging—a reciprocity in anguish. In the words of W.B. Yeats, the poet who helped to immortalize the Irish uprising of 1916:

A terrible beauty is born…
Too long a sacrifice
Can make a stone of the heart.
O when may it suffice?
That is Heaven's part…
What is it but nightfall?…
No, no, not night but death;
Was it needless death afterall?…
A terrible beauty is born.

The uprising of Easter 1916 was the Irish *intifādah*. Is there a global intifadah now under way? If so "a terrible beauty is indeed born." God help us.

NOTES

1. For one report lamenting the end of the African "safe haven," see *New African*, 367 (October 1998), pp. 16-17.

2. This action is discussed in P. Wapner, "Problems of US Counter-Terrorism: The Case of Libya," *Alternatives*, volume 13, Number 2 (April 1988), pp. 271-289.

3. According to the *World Press Review*, "The U.S.-led strikes on Afghanistan provided the backdrop for a weekend of violence in the northern Nigerian city of Kano in mid-October, with estimates of up to 200 people killed." See Sarah Coleman, "Nigeria Religious Riots," *World Press Review*, volume 48, no. 12 (December 2001).

4. A Human Rights Watch report pointed out that country leaders were taking advantage of the anti-terror campaign to suppress dissent and abuse human rights; see *The Washington Post* (January 18, 2002), p. 12. Attending a conference in Malaysia in August 2002, President Robert Mugabe of Zimbabwe was reported to have made comments about the United States' government refusal to recognize the result of the March 2002, presidential election which he won. President Mugabe was reported to have said: "I say Mr. Bush, you of all, refusing the results of my election whereby people voted. Who voted for you? We want to know whether or not you won the election... To this day, I do not know if he [President George W. Bush] is legitimately a president. It has to take a supreme court of the United States to pronounce that he has won, and the supreme court where his party holds the majority support. There you are." See "Mugabe mocks Blair, Bush from Malaysia," *Mail&Guardian* (South Africa) (August 5, 2002).

5. Barbara Crossette of the *New Your Times* reports of the United States handling of this issue that: "What is new is that the detentions are shrouded in secrecy: for the first time, the United States—like countries whose human rights policies it has long criticized—is withholding the names of detainees. A federal judge ordered the Bush administration to release the names by Aug. 17, but it filed a stay on Aug. 8 to challenge the ruling, arguing among other things that the White House does not want to give

Al Qaeda a road map to the investigation by letting it know who has been interrogated." See Barbara Crossette, "In the Secret-Detentions Club," *New York Times* (August 11, 2002).

6. According to the *Washington Post*, "The 1,200 detainees rounded up after September 11 and held in secret were mainly Muslim with immigration problems. So were the people the government tried to deport in closed hearings." See "The War on Civil Liberties," *Washington Post* (September10, 2002).

7. For one discussion of the issues at Nuremberg, consult Alan S. Rosenbaum, *Prosecuting Nazi War Criminals* (Boulder: Westview Press, 1993).

8. See Alan Gelb and Ian Goldin, "Attacks on US Hurt Africa," posted on AllAfrica.com on October 10, 2001.

9. Gelb and Goldin, *Ibid.*

10. Warren Vieth, "U.S. Exports Misery to Africa With Farm Bill," *Los Angeles Times* (May 27, 2002).

11. Franklin Huang and Matt Stremlau, "Disease Researchers Negleting World Poor," *Los Angeles Times* (April 30, 2002).

12. Sarah Boseley, "Aids Drugs Scandal: Toll Soars," *The Guardian* (London) (July 3, 2002).

13. Jeremy Rifkin, "There's Bone to Pick With Meat Eaters: Growing grain for feed instead of food may be humanity's greatest evil yet," *Los Angeles Times* (May 27, 2002).

14. Larry Diamond, "*Compassionate Conditionality for Africa,*" Weekly Essay, posted on *hoover.org* (July 24-31, 2000).

15. Femi Akomolafe, "What am I doing in Holland?" 1994. *(http://www.hartford-hwp.com/archives/30/011.html.)*

16. Paul Blustein, "In Uganda, O'Neill and Bono Disagree About Success of Aid," *Washington Post* (May 28, 2002), p. E01.

17. Joseph A. D'Agostino, "7,000 Men Recently Entered from Al Qaeda 'Watch' Countries," *Human Event Online* (Week of December 17, 2001).

18. "EU nations split over linking aid to migration curbs," *Singapore Strait Times* (June 19, 2002).

CHAPTER THREE

THE THIRD WORLD
AND INTERNATIONAL TERRORISM[1]

R aymond Aron once analyzed contemporary warfare in terms
of a triad of violence. The three types of warfare were symbolized by the hydrogen bomb, the tank, and the sten-gun.
The most comprehensive of these three types of warfare was, of course,
nuclear war, with its power of massive destruction and capacity to
encompass widely dispersed areas. The age itself is called the nuclear
age, and yet the warfare represented by it is the least experienced
within that age. Numerous outbreaks of violence and a variety of
battles have erupted in different parts of the globe since World War
II. The range is from the Vietnam War in the Far East to the football
war in Latin America early in 1970. Yet a nuclear war as such is still
outside direct human experience. It is the fear of nuclear war, rather
than its experience, which has affected the age.

By contrast, warfare symbolized by the tank and by the sten-gun has been very much part of the post-World War II period. The tank signified what is sometimes called conventional warfare, though what is conventional is itself subject to the mutations of time. The most important outbreaks of conventional war since World War II include the Korean War, the Suez adventure of 1956 when Israel, Britain, and France attacked Nasser's Egypt, the June war of 1967 between Israel and the Arabs, the more recent Iran-Iraqi conflict, the clashes between India and China and India and Pakistan, the Israeli intrusions into and invasions of Lebanon over the years, the Vietnamese occupation of Kampuchea, the Soviet occupation of Afghanistan, the American invasion of Afghanistan and the two American wars against Iraq. An even older form of conventional warfare is civil war. African experiences include Chad, Nigeria, Eritrea, Sudan, Angola, and others. Many of these are conventional both in being intra-territorial and in the armaments used.

A third type of warfare in Aron's triad of violence is that waged by guerrilla and terrorist movements. These are symbolized by the sten-gun, the stealthy steps in the stillness of the forest, the sudden spurt of fire on an unsuspecting target. Among the most notable guerrilla wars since 1945 have been anti-colonial wars of national liberation in south-east Asia (especially Indonesia and Vietnam) in the immediate post-World War II period, in Africa (especially Algeria, Kenya, and Southern Africa) from the 1950s to the present time, and in Palestine especially since Israeli occupation in 1967. Then there have been revolutionary guerrilla wars against corrupt elites, e.g., Castro's revolution against Batista in Cuba, the Sandinista revolution against Somoza in Nicaragua and the various uprisings against Mobutu in Zaire.

It should be noted from the start that the term 'terrorism' in this chapter is value-free in the same way as the term 'war' is. As far as this analysis is concerned, terrorism is a form of warfare and can be 'perpetrated' either by revolutionary movements or by governments. 'Terrorism' is the deliberate creation of specialized terror among civilians, through the use of violence, in order to promote political

ends, whether it is revolutionary terrorism by opponents of governments or state terrorism by governments themselves. What are the
purposes of politicized, conspicuous terrorism? Here we must distinguish between ultimate goals and immediate targets. The ultimate
goals include an ambition to gain a hearing for causes that would
otherwise go unheard, and to make a contribution towards the realization of those causes. The immediate target is the manipulation of
fear as a mechanism of combat in the context of wide publicity. This
is particularly so in the case of terrorism 'perpetrated' by revolutionaries instead of by governments.

It is not necessarily the purpose of terrorists to destroy society.
Joseph Kechichian has highlighted the general objectives of revolutionary terrorists:

> Terrorism, broadly defined, is a form of political warfare by
> disenfranchised groups. What most terrorist organizations
> seem to want are rights which they are denied in the exist-
> ing political order. By definition, such a quest indicates an
> awareness of power politics in the international system. It
> is precisely the lack of legitimacy that leads disenfranchised
> groups to the use of political violence in articulating their
> grievances. Thus, the ultimate purpose is not to destroy
> 'civilization' or democratic values but to participate as le-
> gitimate participants in the international system.[2]

TERROR IN THE SKIES: A RETROSPECT

Among the more sensational of terrorist initiatives by revolutionary movements is the use of the skies as a battlefield. A new
version of this last type of warfare was initiated by the Palestine
commandos in the 1970s. This was the tactic of attacking civil aircraft, sometimes on the ground, but more sensationally in mid-air. A
more timid adventure tried in 1970 was that of planting bombs in
aircraft. One blew up in mid-air, killing a number of people, many of
whom had nothing to do with the issue of Palestine. But on 6 September 1970, Palestine commandos took this strategy a stage further.

They hijacked four planes, two American, one Swiss, and one Israeli. According to some reports, the hijacking of the Israeli plane was thwarted by a somersault trick performed by the pilot, which threw the hijackers off balance, and by the intervention of the plane's steward, resulting in one hijacker being killed and the second wounded. One of the American aircraft was taken to Cairo, where, after the passengers had been permitted to disembark, it was blown up in one dramatic explosion.

The remaining two planes went to Beirut and Amman, and passengers were for a while held as hostages as demands were made for the release of other Palestinians held prisoner in different parts of the Western world. Three of these were being held in Switzerland, after being sentenced to serve seven years on charges of attacking an Israeli airliner at Zurich. The Swiss government, after urgent and decisive consultations domestically, agreed to release the three Palestinians in exchange for all the passengers from the Swiss airliner held by the terrorists.

For the remaining passengers, especially the male passengers from the United States, Britain, and West Germany, there were additional demands. Among stipulations reportedly made by the hijackers was the release of Sirhan Sirhan, under sentence of death in the United States for the murder of Robert Kennedy, though this demand was later withdrawn, if it was ever made.

What did these hijacks carried out by the Palestinians really mean in terms of the history of combat tactics? What the world was witnessing in September 1970 was guerrilla warfare transferred from the forests to the skies. The purpose of aerial terrorism is, of course, the same as guerrilla tactics on the ground, the manipulation of fear as a mechanism of combat. The grand design is to undermine morale, not only among the soldiers but also the civilian body. An atmosphere of general insecurity, promoted by spectacular acts of destruction or specially dramatized acts of brutality, is contrived in order to drive the enemy into a desperate readiness to seek a settlement. What the Palestinian commandos were doing in September 1970 was using the international skies as an arena for terrorist activities, since the streets of Israel were not easily accessible to them for domestic terrorism.

There is, however, an important difference between aerial terrorism and domestic guerrilla tactics. Aerial terrorism, as so far illustrated in its initial phases, is by the very nature of things international. Either the plane itself might be traveling across territorial boundaries, or the passengers on board might be nationally mixed, or both these international aspects might be present.

Aerial terrorism is in some important respects symbolic both of the communications revolution and of the conversion of the world into a global village. The communications revolution played its part in the degree to which a hijack attained spectacular publicity, and with regard to the very increase in air traffic and the greater reliance of influential sectors of humanity on air transport. The news aspect of the communications revolution has made aerial terrorism a useful device for attracting world attention to a particular grievance. The traveling aspect of the communications revolution meant heavy air traffic and therefore a wide choice of planes for hijacking. Among the passengers on such planes were men and women from influential countries of the world who were now forced to worry about the implications for their holidays or for their business of this whole new phenomenon in the skies.

The publicity side of aerial terrorism relied in part on the sensationalism of political piracy. By political piracy we mean the forceful takeover of a vessel at sea or in the air for such purposes as attracting publicity, carrying out political revenge, or preparing for a political deal. It had all started in 1961 when a Portuguese revolutionary captain, Henrique Galvao, seized control of a Portuguese ship, the *Santa Maria,* on the high seas in a dramatic assertion of solidarity with the colonized peoples of Angola and Mozambique. This was political piracy in the tradition of tactical publicity.

Will aerial terrorism increase since it is such a guaranteed way of getting international and media attention for otherwise obscure causes? Two trends are pulling in opposite directions. The fact that air traffic in the world will almost certainly continue to increase should expand opportunities for political piracy in the skies. Even more obscure causes may take to the skies, such as the grievances of North Yemenis against Saudi Arabia as manifested in the takeover of a Saudi plane by Yemenis in November 1984. The skyjackers were later overwhelmed by Iranian troops with the help of passengers when the aircraft was at Teheran airport. The international obscurity of the cause was perhaps the most ominous aspect of the whole episode.

Although the expansion of air traffic in the world has increased opportunities for aerial piracy, there have also been simultaneous improvements in the technology of detecting metal weapons, especially since September 11, 2001. There is thus a race between the opportunities provided by expanding air traffic and the controls afforded by improved technology.

Within the Third World it is the expansion of air traffic that is winning. In spite of September 11, technological improvements are significantly slower than multiplication of air passengers and aircraft. At least in the immediate future, aerial terrorism is most likely to increase within the Third World or on aircraft that start in the Third World or pass through it.

There have, of course, always been Third World revolutionaries, including Palestinians, who have been opposed to hijacking. Some have felt that such tactics were bound to be counterproductive and to alienate international opinion. Those who have favored such tactics have sometimes echoed Machiavelli's advice to the prince: 'It is better to be feared than to be loved.' The international community was more likely to want a problem resolved if it threatened its own safety and comfort. The international community might hate the terrorists— but it would still prefer a world without terrorism.

But if world opinion is a factor, is it really better to be feared than loved? Does aerial terrorism attract the right kind of publicity? Questions of this kind miss the whole point of the exercise. In a propaganda campaign to win sympathy in the more influential parts of the world, the Arabs are no match for the Jews. Quite apart from the greater sophistication of Jewish communities in the Western world, there is also the question of access to the influential media of the international system. One cannot escape the issue of comparative Jewish access to the media of communication. Indeed, without such access, Israel itself might never have been created. Any competition by Palestinian commandos for sympathy is handicapped from the start by the massive disproportion between them and Israel in terms of access to mass communications. To elements of the PLO, spectacularly bad publicity is better than no publicity.

For a time (1976-1985), the Palestinian movement seemed to have shelved the skyjacking option. It seems likely that three shocks helped to paralyze this particular arm of the Palestinian struggle. One was the shock of the Entebbe raid (1976)—a spectacular display of Israeli organizational superiority. Israel's reach exceeded its grasp—as the long arm of the Jewish state stretched itself from Jerusalem to the source of the Nile. The blow against Palestinian morale was devastating. The blow against the 'legitimacy' of skyjacking as a mode of Palestinian struggle was even more direct.

After the Entebbe raid, the second great shock for the Palestinian struggle was Anwar Sadat's visit to Jerusalem (1977) and the ensuing events that culminated in the Camp David Accords (1978). Again it was a major blow to Palestinian morale and inaugurated fundamental agonizing about priorities. Should the struggle redirect itself against 'the enemy within' the Arab nation (e.g., Sadat) or 'the enemy without,' namely 'the Zionist entity'? Skyjacking was not appropriate as a method of inter-Arab infighting, so it was widely assumed among Palestinians. Skyjacking against 'the enemy without' was also suspended for the time being.

The third great shock for Palestinians, after Entebbe and the Sadat initiative, was of course Israel's brutal invasions of Lebanon, especially the devastating one of 1982. The invasion destroyed much of the military infrastructure of the Palestine Liberation Organization. But it did not destroy the PLO's capacity for skyjacking and other terrorist activities. Sometimes terrorism increases precisely because other military options have been weakened. About Israeli arrogance it may be true to say that 'power tends to corrupt and absolute power corrupts absolutely.' In the case of the Palestinians the fear is that they are forced to more extreme measures precisely because of weakness. It is after all equally true (in spite of Lord Acton) that *powerlessness* tends to corrupt—and absolute powerlessness corrupts absolutely. New levels of desperation, especially after the expulsion of the PLO army from Lebanon after the Israeli invasion of 1982, in fact, forced segments of the Palestinian movement to return to the days prior to the Entebbe raid.

The first move, however, in a return to skyjacking as a revolutionary tactic came not from the PLO but from Islamic *Jihād*, a Shī'ite fundamentalist group in Lebanon. In June 1985 this group hijacked an American TWA plane and held 42 of its passengers and crew as hostages in Beirut for some weeks. One of the passengers, US Navy diver Robert Stethem, was shot dead. The other hostages and the plane were released after Syria arranged a deal and Israel released 735 Shī'ite Lebanese prisoners being held in Israel (after Israel's occupation of half of Lebanon in 1982-1985).

Then in November 1985 a PLO splinter group opposed to PLO Chairman Yasser Arafat and apparently loyal to Arafat's rival, the Libyan-backed Abu Nidal, hijacked an Egyptian airliner and caused it to be flown to Malta. The Maltese government allowed Egyptian commandos to storm the plane but the operation was bungled and 60 passengers were killed.

On 27 December 1985, Palestinian gunmen, again apparently linked to Abu Nidal and Libya, opened fire on passengers at Israeli airline desks at Rome and Vienna airports, killing 14 people. These attacks were similar in style to the May 1972 massacre of 100 Christian pilgrims at Israel's Lydda airport by the pro-Palestinian Japanese 'Red Army.'

Another type of terrorist action that gained enormous publicity if not sympathy also reappeared in 1985. In October four Palestinians hijacked an Italian cruise liner, the *Achille Lauro,* in the Mediterranean. The group had originally intended not to seize the ship but to land at Ashdod in Israel and mount an attack there. But a ship's waiter spotted them cleaning their weapons in a cabin and, their cover blown, they seized the ship. The hijackers killed Leon

Klinghoffer, an elderly wheelchair-bound American Jewish passenger. Syria refused to accede to the hijackers' request to allow the ship to enter one of its ports but the gunmen were to surrender at Port Said with the promise of an Egyptian plane to take them from Cairo to Tunis, the PLO headquarters. The Egyptian plane was intercepted by US warplanes and forced to land at a US base in Sicily where the Americans handed over the terrorists to the Italian authorities. The hijackers had themselves been hijacked.

POLITICAL KIDNAPPING

Then there is the piracy involving the kidnapping of a specific individual or individuals. This is where political piracy ties in with the more recent phenomenon of political abduction, especially the abduction of foreign diplomats in Latin America. The abduction of foreign diplomats in Latin America involved the diversion not of airplanes in mid-air, but quite often of cars in the street. A car is stopped, and the victim is forced out and taken away in another car; or alternatively an uninvited passenger enters the victim's car, and at gunpoint hijacks the vehicle to another part of the city.

The kidnapping of diplomats of other powers is distinctive of recent times; but the kidnapping of specific individuals as a form of political vengeance or as a prelude to civic justice is part of an older tradition of political behavior. The kidnapping of Westerners in Lebanon by Islamic extremist groups such as the Ḥizb Allāh (Party of God) since 1985, either for ransom or for political bargaining purposes, matches the similar pattern of kidnappings carried out in West Germany and Italy in the 1970s by left-wing terrorist groups. The kidnapping of the US embassy staff in Iran in 1979 by revolutionary students was undertaken partly as an act of revenge for American support for the Shah before and after his fall from power, and partly in an attempt to force President Carter to concede Iranian demands to return the Shah as a prisoner to Iran, together with all his wealth.

State Terrorism

Much terrorism is reactive, a violent response to violence. The attack on Israeli athletes at the Munich Olympic Games in 1972 was a response to Israeli occupation of the West Bank and Gaza five years earlier and harsh rule of these occupied territories. Israel's response to the Munich terrorism was to launch heavy air raids on Palestinian refugee camps and bases in Lebanon as a result of which hundreds of people were killed.

State terrorism is invariably more severe in its consequences than revolutionary terrorism because the state usually has greater force at its disposal than guerrilla forces. Also the purpose of state terrorism is to hit revolutionary terrorists exceptionally hard either to try to destroy them or to deter them from future operations. For example, when in 1978 Palestinian terrorists killed thirty Israeli civilians near Tel Aviv, Israel retaliated by sending 20,000 troops into Lebanon on a 'search and destroy' mission against Palestinian bases. In this operation several hundred unarmed people were killed. In 1981 the French ambassador to Lebanon was murdered by a pro-Syrian gunman and France retaliated by exploding a car bomb in Damascus which killed 110 people. In 1982 Palestinian gunmen shot and severely wounded the Israeli ambassador in London. Israel's reply was to launch a new invasion of Lebanon in which many thousands were killed.[3]

In October and November 1983, Islamic *Jihād* suicide bombers destroyed the American, French, and Israeli military headquarters in Lebanon, killing over 340 soldiers. But an American naval bombardment of the Chouf mountains behind Beirut had already (in September) killed 200 Druze villagers. In March 1985 the CIA was linked to the car-bombing near the home of the militant Shī'ite cleric Shaikh Mohammed Hussein Fadlallah, leader of the Ḥizb Allāh. That car bomb killed 60 people.

Two of the most spectacular examples of state counter-terrorism have been the Israeli attacks on Tunis, seat of the PLO headquarters after the PLO Army was forced out of Lebanon by the Israelis in 1982. In October 1985, after Palestinians killed three Israeli agents in Cyprus, Israeli planes destroyed the PLO buildings in Tunis, killing 45 Palestinians and 25 Tunisians. Then in April 1988 Israeli commandos assassinated the PLO's deputy leader Khalīl al-Wazīr (known as Abū Jihād) in his Tunis home.

In matters of terrorism and counter-terrorism it is difficult to be objective. One person's terrorist is another person's freedom fighter. A president or prime minister may be a terrorist in his actions as much as any guerrilla or hijacker. Israeli prime ministers like Menachem Begin and Yitzhak Shamir were, as young men, revolutionary guerrilla terrorists against British rule in Palestine before they became 'state terrorists' in control of the Israeli armed forces.

So far, we have drawn many examples of terrorism from the Middle East. Neither Islamic fundamentalism nor Shī'ite Islam has been specifically highlighted as a major source of terrorist violence, and for good reasons. First, the most fundamentalist regime among the Arab states is Saudi Arabia, which is not terrorist and is Sunnite, not Shī'itē. Second, the main revolutionary terrorist force in the Middle East, the PLO, is neither fundamentalist nor even Islamic. Most of the Palestinians are Sunnite, not Shī'ite, Muslims and a sizeable minority are Christians, including many in the PLO. Thirdly, Shī'ite Iran is not quite the terrorist state portrayed by the Western media. Iran did hold embassy staff hostage for over a year but none of the hostages were killed and Iran has not significantly engaged in violence outside its own borders. The pro-Iranian Ḥizb Allāh in Lebanon is not controlled by Iran. The Iranian disruption of the *hajj* at Mecca in 1987 was a demonstration, not terrorism. Iran's naval confrontation with the United States in the Gulf in 1987-1988 was not terrorism but conventional warfare—even if on a very limited scale. If Iran is a terrorist state at all, it is so at home, when the Islamic Republic is dealing with its own people, whether it is brutally persecuting the Bahai religious community or crushing internal opposition of all kinds.

If Iran is at present hostile to the United States, it is not necessarily terrorist in its relations with America. Iranian hostility may not even be based on 'religious fanaticism.' Louis René Béres has commented on the problems faced by the United States in its relations with Iran: 'Shi'ite hostility to the USA did not arise in a vacuum. It has its roots in the USA's prior embrace of the Shah, a geopolitical intervention that subordinated human rights in Iran to the present requirements of competition with the Soviet Union.'[4]

The main cause of revolutionary violence and conflict in the Middle East today is neither Islam nor the revival of Shi'ite Islam: it is Israeli occupation of Palestine and the lack of any means other than terrorism for the Palestinians to present their case and make themselves heard.

There are other sources of conflict in the Middle East, such as Sunni-Shi'i rivalry, which has flared up in Saudi Arabia in 1979 (attempted Shi'i coup in Mecca) and 1987 (Iranian demonstrations), in the Iran-Iraq war since 1980 in which over half a million have been killed, and in Lebanon where Shi'ite militia have fought with non-Shi'ite Lebanese and Palestinians. This Sunni-Shi'i conflict, however, tends to be a problem internal to the Middle East and is rarely manifested in the form of international terrorism.

The major Western countries or their citizens seem to be fairly frequent targets of Middle Eastern terrorism because of their support for Israel and also because the Palestinians seem to believe that anti-Western terrorism can lead to the West putting pressure on Israel to grant Palestinian rights. Perhaps only the United States could bring Israel to the conference table with the PLO, in the course of time.

In Latin America and South Africa the United States could have played a major role in reducing conflict but only if it abandoned open or tacit support for state terrorism. In Latin America for several decades the United States contributed to the conflicts and terrorism in that region rather than help reduce them.

In El Salvador the Reagan administration has backed government forces in what Archbishop Oscar Romero described as 'a war of extermination and genocide against a defenseless population.' Some 60,000 people have been killed in the 1980s in the counter-insurgency campaign in El Salvador, most of them being victims of an army organized, trained, and armed by Washington. Right-wing 'death squads,' in practice police and army units, have played their part in this slaughter, one of their victims being Romero himself. The root of the problem in El Salvador is the ownership of most of the land by a few families while the mass of the people are landless peasants. Successive US administrations have opposed any significant measure of land reform as a solution, and hence the civil war and the terrorism and counter-terrorism.

Similarly in Guatemala the United States has (since 1954 when it backed a right-wing coup to overthrow President Arbenz who promised land reform) consistently supported the local security forces against left-wing guerrillas. It is estimated that over 200,000 Guatemalans died in the long conflict since 1954.

In Nicaragua, most of the 45,000 people killed in the Sandinista revolution of 1978-1979 that overthrew the right-wing dictator Somoza were victims of atrocities carried out by Somoza's National Guard. President Jimmy Carter supported Somoza at first and then sat on the fence while Somoza was defeated. Reagan's support of the Contra terrorism against the Sandinista government resulted in the deaths of over 10,000 civilians, nearly all of them at the hands of the Contras.

In southern Africa, the Reagan administration followed a policy of 'constructive engagement,' trying to get President Botha of South Africa to dilute apartheid. Reagan persistently opposed the armed struggle led by the ANC and regularly excused state violence. He insisted that opposition to apartheid must always be peaceful. In his notorious press conference on 21 March 1985, President Reagan said that the blacks recently shot by the South African police at Langa were excusable casualties of 'rioting.' Likewise Prime Minister Thatcher of Britain opposed black violence but was too ready to cast a blind eye over state violence.

Reagan and Thatcher did condemn South African army raids on ANC personnel in neighboring Lesotho, Botswana, Mozambique, and Zimbabwe. But such raids continued with impunity. South African state terrorism—outside South Africa itself, where over 3,700 people were killed by the police since 1975—was at its worst in

Angola and Mozambique. Since Angolan independence in 1975 neither the United States nor South Africa accepted the socialist MPLA in Luanda and they assisted Jonas Savimbi and his rebel Unita forces in a long civil war in the southern half of the country. Towards the end of 1988, however, American diplomacy was playing a major role in moves towards a comprehensive peace settlement for both Angola and Namibia, including a mutual withdrawal from Angola of South African and Cuban forces.

American influence over the South African government did not have any impact as far as Mozambique is concerned. Perhaps the United States was less interested in Mozambique because there were no Cuban troops there. However, it is probably in that East African coastal country that South African state terrorism could be observed at its most brutal and destructive.

Mozambique became independent in 1975 after a long guerrilla war and the guerrilla organization, FRELIMO came to power and implemented socialist policies. In 1976 Ian Smith, the leader of the illegal white settler regime in 'Rhodesia,' set up RENAMO or MNR, the Mozambique National Resistance, out of former black soldiers of the Portuguese army. The MNR began to carry out acts of terrorism in Mozambique. In 1980 'Rhodesia' became Zimbabwe and the new Prime Minister Robert Mugabe expelled the MNR from Zimbabwe. However, Prime Minister Botha became the MNR's new patron and South Africa gave a great deal of assistance to the MNR to try to destabilize Mozambique. The MNR received training, weapons, and supplies from the South African army. It had few military successes but it was adept at sabotage and mindless destruction. The MNR destroyed over a thousand schools and clinics, killed many thousands of people, specialized in maiming people by hacking off limbs, and caused 2 million to leave their homes. In late 1988, 1,600,000 were living in refugee camps in Mozambique itself and another 400,000 had taken refuge in Malawi or Zimbabwe.

In one massacre in July 1987, 420 people in the village of Homoine were killed by the MNR. In spite of South African government denials, there was clear evidence of its military assistance to the MNR in the second half of 1988.

State terrorism, according to our examples from the Middle East, Latin America, and southern Africa, is at least as serious a threat to peace as is guerrilla-style terrorism in these regions. Is it time for the major Western democracies to recognize this dual nature of terrorism and to play their part in bringing both forms of it under control? Or will they continue to back state terrorism by propping up repressive and terrorist regimes? Will the Western powers see both sides of the equation in the Middle East and, while supporting Israel's right to exist, join those over 100 states, including NATO members, Greece and Spain, which have recognized the PLO under Yassir Arafat as the official and legal representatives of the Palestinian people? Will the major Western democracies ratify Protocol 1 of 1977, an addition to the Geneva Convention, which provides for the recognition of the role and status of, and protection for, liberation movements even like Hamas and their combatants fighting against colonial and alien occupation and against racist regimes? The United States, Britain, West Germany, and Israel are among the few states that have refused to sign the protocol. Will they undergo an imaginative change of heart or will they continue to reject the protocol as a 'charter for terrorism'?

Even if the leading Western democracies continue to have a one-sided approach to definitions of terrorism and regard the suppression of terrorism as purely or merely a law and order matter, can they fight terrorism fairly, without resorting to more brutal counter-terrorism? On this issue, Paul Wilkinson recently invoked the spirit of the great seventeenth-century Dutch jurist and founder of international law, Hugo Grotius:

> The true Grotian response by Western states to terrorism must combine firmness with a commitment to act within the framework of the rule of law. Heaven knows this rule of law internationally is pathetically weak. But it is all we have got. If powerful Western states disregard the inhibitions of

international law and use means against terrorism which are totally disproportionate to the threat, they will risk increasing the very anarchy in which terrorists flourish.[5]

A further step would be to tackle some of the injustices that encourage terrorism, because that is the only long-term protection against terrorism. As Louis René Béres recently put it: 'To protect itself against terrorism, the USA will have to return to its own best traditions, reaffirming that human rights are valuable everywhere, and that they are valuable in themselves.'[6]

NOTES

1. This chapter first appeared in "The Third World and International Terrorism: Preliminary Reflections," *Third World Quarterly*, Vol 7, No. 2 (April 1985), pp. 348-64. A revised version of that article is to be found in Ali A. Mazrui, *Cultural Forces in World Politics* (Oxford: James Currey, 1990), pp. 227-236.
2. J. Kechichian, *Terrorism and the Search for Power*, in A. Gauhar (ed.), *Third World Affair 1988* (London: Third World Foundation for Social and Economic Studies, 1988), p. 56.
3. See "Chapter 8: On Race and Conflict: Zionism and Apartheid," in Ali A. Mazrui, *Cultural Forces in World Politics* (Oxford: James Currey, 1990), pp. 145-163.
4. Louis René Béres, *Understanding Terrorism*, in A. Gauhar (ed.), *Third World Affair 1988* (London: Third World Foundation for Social and Economic Studies, 1988), p. 13.
5. From N. O'Sullivan (ed.), *Terrorism, Ideology and Revolution* (Brighton, England: Wheatsheaf Books), p. 222.
6. L. Béres, *Understanding Terrorism*, in A. Gauhar (ed.), *Third World Affair 1988* (London: Third World Foundation for Social and Economic Studies, 1988), p. 13.

CHAPTER FOUR

GLOBALIZATION BETWEEN THE MARKET AND THE MILITARY
A THIRD WORLD PERSPECTIVE[1]

A TALE OF THREE WORLD WARS

The globalization of warfare has been a much more recent phenomenon than the globalization of religion, technology economy or empire. The globalization of Christianity and Islam goes back at least a millennium. The globalization of the economy goes back to the trans-Atlantic slave trade. The globalization of technology goes back to the flowering of the first industrial revolution. The globalization of empire is to be traced to the finest hour of the British Empire. But the globalization of war did not occur until the twentieth century. As indicated in our chapter entitled "Globalization, Islam, and the West," that was the century when for the first time the human race experienced world wars.

For the Third World the short-term consequences of the world wars were disruptive and sometimes devastating. The long-term consequences, on the other hand, were more than benign. They were often positively benevolent. World War I killed millions more Europeans than anybody else. It was a Euro-masochistic war. Long-term gains for the Third World included the birth of the first experimental world body, however imperfect—the League of Nations. The Third World also gained when the First World War ended the brutal German Empire in Africa (Tanzanyika, Cameroon, Togo and South West Africa), and inaugurated a system of Mandates of the League of Nations (later Trusteeships of the UN). The Treaty of Versailles (though short-sighted in handling the defeated Germany) was prophetic about giving more legitimacy to the principle of self-determination. World War II was also a case of devastating short-term consequences for both the North and the South. But the longer-term consequences for the Third World were not only benign; they were also benevolent.

The Second World War weakened Great Britain's imperial will—the will to hold on to the Empire. Within two years of the end of World War II India and Pakistan were liberated from the British Raj. Other colonies followed. Ghana became independent in 1957—almost exactly ten years after India and Pakistan.

Since France had been defeated by Nazi Germany, World War II diluted the mystique of France and undermined the myth of French invincibility. Within less than ten years of the liberation of France from the Nazis, Vietnamese defeated French soldiers at Dien Bien Phu in 1954. World War II was therefore a liberating experience for Third World countries. African soldiers who served in Burma came back home with expanded horizons and with greater awareness of the failings of the white man in battle conditions. World War II also gave birth to the United Nations—a much stronger world-body than the League of Nations.

The rhetoric of the Allies against Hitler was also inspiring to colonial subjects. The Atlantic Charter between Franklin Roosevelt and Winston Churchill in 1942 gave new impetus to colonial nationalists in their demands for self-determination from Britain. On balance, horrendously destructive as World War II was for Europeans, it was on balance a liberating experience for the colonial subjects in European empires.

Then came the Cold War not long after World War II. It was also a globalizing conflict in its own more subdued ways than the two militarized world wars.[2] Competition between the superpowers—the United States and the Soviet Union—once again combined both short-term disadvantages and longer term assets for the world. For Southern Africa the white socialist countries helped Black liberation fighters with weapons. Gamal Abdel Nasser had his Aswan Dam built by the Soviets. The rivalry between the superpowers enabled small countries to compete for concessions from big powers.[3]

Now a major point to note is that World War I, World War II and the Cold War—though global in their consequences—were primarily conflicts between Northern powers. The confrontations were either between different European powers or between the United States and the Soviet Union. Fundamentally these were inter-Northern (or intra-Northern) conflicts.

Is George W. Bush right that the struggle against terrorism is the first war of the twenty-first century? Or should we view it as the first global war which is South against North rather than North against North and with the South as the initiator? Is it also the first global conflict in which one side consists of *non-state* actors (e.g., Usamah bin Laden and Al-Qaida) and the other consists of states?

GLOBAL VIOLENCE AND THE WARRIOR PRESIDENT

But while globalization has afforded Africa a more visible role in diplomacy, it has also made Africa vulnerable when diplomacy degenerates into violence. The dates August 7, 1998, and September 11, 2001, dramatized this transition to violence.

Usamah bin Laden may or may not be the man behind the atrocities committed against the United States, in East Africa on August 1998 and in America on September 11, 2001, but he has become a symbol. It may be time to divide the passions between

Usamahphobia, the hate or fear of Usamah and what he stands for, and *Usamahphilia,* the secret admiration he definitely enjoys among the frustrated and desperate masses of those humiliated by either Israeli policies or American power and global reach.

The politics of Usamahism have affected me in four ways—in my capacities as a Kenyan national, as a long time resident American African, as a Muslim and as a human being (hopefully citizen of the world). The destruction of the U.S. Embassy in Nairobi on August 7,1998 killed over two hundred Kenyans and twelve Americans—the brunt of the attack was therefore borne by my Kenyan compatriots. Nairobi and Dar es Salaam in 1998 were ghastly dress rehearsals for New York and Washington three years later.[4]

My eldest son is a U.S. citizen working for the U.S. Federal Government in Washington, D.C. My son works for a department other than Defense, but hypothetically he might have been visiting a friend at the Pentagon. However, that morning he happened to be at his own desk at a safe distance. He and I grieved for those who were at the Pentagon. I am a Muslim, Chairman of the Center for the Study of Islam and Democracy in Washington, D.C. and a member of the Council of the Center for Muslim-Christian Understanding at Georgetown University, Washington, D.C. I am also one of the Directors of the American Muslim Council in Washington. All the Islamic organizations to which I belong in the United States promptly distanced themselves from the atrocities on the World Trade Center and the Pentagon. American (immigrant) Muslims had, ironically, voted overwhelmingly for George W. Bush in the presidential elections of November 2000.[5]

In my capacity as a citizen of the world, I have seen the phenomenon of terrorism become globalized. Innocent pedestrians on a street in Nairobi were killed in the hundreds in 1998 because a Saudi sympathizer of oppressed Iraqis and Palestinians, orchestrating world conflict from Afghanistan, held the United States responsible for the deaths of innocent children in Baghdad and Gaza. This was real international complexity. But this is also assuming Usamah bin Laden was indeed responsible for the destruction of the U.S. Embassies in

East Africa.

It is estimated that among the dead in the World Trade Center in 2001 are dozens of Africans and hundreds of Muslims—ranging from Nigerian and Arab investors to Bangladeshi restaurant waiters.

However, it is not just terrorism that has become globalized. It is also its causes—the frustrations and desperation of people affected by decisions made in Washington, New York, Paris, London and Moscow. A global coalition against terrorism would only make sense if it included addressing the causes of terrorism.

The single most explosive cause of anti-American terrorism is the perceived alliance between the United States and Israel against major Muslim concerns. The world needs a coalition to seek a permanent solution to the Middle Eastern conflict, especially the Arab-Israeli core. Palestinians and Israelis cannot solve their problems on their own. The United States is too pro-Israel to be an honest broker. We need a coalition of representatives of the European Union, the United States, the Organization of the Islamic Conference, the League of Arab States, and Russia to help the Palestinians and Israelis find a permanent solution to the problem. Without such a solution we can forget about a world without terrorism.

There was a time when the Zionist movement considered establishing a Jewish state in East Africa. At the turn of the 20th century Joseph Chamberlain, Britain's colonial Secretary, offered Theodor Hertzel parts of what is today Kenya and Uganda. The real estate offered to the Jews included what were later known as the White Highlands of Kenya. Fortunately for East Africa the Zionist movement could not reach consensus. Britain's offer to the Jews was turned down.[6] In order to recover the White Highlands, Africans in Kenya had to wage a guerrilla war, denounced by the British as terrorist.[7] The Mau Mau war nearly became a war against the Jewish Highlands of Kenya.

While terrorism has since then been in the process of globalization, the concept of an "act of war" has by no means found a global standard. How many Americans would acknowledge that the Anglo-American no-fly zones imposed on Iraq for the last decade were a continuing act of war? Iraqis were not allowed to fly planes in their own air space. And yet the no-fly zones over Iraq had no United Nations authorization or legal validation.[8] Iraqis were bombed if they challenge American or British planes over Iraqi territory. African territory was bombed by President Ronald Reagan (Libya) and President Bill Clinton (Sudan).

How many members of the Bush administration would accept that the Israeli occupation of the West Bank and Gaza are what a Foreign Minister of India once described as "permanent aggression"? Indeed, are not the Israeli settlements on occupied land illegal and tantamount to belligerency? President George W. Bush's father came close to declaring them as such.[9]

Every American president since Franklin D. Roosevelt has engaged in some act of war or another. Roosevelt was inevitably embroiled in World War II; from Harry Truman onwards the United States military casualties have been primarily in the Third World. Truman helped to initiate the Korean War; Dwight Eisenhower ended the Korean War but started planning for the Bay of Pigs operation on Cuba; John F. Kennedy unleashed the Bay of Pigs operation and helped to initiate the Vietnam War; Lyndon Johnson escalated the Vietnam war; Richard Nixon bombed Cambodia; Gerald Ford sent the Marines in a disagreement with Cambodia over a U.S. cargo-ship, the Mayaguez; Jimmy Carter attempted to thwart the Iranian revolution and paid heavily for it; Ronald Reagan perpetrated acts of war in Lebanon, the Caribbean, Libya and in shooting down a civilian airline in the Persian Gulf; George Bush Senior invaded Panama and is most famous for Desert Storm in the Persian Gulf; Bill Clinton led military action against Yugoslavia over Kosovo and bombed Sudan and Afghanistan; George W. Bush, inherited a decade of bombing Baghdad and subsidizing half a century of Israeli militarism against Palestinians. Now this younger Bush has embarked on what he calls a "crusade against terrorism," starting with the bombing of Afghanistan and proceeding to the invasion and occupation of Iraq. Apart from former Yugoslavia, all casualties of U.S. militarism have been in the Third World.

Every American president since Franklin Roosevelt has regarded an act of war as the equivalent of a "rite of passage." The Commander-in-Chief has to "act presidential." His popularity dramatically rises.[10] Americans love the warrior president. And yet the United States hardly ever calls these engagements "acts of war." Even the war in Vietnam which cost nearly sixty thousand American lives and millions of Vietnamese lives, was never officially declared by the United States.[11] America needs to find more humane rites of passage for its leaders. Why are presidents at their most popular when they find a war to fight?

Terrorism is getting globalized, but the definition of an "act of war" is not. Such a definition is still highly selective, depending upon the power of the perpetrator or the status of the victim. For the immediate future it may also depend upon making sure that Usamahphobia does not degenerate into Islamophobia. The blood of the innocent cries out not just for a coalition against terrorism but for a coalition in search of genuine peace. The West has saved millions of lives through medical science and technology. Let us not destroy those lives through Western warfare and new forms of starvation. I grew up in a Kenya engulfed in a war of liberation that the British called "terrorist"—the Mau Mau war of the 1950s. I have personally met people like Nelson Mandela and Yassir Arafat, men once denounced as terrorists, but who lived to win the Nobel Prize for Peace. Some of their acts of war were in the past localized and regional. But now it is not just terrorists "who can run but cannot hide." Such a situation has become the human condition itself.

What happened at the World Trade Center has no excuse. Even terrorism as a style of war ought to have rules. It is a pity there is no Geneva Convention laying down the rules and ethics of terrorist engagement. For example, the terrorists could have avoided hitting the World Trade Center at the peak hour of 9 o'clock in the morning, and attempted instead to highjack an evening flight at 9 o'clock at night, thus cutting down the casualty rate by three quarters. Or more ethically the terrorists could have avoided the World Trade Center altogether, and gone only for the Pentagon. Just as there is sometimes honor among thieves, there ought to be restraint among terrorists. Any ethical rules of engagement would surely have regarded an attack on the World Trade Center, at a rush hour of the day, as a dastardly act without honor or humanity. However, it is not possible to have a Geneva Convention prescribing rules for legitimate terrorism. Instead, we must both deal with the causes of terrorism and punish perpetrators when we catch them.

PEACE-MAKING AND THIRD WORLD LEADERSHIP

Meanwhile, globalization has also permitted the emergence of Black and African moral leadership on a world scale. It began with the Nobel Prize winners for peace. Over the years these have included Ralph Bunche (1950), Albert Luthuli (1960), Martin Luther King, Jr. (1964), Anwar Sadat (1978), Desmond Tutu (1984), Nelson Mandela (1994), F.W. de Klerk (1994) and Kofi Annan (2001). Black Nobel prizewinners in literature or economics are not necessarily moral leaders.

Globalization has also witnessed the rise of Africans to positions of leadership in global organizations. But here it may be worth distinguishing between Africans of the soil and Africans of the blood. Boutros Boutros-Ghali, the first African Secretary General of the United Nations, was an African of the soil. Kofi Annan, the second African Secretary General, is an African of the blood. North Africans like Boutros-Ghali belong to the African continent (the soil) but not to the Black race (the blood). On the other hand, African Americans are Africans of the blood (the Black race) but not of the soil (the African continent). Sub-Saharan Africans like Kofi Annan are in reality both Africans of the soil (the continent) and of the blood (the race). Globalization has given Africans of the soil and of the blood new opportunities for leadership at the global level itself.

Even before the two African Secretaries-General of the United Nations, Africa had already produced a black Director-General of UNESCO in Paris (the United Nations Educational, Scientific and Cultural Organization). He was Amadou Mahtar M'Bow, an African

of the blood from Senegal. His openly pro-Third World policies infuriated the United States, which finally withdrew from UENSCO in
1985, followed by its compliant ally, the United Kingdom. The United
Kingdom returned to UNESCO in 1997 after the sweeping victory
of the Labour Party in the 1996 elections.

With regard to the United Nations itself, Africa is the only region of the world apart from Europe to have produced more than one
Secretary-General for the world body in the twentieth century. Europe has produced three Secretaries-General, Africa two, and the other
regions of the world have produced either one each or none so far.

The International Court of Justice at The Hague elected in 1994
an African of the soil for its President—Mohammed Medjauni of
Algeria. The World Bank in the 1990s has had two African Vice-
Presidents—Callisto Madivo, an African of the blood from Zimbabwe, and Ismail Serageldin, an African of the soil from Egypt. In
1999, Serageldin was also a serious candidate to become the first
UNESCO Director-General of the new millennium.[12]

The Commonwealth (former British Commonwealth) had Third
World Secretaries-General for two decades—Ramphal of Guyana and
Emeka Anyouku of Nigeria. Ralph Bunche and Martin Luther King,
Jr. were of course African American Peace Laureates and therefore
Africans of the blood in our sense, but not of the soil. Anwar Sadat
and F.W. de Klerk were as Peace Laureates Africans of the soil but
not of the blood. Albert Luthuli, Desmond Tutu and Nelson Mandela
were Africans of both the soil and the blood. All three were South
Africans, as was F.W. de Klerk. But we should note that F.W. de
Klerk is an "African of the soil" by adoption rather than by indigenous roots to the continent. Most North Africans, on the other hand,
are indigenous to the continent, although there has been considerable racial mixture with immigrants over the centuries.

As the twentieth century was coming to a close Nelson Mandela
achieved a unique status. He became the first truly universal Black
moral leader in the world in his own lifetime.[13] Martin Luther King,
Jr. achieved universal status after his death. When Dr. King was alive
half of mainstream America rejected him and regarded him as a

troublemaker. Mandela was fortunate to have achieved universal moral admiration without having to undergo an assassination beforehand. No other Black man in history has pulled off such a "pre-humous" accomplishment (as distinct from a posthumous elegy). In the recognition of Mandela the human race may have taken one more step forward in the search for universalized ethical sensibilities.

Mandela languished in jail for 27 of the best years of his life—ostensibly punished for acts of terrorism. He later won a Nobel Prize for Peace. Usamah bin Laden is unlikely to win the Nobel Prize for Peace, but he should be tried by an International Tribunal like the fate of Milosevic of Yugoslavia, rather than tried by his enemies as Nelson Mandela was.

Above all we need to learn from our disasters, as well as from triumphs. To paraphrase an English poet:

Deign on the passing world
To turn thine eyes
And pause a while from the flag
To be wise.[14]

NOTES

1. This chapter is a revised version of an address at the annual meeting of the Association of Third World Studies held in Savannah, Georgia, October 12-13, 2001.
2. For an overview of the Cold War, consult Michael Kort, *The Columbia Guide to the Cold War* (New York: Columbia University Press, 1998).
3. For overviews of the African stage for the superpower rivalry, see Fred Marte, *Political Cycles in International Relations: The Cold War and Africa, 1945-1990* (Amsterdam: VU University Press, 1994), and Zaki Laidi, *The Superpowers and Africa: The Constraints of a Rivalry, 1960-1990* (Chicago: University of Chicago Press, 1990).
4. For one report lamenting the end of the African "safe haven," see *New African*, 367 (October 1998), pp. 16-17.
5. American (immigrant) Muslims backed Bush in several ways;

for instance, in the 2000 Presidential Elections, a Muslim Political Action Committee endorsed Bush; see the *Christian Science Monitor* (November 2, 2000), p. 18.

6. This issue is discussed in David J. Goldberg, *To the Promised Land: A History of Zionist Thought from its Origins to the Modern State of Israel* (London and New York: Penguin Books, 1996), pp. 83-89.

7. Consult Maloba, *Mau Mau and Kenya* and Marshall S Clough, *Mau Mau Memoirs: History, Memory, And Politics* (Boulder, Colo.: L. Rienner, 1998).

8. The United Nations has objected to the implicit authority claimed by the United States; see the discussion in Jules Lobel and Michael Ratner, "Bypassing the Security Council: Ambiguous Authorizations to Use Force, Cease-Fires and the Iraqi Inspection Regime," *American Journal of International Law*, vol. 93, no. 1, (Jan., 1999), p. 126 and pp. 132-133.

9. An account of the Bush Sr.'s administration's attempts to oppose the settlements may be found in Donald Neff, "Settlements in U.S. Policy," *Journal of Palestine Studies*, vol. 23, no. 3. (Spring, 1994), pp. 62-63. The current Bush Jr. administration appears to be unwilling to "draw a line in the sand" on the Israeli expansion of settlements.

10. At the beginning of the war on terrorism, George W. Bush's popularity was in the 80 percent range.

11. The Vietnamese numbers are controversial. One study has a lower estimate; Charles Hirschmann, Samuel Preston, Manh Loi Vu, "Vietnamese Casualties during the American War: A New Estimate," *Population And Development Review* 21,4 (December 1995), pp. 783-812, estimates the combined Vietnamese toll as approximately one million, with a margin of error of about 175,000 between 1965-1975; the lowest figure is about 415,000 while Hanoi claims there were two million deaths between 1954-1975. In contrast, there were about 58,000 American military fatalities; also see Spencer C. Tucker,ed., *Encyclopedia of the Vietnam War,* Volume One, Santa Barbara,CA: ABC-CLIO, 1998), p. 106.

12. See the report in the *New York Times* (August 18, 1999), p. 8 on Serageldin's candidacy.

13. These lines are stimulated by Samuel Johnson's poem, "The Vanity of Human Wishes," (London, 1749); see J. D. Fleeman, ed., *Samuel Johnson: The Complete English Poems* (New Haven and London: Yale University Press, 1971).
14. These lines are stimulated by Samuel Johnson's poem, "The Vanity of Human Wishes," (London, 1749); see J. D. Fleeman, ed., *Samuel Johnson: The Complete English Poems* (New Haven and London: Yale University Press, 1971).

SECTION TWO

OCCIDENT-ORIENT: THE CULTURAL DIVIDE

CHAPTER FIVE

HAS A CLASH OF CIVILIZATIONS BEGUN?
FROM THE COLD WAR OF IDEOLOGY TO A HOT WAR OF RELIGION

When Harvard Professor Samuel Huntington first published his article "A Clash of Civilisations" in the American journal *Foreign Affairs* in 1993, the idea sounded remote to many people. Muslims especially did not like Huntington's thesis that a confrontation was on the horizon between the West and Islam. Since September 11, 2001, however, it is no longer inconceivable that we are heading for escalating tensions between the United States and its allies, on one side, and much of the Muslim world, on the other.

The Cold War between the Soviet Bloc and NATO was a contest of ideology within the same European civilization and its offshoots. Both American liberal capitalism and Russian communism were born out of European culture. There is now a danger of a hot war of religion to succeed the old Cold War of Ideology. People of good will should try and prevent the new trend between America and its allies, on one side, and such Muslim countries as Iraq, Iran, Libya, Sudan and Somalia.

The Western world as a whole has previously clashed with other civilizations long before the Cold War of Ideology. There was genocide against the native ancient civilizations of the Americas. There was later enslavement of millions of Africans for use in the so-called New World. Thirdly, there was the phase of European imperialism and colonization of most of the world.

The question that arises is whether the fourth phase is that of the United States as an imperial superpower. Is America now a new form of empire, controlling millions of people through a variety of inducements and intimidations? For Kuwait the United States extends the carrot of security against Saddam Hussein's aggression. For Egypt the United States extends a billion dollars a year to keep Egypt out of any military coalition against Israel. For Saddam Hussein the United States wields the stick of military power. For most of the world the United States declares a doctrine of perpetual American supremacy. Never in history has any nation been so far ahead of its nearest rival in economic, military, technological and political power. For better or worse, the United States is truly without a peer—the first among unequals. Let us now take a closer look at these four stages of clash of civilizations and their finale.

FROM GENOCIDE TO GLOBALIZATION

Has Samuel P. Huntington been vindicated by the events of September 11, 2001, and the ensuing Bush war on terrorism? Are we witnessing a clash of civilizations unfolding—especially between the world of Islam and the Western world?

In his article in *Foreign Affairs* in 1993 Huntington had argued that now that the Cold War had ended, future conflicts in world politics would be less and less between states or ideological blocs and more and more between civilizations or coalitions of cultures. The

70

article caused an intellectual explosion at the time. It was debated from New York to Kuala Lumpur and from Cape Town to Stockholm. Since Huntington argued that the most likely civilizational conflict was between the West and Islam, his article was even debated close to Mecca and Medina, with Huntington in attendance. Two years later Samuel Huntington completed a whole book on the subject and published it. Most Muslim and Third World critics of Huntington argued that he got it all wrong. We were not headed for a clash of civilizations. Some insisted that the primacy of the state as the final international actor was not in doubt.

The question arises whether the significance of September 11, 2001, the attacks on the United States, the devastation of Afghanistan, the Israeli onslaught on the Palestinian homeland, the plans to invade Iraq and Somalia, and American troops fighting Muslim militants in the Philippines and former Soviet Georgia, all add up to an unfolding conflict between the United States and its closest allies (Israel and Britain especially) on one side, and more and more Muslim countries, on the other. If that is what has been happening, what has been the role of the media in this unfolding war of nerves? Have the media in the United States been a major theatre of the civilizational conflict? Have the media in Western Europe been part of the healing process between Muslims and Westerners? Or does the Atlantic divide make no difference in the role of the media?

The worst mistake that Huntington made was not conceptual (such as the meaning of "civilization") or factual (whether the role of "the state" would decline). The central error he made was temporal, the assumption that clashes of civilizations were part of the future, rather than inseparable from the past and the present of the human condition. There have been clashes of civilizations between the West and other societies and cultures for at least four hundred years. The stages of these conflicts include the following:

THE GENOCIDAL PHASE OF CLASH OF CIVILIZATION
These were the early years of the European migration and settlement of the Americas. Europeans clashed with civilizations like those

of the Incas and Mayas and effectively destroyed or weakened them. Was there a "world opinion" in that era? Clashes of civilizations are partly about influencing perceptions and constructing stereotypes. In those days, the mass media consisted of the pulpit and church congregations. Distances were long and the time-span of travel immense. The genocides received little criticism from the media of the day.

THE ENSLAVING PHASE OF CLASH OF CIVILIZATIONS

Millions of Africans were exported to North, South and Central America and to the Caribbean. Again there was no such thing as "world opinion." The Print Media was not relevant during the height of enslavement, but it became important during the abolitionist movement. The victims had next to no access to international opinion-formation.

THE IMPERIAL PHASE OF CLASH OF CIVILIZATIONS

The West colonized or semi-colonized more than three quarters of the globe. Westerners settled in some parts of the world, governed in others, and controlled wherever they could.

THE HEGEMONIC GLOBALIZATION PHASE

This is the new phase of America as Empire with worldwide power, the Gulliver of the Globe:
1. Economic Globalization under American dominion.
2. Information globalization under American influence: The Internet, the computer, and the information superhighway
3. Comprehensive globalization as the villagization of the world.
4. One superpower as a security system for the globe.
5. The first among unequals: The United States is so far ahead of its nearest military rival, Russia; its nearest economic rival, Japan; its nearest technological rival, Germany; its nearest linguistic rival, France.

CONTRASTING IMAGES OF ISLAM

Negative	Positive
√ Oppressed women	√ Female Heads of State
√ High Political violence	√ Low street crime
√ International terrorism	√ National terrorism in Sri Lanka, Colombia, Basque Spain, Northern Ireland

THE SINS OF THE PRESS IN THIS ERA OF HEGEMONIC GLOBALIZATION

Clashes of civilizations are also wars of images and the control of opinion. In this hegemonic phase the media are subject to sins.

SINS OF COMMISSION

1. Distortions of stories—such as the American smart weapons during the Gulf War of 1990s
2. Damaging selectivity—such as underplaying "collateral damage" by U.S. dominated news coverage
3. Headlines like "Three Israelis Killed" are common in the American media but never a headline which says "Hundreds of Palestinians feared killed by Israelis"
4. Islam is associated especially with terrorism when in fact the only reason why terrorism by Muslims is widely publicized is because it is international and anti-Western. National terrorism in Sri Lanka, Colombia, the Basque region of Spain, Sierra Leone, and Northern Ireland got far less global publicity.

SINS OF OMISSION

The Taliban story generated comparisons with treatment of women in Saudi Arabia. That was fair enough. However, the gender issue in the Taliban story did not generate contrasts of positive Islamic images—such as the fact that Indonesia, Pakistan, Bangladesh and Turkey have each had a woman Head of Government long before the United States, France, and Russia have had a woman president or Germany had a woman Chancellor. While Muslim countries are more prone to political disturbances than Western, the streets of Muslim cities like Teheran, Cairo and Riyadh are far safer from muggers and rapists than the streets of New York, Detroit and Washington, D.C.

SINS OF SUBMISSION

This sin is submission not to the dictates of the truth but to the warnings of politicians or the demands of advertisers in newspapers or censorship imposed by subscribers to National Public Radio. In my own television series *The African: A Triple Heritage,* PBS in the United States censored my metaphor of Karl Marx as the last of the great Jewish Prophets. PBS was afraid of offending Jewish subscribers and other donors. However, viewers in Britain, continental Europe, Latin America and even Israel heard me describe Marx as "the last of the great Jewish prophets." Another illustration of a sin of submission is when the Bush White House summoned CNN and other network editors to warn them not to replay the Al-Qaeda and Bin Laden videos from the Arab television network *Al-Jazeera.* What happened to editorial independence?

The American Press has also been covering the horrendous story of sexual abuse by some Catholic clergy—priestly pedophilia. In Ariel Sharon's armed forces, there is a tendency that is equally horrendous—a *de-facto pedophobia* against Palestinian youth. This is behavior that causes a lot of damage to children and young people on the West Bank and Gaza Strip. Among Israeli soldiers is a profound dislike of Palestinian youth because it is from among them that suicide bombers are recruited. On the contrary, Palestinian youth are tempted by the martyrdom mystique of the suicide bombers because they are already driven to desperation by humiliation, joblessness, alienation, and brutalization by Israelis and by neglect by fellow Arabs and fellow Muslims.

The Western Press tells us a lot about Catholic priests' *pedophilia.* But there is little mention of Israeli soldiers' *pedophobia* as the soldiers brutalized the Palestinian youth and children. There is also the highly selective use of the word "terrorism." According to Western usage, it is not terrorism if you kill innocent civilians provided you yourself are wearing a uniform, driving a tank and sparing your own life. But it is terrorism if you are prepared to blow yourself up and are not wearing a uniform and you also kill innocent civilians of the other side. "Civilians," yes—but who is innocent on either side? The Israeli government seems to assume that almost no Palestinians is innocent since the militants live among the passive. But why should not Palestinians equally argue that all Israelis of military age—whether in uniform on a particular day or not are part of Israel's continuing war machine?

If Jews blame Germans for electing Hitler, and if Jews find Hitler's supporters accomplices in the Holocaust whether they are civilians or not, why should not Palestinians regard Israeli electors of Ariel Sharon accomplices in the murder of innocent Palestinians? When should democratic electors of brutal rulers be held accountable for the blood those rulers shed? Are Americans in turn accomplices in the killing of Palestinians twice removed? President Bush orders Israeli troops to withdraw from Palestinian towns "NOW." Sharon fails to do so. President Bush congratulates him for being "a man of peace"!! If there was indeed war crimes perpetrated in Jenin in April 2002, was President George W. Bush an accomplice before the fact— or after? Was this a case of the Emperor's New Clothes?" Was Uncle Sam naked as an influence on Israel's behavior? Or was this a case of Uncle Sam winking with his green-eye to give Sharon "the go-ahead?" Are Americans innocent of the massacres perpetrated with their financial knod and their military wink? When is Uncle Sam an accomplice?

THE CULTURAL CONTEXT OF VIOLENCE

We need to distinguish between cultures in which the paramount political value is liberty from cultures in which the paramount political value is dignity. Such cultural differences need not lead to a clash of civilizations, but they can do so if either liberty is collectively denied to those who glorify it or dignity is collectively denied to those who worship it.

Beduin culture in the history of the Arabs had a highly developed mythology and nexus of dignity and honor. These dignitarian concepts penetrated the wider culture of the Arabs, and had enormous consequences on the gender question and issues of war and peace. Arab culture in turn had considerable influence on the religion of Islam worldwide.

Samuel Huntington has argued that there are more violent situations involving Muslims in the world than situations involving members of any other civilization. Huntington does not distinguish between situations where Muslims are primarily victims (as in Chechnya, Kashmir and Palestine) and situations in which Muslims are primarily perpetrators (as in Sudan). In those cases where Muslims are in rebellion against the status quo, a substantial cultural reason for the rebellion is perceived collective indignity. This is true of rebellions of Muslims in Chechnya, Palestine, Macedonia, Kashmir, Kosovo, and even Nigeria

A clash of cultures did occur when President George W. Bush used to the Taliban the macho language of ultimatum and no negotiation over surrendering Usamah bin Laden. "Just hand over Usamah bin Laden and his thugs. There is nothing to talk about." It sounded great to the constituency of George W. Bush—a constituency which admires hard fighting talk from a Warrior President. On the other hand, such language was calculated to humiliate the Taliban. George W. Bush did not give the Taliban any line of dignified retreat. Bush was trying his best to get the Taliban to say "No" to the request for the head of Usamah bin Laden so that Bush could then embark on his long-awaited military action.

If the side of the coalition was using a "good cop, bad cop" strategy on the Taliban, the good cop should have been of the stature of Prime Minister Tony Blair of Great Britain rather than the vulnerable military ruler of Pakistan, General Musharaff. Musharaff was no cop at all. In any case the "good cop, bad cop" style of negotiation does not go well in the full glare of international publicity. George

W. Bush simply was not interested in saving lives by permitting the Taliban room for surrendering Al-Qaeda militants with some semblance of dignity. The old Chinese concept of "saving face" has its Islamic equivalent of dignified surrender. A similar story happens to Iraq under Saddam Hussein. The threat of weapons of mass destruction from North Korea seemed as real as the threat from Iraq. But North Korea is tempted more with carrots than threatened with sticks by the United States. Iraq was threatened with sticks and almost never tempted with carrots.

By the 20th century women in the Muslim world were accorded more dignity and less liberty than women in the West. And women in the West were correspondingly accorded more liberty than dignity than women in the Muslim world. In the Muslim world there was far less prostitution than in the West, far less use of female sex appeal to sell commercial products, almost no beauty competitions in the Muslim world, and too much protection of women from the rat race of the market place.

Sons in the Muslim world respect their mothers more than sons in the West—because Muslim mothers are accorded higher dignity. But husbands in the Muslim world respect their wives less than husbands in the West—because Muslim wives enjoy less liberty.

If the Western world has a nexus of liberty, its center in the course of the 20th century become the United States. The Muslim world has always had a nexus of dignity—and the center of the Muslim world has for centuries been the Middle East. Throughout much of the first half of the twentieth century the United States stood up for the dignity of the colonized people of the Muslim world elsewhere. Even as late as the 1960s, John F. Kennedy as President was emphasizing that "Africa was for the Africans"—and not for entrenched white settler interests and white minority governments. The Americans saw their anti-colonialism as a defense of liberty everywhere. But the fight against European colonialism and racism was above all a struggle for human dignity.

Meanwhile, a Jewish state had been created in a region that for a thousand years had been overwhelmingly Muslim. What is more, it was created in ways that violated dignity. There was an ethnic cleansing which displaced thousands of Palestinians to make room for Jews. An ideology was put in place in which someone from the Ukraine who claims to have had a Jewish ancestor two thousand years ago had more right under Israel's Law of Return than a Palestinian who ran away from within the Israeli borders in 1948. No wonder there had been a raging debate as to whether Zionism is a form of racism.

To add insult to injury (and "insult" is offensive to dignity) the new State of Israel turned out to be militarily brilliant and capable of inflicting one humiliating defeat after another to people sensitive to issues of dignity. And just when European colonialism and occupation of Arab and Muslim lands was coming to an end, an alien expansionist power was created in the heartland of the Arab nation. What is more, the Jewish state was protected by the West from the odium of being called either "colonialist" or "imperialist." Yet in reality more people have been killed in the fight against Zionism and Israeli occupation than were killed in the fight against British colonialism in Africa in the preceding fifty years. The Nazis in Germany had once refused to recognize Jews as proper children of Western civilization. The tragedy for the Jews in Israel today is that they are regarded by Arabs as nothing but children of Western civilization—in all its aggressive imperfections. The Nazis would not let the Jew wear the badge of Western identity. The Arabs would not let the Israeli take off that Western badge of identity.

Hercule Poirot—Agatha Christie's Belgian detective—has repeatedly reminded us that part of the explanation as to why a murder has been committed lies in the victim. A central clue towards solving a premeditated murder investigation lies in knowing more about the victim. We have been so busy trying to understand what is wrong with the terrorists that we hardly ever ask whether there is anything sufficiently provocative in Western behavior to make those of us who live in the West the targets of international terrorism. We shall never understand the causes of international terrorism unless we also ask why they are picking on the West. What is wrong with the targets of terrorism can never be a moral excuse for the terrorism, but it

78

may be part of the objective explanation. The Western world is powerful. "The vices of the powerful acquire some of the prestige of power." The West is not only a target of terrorism from time to time. The West has also been a role model of violence across the generations.

CHAPTER SIX

PAX ISLAMICA
MUSLIM VALUES BETWEEN WAR AND PEACE

Two concepts have been important in the history of war in Muslim experience—the medieval distinction between *Dār al-Ḥarb* (the Abode of war) and *Dār al-Islām* (the Abode of Islam). An even more ancient relationship has been between *Jihād* (the sacred struggle in the path of God) and *Shahīd* (the martyr as a sacrifice to God). All these four concepts have influenced perceptions of war in the Muslim imagination.

Three other concepts have been important in the history of *peace* in Muslim experience—*Dār al-Ṣulḥ* (the Abode of Contractual Peace or Peaceful coexistence), the Qur'ānic principle *"lā ikrāha fi 'd-dīn"* ("There is no compulsion in religion") and the ecumenical principle of *ahl al-Kitāb* (the people of the Book).

Contrary to popular Western perceptions, *jihād* does not mean "holy war." But it does mean "sacred struggle." The struggle can be armed struggle or peaceful striving, a struggle against others or against demons in oneself, a physical struggle or an intellectual one, a self-regarding struggle or an other-regarding confrontation. A struggle in the path of God (*fī sabīli 'lāh*) can be a *jihād* for peace rather than against peace. It is not a contradiction for a *mujāhid* (or a jihadist) to be in quest of peace. The Islamist goal could be peace rather than the establishment of an Islamic state, for example.

An armed *jihād* of Muslim against Muslim is widely regarded as inadmissible, but an armed *jihād* of Arab against Arab is a return to the origins of warfare in Muslim history. The November 2003 bombing of a residential complex in Riyāḍ was Islamically reprehensible because, first it was an act of naked terrorism; secondly, it used suicide as the means of implementation; third, it was Muslim against Muslim; and fourthly it was perpetrated during the holy month of Ramadhan.

The fact that the bombing in Riyadh was Arab against Arab was not Islamically significant, even if it was politically fundamental. The very first armed *jihāds* in Muslim history, including the Battle of Badr during the Prophet's own lifetime, were basically Arab against Arab. They were between newly Islamized Arabs on one side, and Arabs hostile to Islam, on the other. In other words, the very first armed *jihāds* in the history of Islam were basically inter-Arab civil wars.

Those who bombed the Riyadh residential complex in November 2003 may have seen themselves as engaged in a modern version of the Battle of Badr—a *jihād* in the path of God. Doctrinally it was not really a *jihād*. But politically it could have been a harbinger of an Arab civil war. As a civil war it echoed the Battle of Badr but not as a *jihād*.

WAR AND INTER-RELIGIOUS RELATIONSHIPS

As for the medieval distinction between *Dār al-Ḥarb* (the Abode of War) and *Dār al-Islām* (the Abode of Islam), these were geographically overlapping categories. In *Dār al-Islām* amity and cooperation on Islamic principles were supposed to prevail—and *Pax Islamica* was triumphant. *Dār al-Islām* included not only Muslims but also non-Muslims under the protection of *Pax Islamica*. They were protected against internal insecurity and external aggression.

Dār al-Ḥarb was not necessarily an arena of direct military confrontation. It comprised lands of non-Muslims who were often hostile to Islam, constituting the sort of situation which the English philosopher Thomas Hobbes was much later to describe as a "state of war," a state without a shred sovereign. Muslim jurists after the Prophet Muhammed developed the concept of *Dār al-Ḥarb* in relation to countries that did not agree on the sovereignty of God.

But over the centuries it became clear that the arena of *Dār al-Ḥarb* was to be conceived in degrees of relationships. We came to know that religions could relate to each other under different degrees of amity or enmity. By the twentieth century inter-religious peaceful co-existence could be illustrated by the relationship between Islam and Buddhism, in spite of the Taliban's destruction of the huge monuments of the Buddha, and in spite of the relationship of Buddhists and Muslims in Thailand. On the whole Muslims do not feel any antipathy towards Buddhists as adherents of a different belief-system.

In addition to inter-religious peaceful co-existence, there is inter-religious rivalry. This is particularly relevant to Christianity and Islam, in areas like Africa where they are in competition for the soul of a continent. Since Christianity and Islam see themselves as universalist religions intended for the entire human race, they are often caught up in competitive proselytism and competitive evangelism.

The third kind of inter-religious relationship is adversarial. In South Asia Hinduism and Islam have become adversarial, mainly because of the consequences of the British Raj and of the partition of India in the wake of decolonization.

Since the creation of the state of Israel Islam and Judaism have also become adversarial partly because of the displacement of Palestinians to accommodate Jews, partly because of Jewish expansionism beyond Palestine, such as the annexation of the Golan Heights, partly because of the brutal Israeli occupation and colonization of the Palestinians and partly because of the debate about competitive sovereignty over Jerusalem as a sacred city for Jews, Christians and Muslims.

In addition to religious relationships of co-existence, rivalry, and adversary, is there a religious relationship of cooperation? Samuel Huntington, in his clash of civilization thesis, has been concerned about cooperation between the world of Islam and the world of Confucianism in China and its extensions in East Asia. Is there room for special kinds of cooperation between China and the Muslim world?

The fifth type of inter-religious relationship is religious interpenetration. This is the relationship between Islam and indigenous religions, such as the ancestral creeds of Black Africa. While Christianity and Islam are mutually exclusive religions in that one cannot be both a Muslim and a Christian at the same time, Islam and African traditional religions are often syncretized. Many Africans are at one and the same time both Muslim and believers in African Yoruba religion or African Bantu religions. In Indonesia there may also be syncretism between Islam and neo-Hindu continuities. More purist Muslims may not accept sociological syncretism, but historically Muḥammad's own Islam was Judaism, Christianity and the special distinctive message of Muḥammad, peace be upon him.

IN SEARCH OF ECUMENICAL TOLERANCE

This concept of a synthesis of the teachings of Moses, Jesus and Muḥammad is part of the ecumenical message of Islam. Islam is a fusion of three religious traditions—Judaic, Christian and Muḥammadist. In a sense, Islam has more in common with Judaism and Christianity than Christianity and Judaism have with each other. Islam accepts Jesus as the Messiah *(al-Masīḥ)*, but Judaism does not. Islam accepts the miracle of the arrival of Jesus through the virgin birth—but Judaism does not. Islam attributes more miracles to Jesus (such as miraculous healing of the sick) than Islam attributes to the

Prophet Muḥammad, but Judaism conceded no such prophetic miracles to Jesus. Islam accepts the physical bodily ascent to heaven of Jesus at the end of his earthly career, but Judaism does not. Doctrinally, Islam is the religion that bridges the gulf between the Old Testament and the New, between the legacy of Moses and the heritage of Jesus.

Out of this fusion of Moses, Jesus and Muḥammad in Islam there developed the concept of *ahl al-Kitāb*, or the people of the Book. Jews and Christians were regarded as monotheistic brothers and sisters to Muslims, with special bonds of solidarity. A Muslim could marry a Jew or Christian without conversion provided the children were brought up as Muslims. In Muslim history, Jews and Christians rose high to positions of political power and influence.

Right up to modern times Boutros Boutros-Ghali—a Christian married to a Jew—could rise high enough in the Egyptian foreign service to be eligible for election as Secretary General of the United Nations. In Saddam Hussein's Iraq, Tareq Aziz—a Christian—could be Foreign Minister and later Deputy Prime Minister. No Christian country in the Western world has ever permitted a Muslim to rise as high as Foreign Minister, let alone Deputy Prime Minister. And yet the percentage of Muslims in European countries like France or Russia is higher than the proportion of Christians in Iraq or even Egypt.

In Africa the concept of *ahl al-Kitāb* as an organizing ecumenical principle has been carried further than anywhere else. In Senegal the percentage of Muslims is higher than the percentage of Muslims in Egypt. Senegal is at least 94% Muslim—which is higher than the percentage of Muslims in Egypt. And yet for twenty years (from 1960 to 1980) Senegal had a Roman Catholic President, Léopold Sédar Senghor, without demonstrations in the streets of Dakar proclaiming *Jihād fī Sabīl Allāh* (*Jihād* in the path of God).

This was followed from 1980 to 2000 by a Muslim president of Senegal, Diouf, married to a Christian First Lady. Imagine one of the presidential candidates in the United States admitting on LARRY KING LIVE that he or she was engaged to a Shī'ite Muslim. That would bury his or her chances in the primaries—and certainly in the general elections.

Neither Christianity nor Judaism has a doctrine of *ahl al-Kitāb*. I do not expect a Muslim Vice-President of the United States or Muslim Chief Executive of any of a continental European country, in the foreseeable future. As for a Muslim Prime Minister of Israel, that is virtually a contradiction in terms. A Jewish state cannot possibly have a Christian, let along a Muslim, Prime Minister. Yet Tanzania has had a virtual religious rotation of the Head of State—Christian Julius K. Nyerere, Muslim Ali Hassan Mwinyi, Christian Benjamin Mkapa and hypothetically Muslim Salim Ahmed Salim in the future.

The United States—deprived of the doctrine of *ahl al-Kitāb*—has never had a non-Christian President, not even a Jew. Indeed, the United States has only once departed from the Protestant fraternity for President. It was not even clear that John F. Kennedy—like George W. Bush—was really elected. We only know they became Presidents.

Combined with the ecumenical principles of *ahl al-Kitāb* (people of the Book) is the tolerant principle of *lā ikrāha fi 'd-dīn* (there is no compulsion in religion), which is part of the Qur'ān itself. Again the Arabs as the first Muslims have implemented that imperative of religious tolerance less well than have other Muslims in other parts of the world.

In Africa a father may be a Sunni Muslim, the wife a follower of indigenous religion, while two daughters are Bahai, two sons are Roman Catholic, and the oldest Son is a Shī'ite Muslim. The supreme ecumenical family is to be found in Black Africa. While Idi Amin was a Muslim President of Uganda, he did consider having one of his sons trained for the priesthood in the Roman Catholic Church without butting an eyelid. Idi Amin's ecumenicalism was perhaps extreme, but it was symptomatic of Africa's religious openness.

On Martyrdom: Submissive and Combative

As for *Shahīd* (martyr) as a Muslim concept, it is often related to *mujāhid* who has paid with his life (or her life), for the cause:

Qad māta shahīdan man māta fidā'an li 'llāh.
He has died a martyr he who has died as a gift to God.

However, within the concept of martyrdom, there are two subdivisions. Submissive martyrdom is a martyrdom of resignation. The classic illustration is the Christian account of the death of Jesus. According to Christian tradition, Jesus carried the very cross on which he was to be crucified. Apart from a brief moment of weakness when, from the cross, he cried out to God "Why have you forsaken me?" Jesus according to Christian tradition accepted his crucifixion as "mission accomplished."

Although Muslims revere Jesus as a great prophet of Islam, they do not believe he was crucified:

Wa mā qatalūhu wa mā ṣalabūhu wa lākin shubbiha lahum.
They did not kill him, they did not crucify him. It was only made to appear so.

Nevertheless, the Christian version of the death of Jesus is a classic example of martyrdom with resignation. When less than a century later, Peter the Apostle was sentenced by the Roman Emperor Nero to die by crucifixion, St. Peter was ecstatic. "To die as the Lord did? It is more than I deserve." Tradition has it that Peter was crucified in 55 A.D. in Rome. This was another great illustration of submissive martyrdom. Nero seems to have crucified him upside down to deny him full comparison with Jesus.

Combative martyrdom, on the other hand, is when a believer dies as part of a combat to defend either his religious beliefs of his religious identity. Muslim populations under direct military occupation right now include Iraq, Afghanistan, Palestine, Kashmir, Chechnya and Kosovo. Many of the casualties in combat are seen as *mujāhidīn,* jihadists, each of which becomes a martyr when killed.

In terms of killing, Muslims are a people currently more sinned against than sinning. Since the Iraq war began thousands more Iraqis have been killed than have members of coalition forces. In the last three years, hundreds more Palestinians have been killed than Israelis, hundreds more Chechens than Russians, hundreds more Kashmiris than Indian forces, thousands more Afghans than members of coalition forces. Many of the dead in these victimized Muslim societies are seen as combative martyrs. This is quite apart from Muslims who were herded into concentration camps in Bosnia in the 1990s and Muslims in Kosovo who were brutalized by the Serbs until the North Atlantic Treaty Organization decided to intervene. World coverage of Muslim news tends to portray Muslims as the aggressors against other people—when in fact Muslims are more often victims rather than villains.

Suicide as a mode of combat has now taken new forms. But in principle combative suicide is not something new. Jewish mythology traces it to at least the Biblical Samson who brought the whole temple down knowing it would kill him, his enemies and a lot of bystanders. Israel's decision to go to nuclear has been described as "the Samson option." If necessary Israel would be prepared to fight a nuclear war and bring the whole region of the Middle East down, including itself—rather than abandon the principle of a Jewish state. It would be a form of collective combative suicide writ large. Another glorified ancient suicide in Jewish history is Masada, the site of the final Jewish resistance to the Romans after the fall of the Temple. In the year 70 of the Christian era the final Jewish defenders are said to have committed suicide as a final direct challenge to the Romans. In present day Israel Masada is idealized and glorified and is a popular site for both religious tourists and Israeli patriots.

THE GENDER OF WAR AND TERROR

"Terrorism" is a new word, but the deliberate killing of innocent civilians, almost at random, is a much older phenomenon. Certainly terrorism perpetrated by rulers or the state goes back to Gengis Khan, the Mongols and beyond. Large-scale terror in the twentieth century flourished under the Nazis and under Stalinist Russia.

Neither Islam nor Judaism nor Christianity deals with "terrorism" as we know the concept today. Islam is clearer in forbidding the killing of women and children than in forbidding the killing of men who are perceived as threats. Although the Prophet Muhammad's widow 'Ā'ishah set the precedent of Muslim women in combat roles on the battlefield there is general consensus among Muslim jurists that killing women or children is beyond the pale. This has to be seen in the context of three varieties of sexism evident in human behavior, not uniquely Islamic. Benevolent sexism is a form of gender discrimination that selectively favors the otherwise disadvantaged gender. For example, when in 1912 the captain of the Titanic decided that the limited space on the lifeboats was to be reserved for women and children, that was a form of benevolent sexism with which most cultures would agree. The safety of women and children come first.

Most cultures would also agree that while women may have a duty to die for their faith or for their country, women do not have a duty to kill for their faith or their country. Even in the West drafting women for direct combat has been culturally repugnant. Forcing women to go and kill has tended to be avoided in most cultures, including Western and Islamic.

In spite of 'Ā'ishah's role in the Battle of the Camel, benevolent sexism in Islam has spared women obligatory combat roles. In addition to benevolent sexism, there is benign sexism. This benign sexism is of differentiation rather than of discrimination. A policy of different dress codes for men and women has been part of the sexism of differentiation in Islam. There are different rules of modesty for male and female. In most cultures women are expected to cover more of their bodies than men. Malignant sexism is another kind of sexism. This is the kind of gender discrimination that results in sexual exploitation, economic marginalization, cultural subordination or political disempowerment. Although many Muslim countries are guilty of such versions of malignant sexism, there are paradoxes in the Muslim world. In no Muslim country are women more liberated than women are in the United States, but in some Muslim countries women have been more empowered than women have been in the United States.

Right now two Muslim countries have women as heads of state or heads of government. Indonesia, the largest Muslim country in population, has a woman as President—Megawati Soekarnoputri. In Bangladesh, both the Head of Government and the leader of the Opposition have been women—Sheikh Hassina and Begum Khalida Zia have alternated in political power for more than a decade. Two other Muslim countries have had a woman chief executive at the top of the political process. Benazir Bhutto has been Prime Minister of Pakistan twice. And Ms. Ciller has been Prime Minister of Turkey. All these cases of Muslim women at the top have occurred long before the United States has had a woman president, or Germany a woman Chancellor, or Italy a woman Prime Minister, or Russia a woman President.

While serving as heads of government, such Muslim women in those countries have been *de facto* Commanders-in-Chief. Were they continuing in the tradition of the Prophet's widow 'A'ishah in the middle of the Battle of the Camel way back in the fist century of the Hijrah calendar, the seventh century of the Christian era?

Have any of these Muslim women in power had to contend with terrorism by fellow Muslims? Bangladesh has had conflicts, coups and assassinations over the years, but neither Sheikh Hassina in power nor Begum Khalida Zia has had to fight terrorism. On the other hand, Megawati Soekarnoputri in Indonesia has been under enormous pressure to act against Islamic militants, especially since the devastating terrorist bombs in the resort town of Bali.

Muslims are not unique in resorting to terrorism in a bid to redress wrongs perpetrated against them. However, terrorism by Muslims gets far more publicity as a rule than terrorism by others. What all cultures and all religions are being forced to scrutinize more closely than ever are the detailed ethics of terrorism. One possible framework for such scrutiny could be the following:

TERRORISM: THE MEANS AND ENDS CRITERIA
1. Terrorism Heroic:
    a. Goals are more than legitimate. They are laudatory, like defending one's faith or one's country.
    b. Means are illegitimate.
2. Terrorism Horrific:
    a. Goals are illegitimate and perhaps even evil (like defending a tyrant or an evil ideology).
    b. Means are illegitimate and perhaps evil.

CRITERIA OF COMPARATIVE INSPIRATION
1. Inspiration
    a. Racially inspired terrorism (like Ku Klux Klan).
    b. Religiously inspired terrorism (like Al-Qaeda, Irish Republican Army).
    c. Nationalistically inspired terrorism (Serbs in Bosnia).
    d. Ideologically inspired terrorism (Marxist or Fascist inspiration).
2. Agency of Terror
    a. Individual agency—(e.g. Palestinian suicide bombers).
    b. Radical movement—Al-Qaeda, Irish Republican Army.
    c. State Terrorism—Stalinism in USSR, the Nazis in Hitler's Germany, Israel under Sharon.

SYSTEMIC VERSUS EPISODIC TERROR
1. Systemic
    a. Nazi Germany as a system of terror
    b. Stalin's USSR as a system of terror
    c. Apartheid in South Africa as a system of terror
    d. North Korea as a system of terror
2. Episodic
    a. Israeli acts of targeted assassinations
    b. Palestinian suicide bombers
    c. New American culture of assassinations

    d.   African National Congress and necklace executions, in apartheid South Africa

NEW FORMS OF TERRORISM

1.   One form of terrorism is taking advantage of disproportionate technological superiority or disproportionate disparity of scale, such as using state of the art surface-to-surface rocket against 3 African warriors with spears. US shares with traditional terrorists the tendency to prefer soft targets. American conventional might against Iraq was the equivalent of a surface-to-surface rocket against three warriors with spears. The last time the USA challenged a country approximating equality of power was with the USSR over the Cuban missile crisis in 1962. USA is now drifting towards becoming a global empire of technological terror.

2.   Unmanned American weapons or unmanned American aircraft used against defenseless adversaries is in principle also a form of terror.

3.   "Innocent civilians"—not all civilians are innocent. Apart from children, are there any innocent civilians left in Israel? Are Palestinian suicide bombers terrorists or soldiers? In or out of uniform, almost every adult Israeli is "an enemy combatant."

A CONCLUSION

The whole world is now becoming *Dār al-Ḥarb*, the abode of war. Muslims have been targeted by Muslims almost on the outskirts of Mecca. The victims are sometimes perceived as traitors to Islam. As the United States emerges as a new kind of global empire, ready to use its military might repeatedly against such Muslim countries as Iraq, Afghanistan, Libya, Sudan and potentially Syria and Iran, the ultimate *Dār al-Ḥarb* (the abode of war) has become the American Empire.

Ironically, President Bush is emerging with a dichotomy of his own. To him *Dār al-Ḥarb*, the abode of potential war and instability, are the countries without democracy. The new doctrine of George W. Bush is that the world is divided between the Abode of Democracy, where there need be no conflict, and the Abode of War, where democracy has yet to take root. American political scientists are giving the Bush doctrine intellectual ammunition. Political scientists have been making the case that democratic countries do not go to war against each other. Democracies may commit aggression against non-democracies, but American political science is fuelling the thesis that democracies do not militarily fight each other.

Muslims who enunciated the old dichotomy between *Dār al-Ḥarb* and *Dār al-Islām* used to believe that only when the whole world was Islamized would there be world peace. The Bush doctrine today argues that only when the whole world is democratized will there be world peace. While we wait, however, democracies reserve the right to declare war on non-democracies whenever democracies feel like it. Unfortunately the non-democracies that are most vulnerable to such Western military initiatives are now disproportionately Muslim countries. Between the Gulf War of 1991 and the Iraq War of 2003, over a million Muslims have been killed either by direct Western military action, or through Israeli action, or by increasing Muslim infant mortality through Western economic sanctions, as was the case in Iraq for twelve years.

If the main theatres of war are now in Muslim lands, has *Dār al-Islām* now become indistinguishable from *Dār al-Ḥarb?* Have the two concepts entirely merged? Both the old medieval dichotomy of Muslim jurists and the new Bush doctrine of *Dār al-Democraciyyah* have to go back to the drawing board of history. As the poet put it:

> The blood of experience meanders on
> In the vast expanse of the valley of time
> The new is come and the old has gone
> And life abides a changing clime.
> Let the drums of war be silent;
> Let the bells of peace be eloquent;—;
> And let the song of justice be heard.

CHAPTER SEVEN

TERRORISM
AND THE GLOBAL IMAGE OF ISLAM
POWER, PASSION AND PIETY

O f all developing areas of the globe, the Muslim world has been both vital to the survival of Western power and a great threat to the persistence of Western hegemony or domination. Western power depends disproportionately on Muslim oil. Western domination is threatened disproportionately by Muslim resistance. The organization of the Petroleum Exporting Countries (OPEC) is two thirds Muslim in composition. It includes two of the biggest oil reserves in the world—Saudi Arabia and Iraq. It also includes Islam's most populous country—Indonesia. Africa's OPEC members include Nigeria, Libya, Algeria and (most of the time) Gabon. These OPEC members are primarily Muslim.

With regard to resistance to Western hegemony, Islam has also been unique. No civilization has more persistently challenged Western planetary domination than Islam has done. Some civilizations dominated by the West are older than Islam—such as the Indian civilizations of South Asia and the Chinese/Confucian civilization of the so-called Far East. But no culture in Africa or Asia has been more of a thorn into the skin of Western imperialism than Muslim resistance.

God chose the sacred land of Saudi Arabia as a ground and pre-eminent reservoir of oil for the human race. But has God also chosen Al-Qaeda as a Saudi vanguard of a global *jihād?*

COUNTER-TERRORISM AND GLOBAL APARTHEID

What are the reasons for the great Muslim resistance to Western hegemony? There are a number of factors that have contributed to Muslim readiness to take on the West. Among them is the nature of the emerging global apartheid. The greatest economic victims of global apartheid are Black people everywhere; the greatest military victims are Muslims across the globe. Political apartheid in South Africa has been dismantled; economic and military apartheid on a global scale are alive and well.

Black people are economic victims because of the exploitation of their resources by others; because of unrelenting poverty, destitution and disease; because of the crippling debt crisis threatening the survival of African economies, and because of the marginalizing consequences of globalization for Africa.

Muslims across the world are military victims of the new global apartheid because their resistance against injustice provokes superior fire power against them. The Administration of George W. Bush has already bombed and partially occupied two Muslim countries—Afghanistan and Iran. Members of the Bush Administration have made threatening noises against two other Muslim countries—Iran and Syria.

The image of Muslims across the world is often that of a people who commit atrocious acts of violence. But please look closely, who is killing whom? The number of Muslims who have been killed in

Afghanistan by the American invasion and its aftermath is several times the number of Americans killed at the World Trade Center on September 11, 2001. The number of Iraqis killed in this year's American war on Iraq, both civilian and those in uniform, is unlikely to be less than twenty thousand. In the West Bank and Gaza, the Israelis continue to kill several Palestinians for every Israeli killed. It is a military confrontation totally unequal in power.

Are Muslims more sinned against than sinning? They certainly are in the Middle East. Further north in Chechnya Russian continue to kill Chechens disproportionately. In Kashmir Hindu soldiers kill more Kashmiris than the other way round. Throughout the 1990s Muslims were butchered by Serbs or sometimes herded like cattle into concentration camps. Before the Kosovo war Albanian Muslims were being brutalized by Serb forces under Milosovich. In the Ivory Coast Muslim claims for a fairer distribution of power has provoked a military response, with consequences for both sides. In Africa the only country in which Muslims are more aggressors than victims is the Sudan. Almost everywhere else in Africa Muslims are discriminated against as a minority (as in Kenya) or denied political power commensurate with their numbers (as in Ethiopia, Nigeria and possibly Tanzania). It is in that sense that Muslims across the globe are more sinned against than sinning. All these forces have contributed to extensive Muslim rage and anger, especially against the Western world, whose policies have usually contributed to the sufferings of Muslim people internationally.

Terrorism in postcolonial Kenya has almost never been targeted against Kenyans. It has been targeted at Americans and Israelis. Many Kenyans have died in the crossfire. In order to kill a dozen Americans in August 1998, terrorists killed some two hundred Kenyans. And in order to kill a handful of Israelis at the Paradise Hotel in Mombasa in November 2002, terrorists killed three times as many Kenyans. We are caught up in other people's wars and conflicts. We are being drafted to combat terrorists, but we are given no say in determining the *causes* of terrorism. The more we become part of America's shield against terrorism, the more we may become *targets* of external anti-American terrorist attacks.

What is more, the money we receive from the United States to combat terrorism may tempt our security forces to show results, however spurious. How are we going to use the coming millions of dollars against terrorism? One type of demonstration is to arrest bearded Muslims, or people in Muslim attire or *wananchi* (the average citizens) with Muslim names.

LEGISLATING AGAINST CIVIL LIBERTIES

During the years of the Cold War our liberties were compromised because the West was in conflict with the Communist world. People went to jail for possession of *The Communist Manifesto*. Kenyans in possession of the works of Mao Tse Tung were liable to prosecution. I once saw in a Nairobi dustbin a beautiful gold-bound edition of the works of Mao. I hesitated between the imperative of a scholar to resist the banning of books and the imperative of a citizen to obey the law of the land. Should I now plead the Fifth Amendment against self-incrimination?

If today I saw a work by Usamah bin Laden in a Nairobi dustbin, or a beautiful framed painting of Saddam Hussein on a heap of garbage, should I dare rescue them? Or would I be taking the same risk as I considered taking when I looked at Mao's beautiful edition in the 1970s? In the years of the Cold War under both Kenyatta and Moi, possession of communist literature was often regarded as proof that one was a communist. In the new dispensation after September 11, 2001, is possession of an Al-Qaeda document proof that one is a terrorist?

The trouble with all new African legislation against terrorism is the simple issue of definition—what is a terrorist? Many people are still convinced that one man's terrorist is another's freedom fighter. Was Dedan Kimathi of Mau Mau a terrorist? Is Robert Mugabe in Zimbabwe a former terrorist? Nelson Mandela lost twenty-seven of the best years of his life ostensibly for involvement in "communist terrorism." Is Ahmed Ben Bella, former Algerian leader, and an ex-terrorist in the war of independence fought against France? Was Menachem Begin, the late Prime Minister of Israel, a terrorist against the British mandate in Palestine? There are even debates as to whether Prime Minister Sharon currently in power is himself a terrorist of a different kind. On the other hand, the Kenyan Suppression of Terrorism Bill 2003 turns almost every crime of violence into terrorism. Terrorism is the

use or threat of action which
(1) involves serious violence against a person;
(2) involves serious damage to property;
(3) endangers the life of any person other than the person committing the action....

The word terrorism loses its meaning when it seems to include robbery with the use of a weapon, lovers threatening each other, a crime of passion by a jealous husband. "Terrorism" in the Kenyan draft is a catch-all phrase. We might as well abolish all other criminal laws and have only one law—against "terrorism." There is also considerable threat to civil liberties in the Bill. Under President Daniel arap Moi Kenyans could demonstrate against the American war on Afghanistan without the risk of being accused of supporting the Taliban as a so-called terrorist government.

Even on the more recent war on Iraq Members of Parliament in Nairobi could protest against the war without risking being identified with Saddam Hussein's Ba'ath Party. But the new Kenyan bill is so wide-ranging that the police or the Minister can decide which kind of public demonstrations constituted support for terrorist forces abroad. The particular protest T-shirt a demonstrator wears could be a punishable offense. Or a Muslim elder in robes and a long beard could be regarded as suspicious.

We have all seen pictorial representations of pictures of Jesus Christ. In churches we have seen statues or statuettes of Jesus on the Cross. We have seen movies about Jesus Christ. Jesus had a long beard, and long hair, and often wore robes very much like Muslim robes today. If Jesus walked in the streets of Nairobi with his long beard and Arab-style robes, he would be liable to arrest as a potential terrorist under Kenya's anti-terrorist legislation. Jewish dress and Arab dress were very similar before the Jews were Diasporized and Westernized. The Kenya Bill says that a person who, in a public place, (a) wears an item of clothing or (b) wears, carries or displays an article

> in such a way .... as to arouse reasonable suspicion that he is a member or supporter of a declared terrorist organization shall be guilty of an offense and shall be liable on conviction to imprisonment for a fine not exceeding six months, or to a fine or both.

A Kenyan police officer encountering bearded Jesus Christ in robes near the Norfolk Hotel, Nairobi, could stop him and say, *"Wee, unakwende wapi na ndevu zako?"* ("You! Where do you think you are going with your beard?") An American police officer confronting bearded Jesus could say, "Stop! You have a right to remain silent!" It is worth remembering that Jesus Christ and the Prophet Muḥammad of Islam wore very similar clothes although they were separated by more than five centuries. The Prophet Muḥammad near the Norfolk Hotel would be liable to similar police challenge on grounds of his clothes and beard—if this new anti-terrorist legislation was passed.

In South Africa, the citizens have also been debating anti-terrorist legislation. The South African bill is denounced by its critics as being more anti-terrorist than the laws of the State of Israel—a country that is confronted with political violence almost constantly. South Africa's constitution is the most liberal in the world. Will anti-terrorist legislation destroy its liberal uniqueness? Tanzania passed anti-terrorist legislation with almost no debate in Parliament. In fact the evidence seems to show that Parliament was virtually gagged by the Executive Branch, which in turn was under great pressure from the Americans. The United States was once a force for the democratization of the world. But the new American war on terrorism is beginning to undo that democratization. The United States under the Bush Administration has been eroding its own democratic traditions. Detention without trial—once notorious under colonial and postcolonial dictatorships in the Third World—is now practiced with impunity by the United States. The old Soviet Union used to have Siberia for its worst gulags. The United States has Guantanamo Bay in Cuba as its own gulag of prisoners denied of justice or legal protection.

Under the Patriot Act in the United States my librarian in Binghamton, New York, may be called upon by the FBI to monitor what books I read. The librarian is forbidden to tell me that the FBI is tracking my reading patterns. George Orwell in his book 1984 warned us about a system in which "big brother is watching." Since September 11 such an Orwellian system has been creeping into the United States. The United States may or may not have a right to damage its own democracy in exchange for its own security. Does it have a right to damage the fragile democracies of African countries—in exchange for American security rather than Africa's own well being?

Uganda may need mediation of a kind to help it find a longer-term resolution of its North-South divide. The divide has so far been a stubborn cause of instability and social injustice. Pax Africana Oriental needs to be internalized to deal with domestic tensions within countries. Pax Africana is the kind of peace that is protected, kept or enforced by Africans themselves.

Should Somalia be persuaded to let Somaliland go amicably and become a separate country? This world enables Somaliland to seek international recognition and find its own seat in the African Union and at the United Nations. Somaliland would undergo a more peaceful "Eritrean" style of separation—without the risk of a conflict with the parent country. Former Italian Somaliland needs to be persuaded to let go of former British Somaliland, and let the two become separate states once again.

BETWEEN PAX AFRICANA AND PAX AMERICANA

Peace is disturbed in Africa not always for reasons internal to Africa. Conflicts abroad have often had huge repercussions in Africa. It is still not clear how many Kenyans were involved in the anti-Israeli terrorism which was perpetrated on the Israeli hotel, The Paradise, in my hometown of Mombasa in November 2002. Four times as many Kenyans died as did Israelis. Was it one more moment of convergence between the politics of the Middle East and politics of Islam in Africa?

Here we must distinguish between terrorism at the national level, on the one hand, and international terrorism, on the other. Kenya had won its independence partly as a result of a liberation war that included terrorism at the national level. Both the British colonial forces and the Mau Mau movement resorted to terrorism at the national level in a colonial war. What is different about terrorism in the Middle East is that it is international, intercontinental, and especially targeted at a global super power and its protégé, Israel. In response to the convergence between anti-Americanism and anti-Zionism, some leaders are looking for an alliance between Pax Africana and Pax Americana.

The Israel-Palestinian conflict has been a cause for today's international terrorism. Speedier action is needed to solve the Israeli-Palestinian conflict, both for its own sake, and because it has ramifications and repercussions which destabilize other parts if the world. It is not enough to fight terrorists. It is more fundamental to address the causes of terrorism. Brutal Israeli occupation of Palestinians is a central cause of Mid-East related terrorism.

CONCLUSION

If we place Pax Africana alongside Pax Americana, striking contrasts emerge. Pax Africana is intra-continental, with the African region as the primary arena of peacekeeping; Pax Americana is intercontinental with a global reach. Dimensions of collective love are in confrontation. Pax Africana is militarily weak; Pax Americana is under the auspices of the greatest military power in human history, the Untied States of America. Pax Africana is trying to cope with postcolonial instability, while Pax Americana is trying to deal with post-Cold War uncertainties. Pax Africana is often involved in fragile state building, while Pax Americana is vulnerable to political violence by non-state actors.

One big question for the coming years is whether African collaboration with the United States would help or hinder Pax Africana. Will American resources help to strengthen Pax Africana—or will American power simply turn Pax Africana into a handmaiden or a servant of Pax Americana?

How do we avoid the Americanization of Pax Africana? One solution is for the African Union to evolve a shared position and shared rules of involvement in the war on terrorism. Ideally the United States should deal with a "South Atlantic Treaty Organization" (SATO) consisting of African states that are allied against terrorism, rather than the Untied States dealing with separate African countries. Above all the trend towards establishing American military bases in Africa should be stopped.

As for Kenya, Uganda and Tanzania, they are attempting a resurrection of the East African Community. The old Community limited its agenda to economic issues and developmental concerns. When the Community was confronted with a major problem of instability following Idi Amin's coup of January 1971, the East African Community could not deal with it. It had been created and envisioned as a Community of trade and economic exchange rather than a Community of shared concerns of stability.

The new African Union as a whole should seek to combine a quest for development with a concern for stability, a dream for prosperity with a dream for peace. Pax Africana should enter the official agenda of the new African Union—eager to prevent conflict as well as to end it, eager to mediate as well as to pacify. The new African Union should not only seek to institutionalize the quest for development; it must also be engaged in the pursuit of a more stable Africa at peace with itself and with its neighbors in the Middle East. To paraphrase Kwame Nkrumah and the Bible:

> Seek ye first the kingdom of peace,
> And all else will be added unto you.
> AMEN!

But behind all the scenarios and all the search for solutions, behind the pain and the anguish of Third World terrorism, is the paramount question—are we facing birth pangs in the present crisis? Are we witnessing the real bloody forces of decolonization—as the colonial structures are decaying or collapsing? Is the colonial slate being washed clean with the blood of victims, villains and martyrs? Are the refugees victims of a dying order, or are they traumatized witnesses to an epoch-making rebirth? Is collective love part of the problem or part of the solution?

Moral reform is often a coy mistress in the old style. It is difficult to persuade the reform mistress to come out and be consummated. Love as a metaphor becomes love as a social healing. "Sweet Helen make me immortal with a kiss..." If moral reform is a coy mistress of the old style, we need to give her the same warning that Andrew Marvell, the 17th century English poet, gave his more individualized coy mistress:

> Had we but world enough and time
> This coyness, dear Lady, mere no crime...
> But at my back I always hear.
> Time's winged chariot hurrying near.
> And yonder before us lie
> Deserts of vast eternity...
> The grave's a fine and private place,
> But none, I think, do there embrace!

CHAPTER EIGHT

THE TRUTH
BETWEEN TERROR AND TYRANNY
THE UNITED STATES, ISRAEL AND HEGEMONIC GLOBALIZATION[1]

In our chapter entitled "Has a Clash of Civilizations Begun?" I outlined four stages of clash of civilizations, which started about four centuries ago. There I explored the sins of the press—i.e. those of commission, omission and submission—in the era of hegemonic globalization. In what follows I will elaborate more on the position of Israel in the United States' foreign policy that often discredits Muslim societies.

IS ISRAEL A THREAT TO AMERICAN DEMOCRACY?[2]

There will be no world without terrorism for as long as the Palestinian-Israeli dispute is unresolved. It is by far the biggest trigger of rage against the United States among all issues, in this era of hegemonic globalization.

Muslims are victims of violent injustice elsewhere in the world without the globalization of anger against the United States. Muslims in Kashmir, India, are victims of Indian security forces trying to prevent them from having self-determination. Muslims in Chechnya are victims of Russian security forces trying to prevent them from having self-determination. Muslims in Macedonia are trying to cope with discrimination from Christian Macedonians. Muslims in Kosovo are denied a separate state by the international community and face the risk of reintegration with Yugoslavia against their will. Muslims in Afghanistan faced the Soviet Union before and defeated it. The Afghans have now experienced military action by the United States.

If Muslims have been victimized elsewhere by other powers, why is the victimization of Muslims in the Middle East such a powder keg? Hegemonic globalization globalizes its own opposition. Rage against the United States has become globalized. British publications like *The Independent, The New State-Man* and even *The Economist* have started accusing Israel of war crimes while President Bush praises Sharon as a man of peace.

A Zionist Shadow on the U.S. Constitution

Israeli militarism, occupation of Arab lands and repression of Palestinians are the main causes of not only anti-Israeli terrorism but also anti-American terrorism. No issue in the world since apartheid in South Africa has caused greater international rage than Israeli repression of Palestinians.

Even in dusty Khartoum—the *New York Times* reports—several hundred thousand people have marched in the streets denouncing Israel and the USA—and some cheered Usamah bin Laden. On April 17, 2002, President Husni Mubarak of Egypt declined to see Secretary of State Colin Powell and sent Egypt's Foreign Minister instead to meet him. Mubarak had a diplomatic cold.

If Israeli repression and militarism provoke suicide bombers and give rise to movements like Hamas and Al-Qaeda, Israeli political culture becomes increasingly racist—and the Attorney General of the United States begins to curtail civil liberties in the United States. Global issues are damaging American democracy, and American media are lukewarm in defense of democratic values. And now steps are being taken towards militarizing domestic life in the United States. New military reforms establish a military command for within the United States.

If Israeli atrocities and repression cause terrorism in the United States, and terrorism in turn threatens civil liberties in America, a chain of causation is established. The behavior of the state of Israel threatens not merely democracy within the Jewish state. Israel threatens democracy in America as well. Hegemonic globalization not only threatens conflict between civilizations. It also threatens civilized standards of governance.

We keep on hearing that Israel is the only democracy in the region. But is it not in the interest of the United States that Israel should be the only democracy? Because of Israeli intransigence, Arab public opinion is more anti-American than are most Arab dictators. Had the Arab world been more democratic, their governments would have had to be more militantly anti-Israel and anti-American than they are.

The United States has a vested interest in an Arab world that is not democratic. For Arab dictators are a safety valve to keep their populations less explosively anti-American. Almost all the 20 Arab governments of the Arab League apart from Syria, Iraq, Libya and Sudan are obedient to the United States. But such pro-American obedience would have been voted out of office had the Arab word enjoyed free elections.

Similarly, only a military regime in Pakistan under General Musharaff could have cooperated so fully with the United States in its invasion of Afghanistan. No elected government in Pakistan would have been able to defy the pro-Islamic and pro-Taliban segments of Pakistani opinion with such impunity.

The United States gained from lack of democracy in Pakistan. Into the Arab heartland Western powers decided to create a Jewish state in 1948—with President Harry S. Truman playing a critical role in making it happen:

1. It did not stop with the creation of the Jewish state;
2. Israel expanded after the 1948 war;
3. Eisenhower prevented expansion in 1956;
4. Further Israeli occupation of Palestinian territory after 1967 war;
5. Annexation of Jerusalem by Israel in 1967;
6. Creating Jewish settlements on Arab land continually;
7. Blowing up and destroying Arab homes as a hidden strategy of ethnic cleansing.

Why is the U.S. being blamed for Israeli policies? Where was Usamah bin Laden's anti-Americanism coming from? We are back to hegemonic globalization. The following points may shed light to our inquiries:

1. Massive economic aid from the United States to Israel in billions
2. Provision of sophisticated American weapons to Israel
3. The United States was shielding Israel from U.N. censure
4. The United States was making U.N. Security Council impotent in punishing Israel.
5. The United States was weakening anti-Israeli Arab forces by buying off the government of Egypt with a billion U.S. dollars every year. Egypt is the largest Arab country and used to be the biggest single Arab threat to Israel militarily. The U.S. largess has bought off Egypt effectively.
6. The U.S. was preventing Iraq from rising as an alternative to Egypt in challenging Israel. Taking advantage of Iraq's invasion of Kuwait to weaken Iraq permanently—whereas Pearl Harbor was not used to weaken Japan permanently, nor was Hitler's aggression used to weaken Germany permanently.
7. The United States is both the main source of military support for the enemy of the Arab World, Israel, and the USA is also the

main destroyer of Arab capacity to rise militarily. This latter policy includes weakening Egypt and enfeebling Iraq.

8.   The American base in Saudi Arabia since 1991 is perceived as turning sacred Islamic soil into an extension of the Pentagon. The American base in Saudi Arabia is seen not as a shield against such external enemies as Saddam Hussein, but a shield against an internal Iran-style Islamic revolution in Saudi Arabia. A situation of gross military frustration has been created, especially in Palestine and Iraq, but also on the sacred sands of Saudi Arabia.

We must solve the Palestine problem if terrorism is to end. To the moralist, terrorism against the United States is born out of evil. To the political analyst terrorism is born out of rage and frustration. The American Press has bought into the good versus evil scenario. It is therefore not critical enough of fanatic John Ashcroft. Solving the Israeli-Palestinian brutal stalemate is indispensable for the creation of a world without terrorism. It is also indispensable for making the United States a more benevolent super power, and Israel a less racist power. Finally, the Jews to whom 1.2 billion Muslims owe a lot doctrinally and to whom a similar number of Christians are equally indebted, will one day re-discover their global role. The Jews—who invented globalization—may one day help to make globalization more humane.

TOWARDS THE RACIALIZATION OF ZIONISM

But for the time being many friends of Israel are anxious that the repressive forces in the Jewish state are getting stronger—and a distinctly Israeli form of racism may be evolving. This is a minority. But within that racially anti-Arab minority there may be a smaller and more ominous sub-group.

There is a school of thought in Israel which is already becoming fascist. This issue is debated more frankly in Israel itself than in the United States. Again the Western press observes a conspiracy of silence. Lovers of democracy in Israel should be alarmed by the fascist trend. There is even an Israeli word for this kind of Semitic fascism. Professor Yeshayahu Leibovitz of the Hebrew University coined it twenty years ago: *Judeo-Nazism*. As editor of the *Encyclopedia Hebraica*, Leibovitz has grappled with many trends in the Jewish experience. But he has now raised the issue of whether the concept of *Judeo-Nazism* is any longer a contradiction in terms.[3]

As Israeli bull-dozers have buried Palestinians alive in Jenin, other critics of Israel have married the word *Nazi* with the word *Zionism—Nazi-onism*. Israelis are warning each other that the unthinkable is not necessarily impossible. Specific sociological conditions in inter-war Germany fostered right wing extremism among the Germans. The history of German extremism started with a people who believed they had been humiliated and humbled. The German Press instilled the German sense of shame.

The Treaty of Versailles that ended World War I created among the Germans a martyrdom complex, which later favored the rise of extreme nationalism. The martyrdom complex—strong among the Israelis today and powerful among the Germans in the inter-war years—can degenerate into paranoia. We now know that lovers of democracy in the German population underestimated the danger. The whole world paid a heavy price for German paranoia. Jews—like the Germans—have been impressive contributors to world civilization. But both people are human, and therefore psychologically vulnerable. The danger of extremism is real. The stages toward extremism through which the German psyche passed were as follows:

1. Martyrdom Complex;
2. Paranoia;
3. Extreme Nationalism;
4. Racial Exclusivity;
5. Militarization;
6. Territorial Expansionism.

It is very unlikely that Israelis will pass through similar stages.

There are in any case major constraints to Zionist extremism. The question nevertheless remains whether the danger of fascism in Israel is real enough to alarm Israeli patriots themselves.

Israel was genuinely born out of the ashes and anguish of the Holocaust. It was a more genuine martyrdom than was the Nazi sense of humiliation in the inter-war years. Our question is "when does the martyrdom complex evolve into paranoia?" In the case of the Jews, the evolution takes the following two stages:

1. Monopolizing the Holocaust as an experience of the Past;
2. Pre-empting imaginary Holocausts of the future.

A 1980's American immigrant into Israel from a religious family in New York prayed for a new persecution of Jews in the Diaspora so that they are forced to go to the fortress Israel:

> The hatred the Gentiles feel towards the Jews is eternal. There never was peace between us and them except when they totally beat us or when we shall totally beat them. Maybe if they will give someone like Sharon the chance to kill...until the Arabs will understand that we did them a favor letting them remain alive.... We are powerful now and power should talk now. The Gentiles only understand the language of power.[4]

Prime Minister Yitzhak Shamir declared in April 1988:

> We say to them, from this hilltop and from the perspective of thousands of years of history, that in our eyes they are like grasshoppers.[5]

Menachin Begin's earlier denunciation of Palestinians as "two-legged animals" has formed part of the same drift towards racist perceptions and perspectives in powerful circles in Israel. Are Israel's racial attitudes towards external Palestinians in the West Bank al-

ready racializing Israeli attitudes towards Palestinians who are Israeli citizens? Is Zionist nationalism stifling Israeli liberalism? Opinion polls of Jewish attitudes to the Palestinian uprising in the occupied territories is one measure. The death of over 500 Palestinians
since the *intifāḍah* began has not alarmed enough Israelis. Indeed,
the majority of Israelis seem to want even stiffer measures against
the Palestinians. This is bound to affect how they view Israeli Arabs
at home. In time there will be as big a percentage of Arabs in Israel as
the percentage of Turkish Cypriots in Cyprus. When is soft Israeli
arrogance towards the Arabs paternalistic? As an Israeli originally
from Aden put it:

> We know that the Arab is an obedient good creature as
> long as he is not incited and no one puts ideas into his
> head.... He just has to be told exactly what his right place
> is.... They must understand who the master is. That's all.[6]

When united to fanaticism and nationalism, arrogance can take
the form of militant racism. Take the case of the young rabbi who
denounced the "filth" of mixed marriages and the "hybrid children"
such marriages produce—a "thorn in the flesh of the Jewish society
in Israel."[7] This rabbi recommended school segregation and exclusion of Arabs from the universities. Echoes of apartheid are unmis-
takable.

As for the trend towards militarization, Israel has indeed become the most efficient war machine since Nazi Germany. In war
after war the Jewish state has demonstrated staggering proficiency
both in the air and on land. The six-day war in June 1967 was its
most dazzling military success. Did this military success increase
territorial appetite?

A state created in the teeth of the opposition of indigenous people
became a state surrounded by hostile neighbors. It was only a matter
of time before the moral cost had to be paid. A Director-General of
Israel Broadcasting Authority (radio and television) during years of
apartheid was a "long time admirer of South Africa and a frequent

visitor there." He even wrote an "emotional article" expressing his preference for South Africa over Black Africa, complete "with citations of research proving genetic inferiority of blacks"—a view which "seems to reflect the feeling of many in the Israeli elite."[8]

The journal of *Mapam* (left wing of *Labour Alignment)* published an explanation of the superiority of Israeli pilots. Blacks and Arabs were inferior in "complex, cognitive intelligence." That was why "American Blacks succeed only in short distance running."[9] Israeli neo-Nazism reversed the scale of genetic values favored by German Nazis. Both forms of extremism exaggerated the impact of the Jewish factor. The Nazis thought the Jewish impact was negative. The Israeli extremists erred the other way.

Why has the United States out-distanced Europe in modern culture? The proportion of Jews in the American population has enhanced American creativity, according to this Israeli school of thought.[10] By implication German inventiveness before the Holocaust was due to the Jewish creative infusion into the German population. An Israeli labour party journal refers to "genetic experiments" at Tel Aviv University—which have shown that "genetic differences among Jewish communities [Poland and Yemen are cited] are smaller than those between Gentiles and Jews."[11]

In earlier years the Rabbinate had cited biblical authority to justify expulsion of the Arabs ("the foreign element") from the land, or simply their destruction, and religious law was invoked to justify killing of civilians in war or raid.[12] A doctrine of "transferring the Arabs" to refugee camps in other Arab countries is gaining support in Israel. American Rabbi Isaac Bernstein argued that religious law gives power and legitimacy to Israel to "dispossess the Arabs of the conquered territories."[13] Another Rabbi, Rabbi Lubovitcher of New York, deplored that Israel did not conquer Damascus during the 1973 October War.[14] A doctrine emerged called "secure and defensible borders." After almost every war Israel attempted to get more territory. Whose secure and defensible borders? Because of Israel's military supremacy, only Israel had such secure borders. The Arabs were easily penetrable by Israeli air and rocket power.

The transition from chosen people to chosen race gathered momentum. Rabbi Elazar Valdman of Gush Emunim wrote in the journal *Nekudah* of the West Bank settlers:

> We will certainly establish order in the Middle East and in the world. And if we do not take this responsibility upon ourselves, we are sinners, not just towards ourselves but towards the entire world. For who can establish order in the world? All of those Western leaders of weak character?[15]

The question that inevitably has now arisen is whether Israel's taste for imperial expansion can long be sustained without hurting Israeli democracy. Can the sadism against Palestinians be long enjoyed without creating Israeli masochism? Is Zionism becoming a cancer not just on the body politic of Arab stability but also on the body politic of Jewish sense of justice?

CAN A STATE BE JEWISH AND DEMOCRATIC?

In the course of this twenty-first century Israel will have to choose between remaining a Jewish state and remaining a democracy. Such a dilemma already exists but it will get worse. The proportion of Arabs in Israel is higher than the proportion of Blacks in the United States. Yet while Blacks in the United States have reached high echelons in the executive branch, Arabs in Israel are marginalized in government. Arab Israelis have done well in the legislative branch, but have effectively been kept out of major executive and judicial positions. There is no Arab equivalent of Thurgood Marshall or Justice Clarence Thomas. The Arab population in Israel—now eighteen percent—is on its way towards becoming a quarter of the population. This will be the equivalent of Turkish Cypriots in Cyprus. There will indeed come a time when Israel has to choose between being a Jewish state and being a democratic state.

More recently there is increasing support in the state of Israel for a policy that is euphemistically called "transfer." The right wing press is popularizing it. It is basically a policy of ethnic cleansing. More and more Israelis are dreaming of a kind "final solution to the Palestinian problem"—the transfer of all Palestinians of the West Bank (and presumably Gaza) to new refugee camps in the rest of the Arab world. What to do with those Palestinians who are already Israeli citizens poses difficult problems for these ultra-Zionists.[16] It is to be noted, however, that American civil liberties and Israeli democracy are not the only victims of the cruel behavior of the State of Israel towards Palestinians. There is also the additional risk of reactivating international anti-Semitism. It is to this dimension that we should now turn.

ISRAEL AS A CAUSE OF ANTI-SEMITISM

The state of Israel was created partly as a permanent asylum for Jews who might otherwise suffer persecution in other parts of the world. The Zionist movement was originally conceived as a quest for a piece of land without people to accommodate people without land. As it turned out, Palestine was hardly "a piece of land without people." Millions of Arabs have remained displaced to accommodate Jews from elsewhere.

Political Zionism was originally intended as a defense against anti-Semitism. Fifty years after the creation of the State of Israel, has Zionism now become a cause of new forms of anti-Semitism? Is the state of Israel becoming a cause of hatred for other Jews around the world?

This appears to be the conclusion that has been reached by the Chief Rabbi of Great Britain. On the last day of February 2002 Dr. Jonathan Sacks urged strong action to prevent "violence and bloodshed" against Jews in England. He argued that the Israeli-Palestine conflict had sparked off levels of anti-Semitism not seen in Britain since the years of the Holocaust. He referred to an increasing number of attacks on synagogues and "virulent anti-Israel campaigns on some English university campuses which have left many Jewish students fearful for their safety" (*The Times* (London), March 1, 2002:2).

The Chief Rabbi complained that the leading liberal newspapers in Britain such as *The Guardian, The Independent* and *The Statesman* had started publishing op-ed articles questioning Israeli's right to exit. According to the Chief Rabbi, the websites of *The Independent* and *The Statesman* had become what he describes as a focus of anti-Semitic discussion. At the University of Manchester, England, Jewish students claimed to have been spat upon and denounced as "Nazis" and "baby butchers" during a bitter dispute at the students' union about whether Israel should be declared an apartheid-state. Rabbi Sacks claimed that until recently he had never experienced anti-Semitism in Britain. But he saw new evidence that anti-Semitism was returning not only to Britain but also to other parts of Europe.

> The fact that I have chosen to speak indicates the depth of my concern. We know from all of history that words turn into deeds, prejudice into violence, and eventually violence into bloodshed... You cannot deny people the right to criticize any nation-state [such as Israel]. But what we are seeing goes beyond that, and has become an attack on Jews, not just the state of Israel ... That Jewish students on campus should have to go in fear is unacceptable. (*The Times* (London) March 1, 2002)

After the massacre in Jenin in April 2002, *The Independent* in London accused Israel of a "monstrous war crime" (April 16). In the correspondence columns of *The Guardian* (London) there have been many letters about whether negative reactions to Israeli policies are leading to a revival of European anti-Semitism. One pained statement came from David Grossman as early as October 22, 2001. He said:

> I am highly critical of Israel's behavior, but in recent weeks I have felt that the [British] media's hostility to it has not been fed solely by the actions of the Sharon government. A person feels such things deeply, under the skin, I feel them with a kind of shiver that percolates down to the cells of

my most primeval memories...[17]

In Black Africa, where Israel had many friends, there is new questioning. John Nagenda has said the following in a Uganda newspaper:

> The Israelis latterly scored over 300 Palestinian deaths to less than 20 against them, but still insisted that it was Arafat and his Palestinians who were the aggressors. Where is God? It must be crystal clear that Sharon's blind rage policy daily leads Israel to more insecurity, not less... By Bush giving *carte blanche*, the American President is a bad, not a good friend of Israel. Does Bush know many Israelis? Did he go to prep school with many of them? Are many of them members of his clubs?[18]

By giving Israel *carte blanche,* the United States was also a bad friend to world Jewry. Is the U.S. feeding into global anti-Semitism?

In April 2002 World Jewish leaders held an emergency meeting in Brussels to discuss what was described as "the rash of anti-Semitic violence that has swept Western Europe." The Secretary-General of the World Jewish Congress said: "We are now facing an unprecedented increase in anti-Semitism on this continent." Israel's military action against Palestinians was identified as a factor (*New York Times,* April 23, 2002). In the final analysis, blind U.S. policy, which is uncritical of Israel, is dangerous to American lives—as well as to Jewish safety. It is also a potential threat to American democracy.

Israel was created as a refuge from anti-Semitic hate. It has become one of the main causes of anti-Semitic rage against innocent Jews in other parts of the world. It is also in danger of compromising its own democratic order, as well as the constitution of its closest friend, the United States of America.

CONCLUSION

The issue of Israel started causing damage to American democracy long before September 11, 2001. Academic and the media were both compromised. Few topics have caused more self-imposed censorship on the American media than any criticism of the State of Israel. Journalists, reporters and editors have to watch carefully what they say about Israel. What is at stake is the potential wrath of the pro-Israeli lobby, and also potential loss of revenue from angry advertisers who withdraw their commercials or angry Jewish subscribers to public television or National Public Radio. The Print media in the United States also routinely censors themselves against any criticism of the State of Israel.

The issue of Israel has also detracted from academic freedom on American campuses. There have been cases when scholars have been denied tenure because of their pro-Palestinian writings or lectures. The United States may be the only country in the world in which it is safer to criticize the host country itself (i.e. the United States) than to criticize a particular external power (i.e. Israel). While some scholars have lost their jobs for criticizing the government of Israel almost no scholar runs much of risk at an American University for criticizing the U.S. administration of the day.

Perhaps Israel ought never to have been created. Millions of Jews were opposed to its creation in the first place. Those Jews have now been vindicated. The creation of the Jewish state has cost thousands of lives and may cost many more. If the world had realized the potential human cost, even the unrepresentative United Nations of 1947-1948 might never have voted for the partition of Palestine.

But now that Israel has been created, there should be no attempt to destroy it physically. Most Israelis today are innocent of the original massive miscalculation, and do not deserve to suffer for that mistake. However, the Jewishness of Israel will be destroyed by its own contradictions. In a few decades Israel will have to choose between remaining a Jewish state and remaining a democracy. The two will be incompatible.

Already the effort to maintain the Jewishness of Israel is racializing Jewish attitudes to Palestinians. Rightwing views in Israel even from Rabbis and religious figures are getting increasingly racist. And under Prime Ministers like Ariel Sharon, Israeli policies are narrowing the gap between the behavior of Nazis towards Jews and the behavior of Israelis towards Palestinians. Terms like the following are entering the vocabulary of international censure of Israel—*Judeo-Nazism* and *Nazi-onism*. Israeli Jews, who were once the unique martyrs of human history, are now becoming just one more oppressor of other people. Human kind is the poorer for this Israeli deterioration.

There is still time to reverse direction. Globalization may be inevitable, but it does not have to be hegemonic. Globalization does not have to be dominated by a single superpower, or even by a single civilization (the West). Israelis may be among the brutal offenders of the last fifty years, but Jews have been the unique martyrs of the last three thousand years. World Jewry should now stop regarding ethnic solidarity with Sharon as more important than humane solidarity with their exceptional history as a moral people. As for the Press, they should correct their sins of commission; fill the gap of their sins of omission, and re-learn the dictates of Press freedom as they transcend the sins of submission.

NOTES

1. This chapter was presented as Keynote Address at the Fifth International Conference of the International Center for Contemporary Middle Eastern Studies, Eastern Mediterranean University, Cyprus, on the theme "September 11 and the Clash of Civilizations: Role of the Media and Public Discourse," April 25-27, 2002. It is an expansion of the author's earlier lecture "Is Israel a Threat to American Democracy?" (Binghamton, New York, April 2002).
2. Based on a presentation at Binghamton University, Binghamton, New York, under the auspices of a "Teach-In" organized by Graduate Students, on Wednesday April 17, 2002.

3. Cited by Noam Chomsky, *The Fateful Triangle : The United States, Israel, and the Palestinians* (Boston: South End Press, 1983).

4. Report by Israel Writer Amos Oz based on interviews and published in *Davar.* Quoted in Noam Chomsky, *The Fateful Triangle*, pp. 446-7.

5. "Search for Partners: Should the US Deal with the PLO?" *Time Magazine*, April 11, 1988. See what is a "Grasshopper," letter to *New York Times*, April 20, 1988.

6. Report by Amos Oz in a series of articles in *Davar*, Ibid. Chomsky, *The Fateful Triangle*, p. 447.

7. Consult report by Eliahu Salpeter, *Ha'aretz*, no. 4, 1982.

8. Benjamin Beit-Hallahmi, "Israel and South Africa" *New Outlook*, March/April 1983; *Hotam*, April 18, 1975 and October 1, 1982.

9. Chomsky, p. 152.

10. *Davar*, September 8, 1981, in Chomsky, pp. 151-152.

11. Charles Hoffman, "A Monkey Trial, Local Style," *Jerusalem Post*, March 22, 1983.

12. Chomsky, *The Fateful Triangle: The United States, Israel and the Palestinians* (Boston: South Press, 1983), p. 153. See also Military rabbinate publications *Peace in the Middle East?* pp. 108-9; Shahak, *Begin and Co.*, Said, *Question of Palestine*, p. 91.

13. Chomsky, p. 153; Bernstein, *Dialogue* (New York) Winter 1980.

14. *Al Hamishmar*, January 4, 1978.

15. Cited by Danny Rubenstein, *Davar*, October 8, 1982.

16. The increasing popularity in Israel of the idea of "transfer" of the Palestinian population was covered in "60 Minutes II," ABC Television (U.S.A.), Wednesday April 10, 2002.

17. "Diary," *The Guardian*, October 22, 2001. Cited in a letter by Arnold Wesker, *The Guardian* (London) March 1, 2002.

18. "Sharon's Blind Rage is Leading Israel to Hell," *The New Vision* (Kampala), February 23, 2002.

CHAPTER NINE

COMPARATIVE TERROR
FROM SHAKA TO SHARON
REVOLUTIONARY, RACIAL, RELIGIOUS AND STATE VIOLENCE[1]

The word "terror" in the political context was probably born out of the French revolution in the eighteenth century. Terror and revolution became intertwined and synthesized. A modern social revolution was born.

A TYPOLOGY OF TERROR

In this presentation we distinguish between firstly, revolutionary terrorism, which went back to the French revolution; secondly, racial terrorism, which in the twentieth century included the Ku Klux Klan in the United States and apartheid in South Africa. And thirdly, there is religiously inspired terrorism, which includes Al-Qaeda but has also manifested itself among Sikhs, Hindus, Christians in Ireland

and Lebanon. It is true that religious zealots from the Islamic background killed Anwar Sadat. We should also remember the religious zealots from the Sikh background who assassinated Indira Gandhi.

There is the question of whether state terrorism is a different category, or whether it is a difference in method. For example, did the apartheid state commit state terrorism—or was it a vision of racially-inspired terrorism? Has Israel been guilty of state terrorism? Ariel Sharon, when he was Defense Minister in 1982, could even engage in surrogate terrorism in Sabra and Chatila. He facilitated the massacre of Palestinians by Phalangist right-wing Christian militia in Beirut.[2] Was this a combination of racial and religious terrorism?

After he became Prime Minister of Israel in 2001 Sharon became similarly reckless with the lives of Palestinian civilians in response to attacks on Israelis by Palestinian suicide bombers. When in July 2002 an F-16 fighter plane fired a rocket into a civilian residential building in Gaza in order to kill one adversary, and killed nearly ten innocent children as well, Ariel Sharon described the Israeli mission as one of Israel's greatest military successes.[3] (His Foreign Minister was more apologetic and circumspect in his utterances.)

There is no doubt that Ariel Sharon's attitude to civilian life on the Palestinian side has a terrorist-style of recklessness. He has been kept in check by the wider democratic culture of Israel, and by the constraints of the opinion of the United States and by the reactions of European allies. Under Sharon Israel has drifted towards periodic state-terrorism and war-crimes.

Having differentiated revolutionary, racial, state and religiously inspired terrorism, we should also note that each of those in turn includes two sub-varieties—heroic terrorism and horrific terrorism. Heroic terrorism is of the kind whose aims are noble and may even be humane, but whose means are morally ignoble and often physically cruel. Horrific terrorism, on the other hand, lacks legitimacy at the level of both the goals being pursued and the means being employed. Both ends and means are ignoble.

In our own day, there is a debate about whether suicide bombing by oppressed Palestinians are a case of heroic terrorism. Many people in the countries that have been bombed by the United States in the last forty years may also wonder whether the attack on the Pentagon on September 11, 2001, was not a case of heroic terrorism—since the Pentagon is widely viewed as a war machine and therefore a legitimate military target.

However, there may be a general international consensus that the attack on the World Trade Center in New York on the same day was a clear case of horrific terrorism. What makes the means being used illegitimate is sometimes the test of proportionality. The means used against the World Trade Center was out of all proportion to the end envisaged—even by the Machiavellian standards of the end justifying the means.

I became politically conscious in colonial Kenya against the background of the Mau Mau war of the 1950s. The British colonial authorities condemned Mau Mau as a terrorist movement. If it was a terrorist movement, it was of a revolutionary variety rather than a racial variety. If Mau Mau was a terrorist movement it has to be regarded as a case of heroic terrorism. Liberation struggles that resort to terror may have disgraced their methods, but surely not their goals.

The trouble with apartheid in the history of South Africa was that both the goals and the means were illegitimate. The goals were racial segregation within each city internally, and the pursuit of territorial ethnic cleansing as a long-term strategy of separate development. The means was an elaborate structure of racial control, and the disenfranchisement and intimidation of all the races but that of European stock. Apartheid started off as tyranny without terror—white dictatorship without daily violent intimidation. But it did not take long before apartheid became tyranny plus terror. The more the internal opposition to apartheid grew, the more the system became a regime of horrific terrorism.

Did the opposition to apartheid also resort to terrorism? The answer is YES. But there were two differences. Firstly, terrorism perpetrated by ANC followers was not systemic to the movement. There were incidents of terror rather than a mapped out strategy of terror. ANC terror was episodic. Necklace burning of presumed Black traitors, for example, was a form of terrorism. But such incidents were often happening in spite of the policies of the ANC and in spite of the preferred goals of the leadership.

The second difference between apartheid terror and opposition terror is that movements like the ANC were seeking to democratize South Africa. The goals remained noble and even humane. The means were occasionally a case of heroic terrorism. Israeli terror against Palestinians is, on the whole, episodic rather than systemic. Occupation of another people is a form of tyranny but not necessarily a form of terror. But Israeli occupation is drifting towards terror, even systemically.

FROM SHAKA TO USAMAH BIN LADEN

Perhaps even more fascinating from this point of view is the significance of Shaka Zulu in the history of terror. Was Shaka the first heroic terrorist of modern African history? Was he also the first revolutionary terrorist of modern Africa?

Shaka was a military genius but also a control freak. Militarily he did have brilliant ideas of formation and organization. He was an innovator in weaponry. But can he be compared with Usamah bin Laden? It partly depends upon the difference between trying to build an empire, and trying to dismantle an empire. Shaka Zulu was a heroic terrorist who had sought to construct a new and glorious Zulu Empire. Was Usamah bin Laden a heroic terrorist who has sought to bring down the American empire? Some have admired Shaka Zulu because he began life as a fatherless child and rose to become one of the great warrior-kings of all time. Others have admired Usamah bin Laden as a millionaire who decided to live in caves in Afghanistan for a cause much bigger than his millions. Shaka moved from the cave to the palace; Usamah moved from the palace to the cave. Shaka Zulu was not, of course, himself a writer. But he has fascinated writers and induced creativity in others. He was a figure of contradiction—an innovator and a destroyer, a man of passionate love and infinite cruelty. Some writers have described Shaka as Africa's answer to Machiavelli—a Prince who truly believed that power stood on the pillars of fear rather than the foundations of love. Shaka practiced what Machiavelli had once preached—that great ends justified any means.

Léopold Sédar Senghor, founder-President of Senegal, composed a dramatic poem for several voices in honor of Shaka, but dedicated to "The Bantu Martyrs of South Africa." In the poem Senghor has a white voice taunting Shaka for the murder of Noliwe. The white voice accuses Shaka of having killed his fiancé in order to escape from his wider public conscience.

Shaka answers:
And you talk about conscience to me? Yes, I killed her, while she was telling of the blue lands; I killed her yes! My hand did not tremble; a flash of steel in the odorous thicket of the armpit.

White voice:
So you admit it Shaka? Will you admit to the millions of men you killed
Whole regiments of pregnant women and children still at breast?
You, provider-in-chief for vultures and hyenas, poet of the Valley of Death.
We looked to find a warrior. All we found was a butcher....

Shaka:
The weakness of the heart is holy....
Ah! You think that I never loved her
My Negress fair with Palm oil, slender as a plume
Thigh of startled otter, of Kilimanjaro snow...
Ah! You think I never loved her!
But these long years, this breaking of the wheel of years,
This carcan strangling every act
This long night without sleep....
[You think I never loved her?]

I wondered like a mare from the Zambezi running and rush-
ing at the stars,
Gnawed by nameless suffering like leopards in the trap
[You think I never loved her?]
—I would not have killed her if I loved her less.[4]

We have here a fusion between the sadism of murder and the
masochism of suicide. He killed Noliwe to escape his own love for
her. He killed many Black people because he was wanted to make
their nation truly great. Shaka betrayed the Black in order to raise
them high. In the words of Senghor's Shaka:

I had to escape from doubt...
From love of Noliwe
From the love of my black-skinned people.[5]

Shaka Zulu has become almost a Muse unto himself—stimulat-
ing poets like Mitshali, scholars like M. Kunene, playwrights like
Wole Soyinka, comparative analysts like Michael Chapman, states-
men like Léopold Senghor, literary pioneers like Thomas Mofolo,
and more recently televesion work like the popular South African
television series (SATV) on Shaka.

Physical destruction is often manure for artistic creation. Jean
Graudoux caught this paradox with a brilliant hyperbole when he
said in 1944:

As soon as war is declared it will be impossible to hold the
poets back. Rhyme is still the most effective war drum.[6]

On the eve of the year 2000 the British Broadcasting Corporation asked me to choose my African of the millennium. I insisted on
choosing two Africans—one great African of thought and one great
African of action. For my African of thought of the last thousand
years I chose Ibn Khaldun, the North African widely regarded as the
founding father of modern social science. His book *al-Muqaddimah*

(written in the fourteenth century) is still widely read in universities worldwide.

Arnold Toynbee, himself a major macro-historian of great distinction, had the following to say about this book by the Tunisian, Ibn Khaldun.

> Undoubtedly the greatest work of its kind that has ever been created by any mind in anytime or place ... the most comprehensive and illuminating analysis of how human affairs work that has been made anywhere. (Toynbee, *The Observer* (London))

If my choice of African of thought of the last thousand years was Ibn Khaldun, my African book of the period would be *al-Muqaddimah*—alongside St. Augustine's *City of God* of the preceding thousand years.

But what was my choice of the African man of action of the last one thousand years? In the BBC interview I chose Shaka Zulu as my African of action of the millennium. As a Western commentator has put it:

> Shaka stands out as the greatest of them all—both Romulus and Napoleon to the Zulu people—and his legend has captured the imagination of both European and African writers, inspiring novels, biographies, and historical studies in several tongues. As a violent autocrat he is both admired and condemned: admired by those who love conquerors, condemned by those who hate despots.[7]

Let us now cross the Atlantic and look more closely at the American experience of terror, much of it going back to Shaka's own lifetime and beyond. Long before Usamah bin Laden America had suffered from terrorists.

KU KLUX KLAN AS A TERRORIST MOVEMENT

The history of terror in the American experience is a transition from individualized terrorism from within the United States to collective terrorism from outside the United States. Individualized terrorism is the tormenting or killing of individual civilians by other civilians for racial, ideological, or other political reasons. Under this definition Ku Klux Klan (KKK) was a terrorist organization—designed to create terror and consternation among particular vulnerable groups in the society.

The Ku Klux Klan was the most durable and longest surviving terrorist organization in the history of the United States. More than a century before Al-Qaeda, there was "Al-Klan." More than a century before Usamah bin Laden there was the Grand Wizard Nathan Forrest. In 1867 the Klan was declared "the Invisible Empire of the South" at a convention in Nashville. Nathan Bedford Forrest was the first Grand Wizard. In the nineteenth century, the KKK started as a social club by Confederate veterans in Pulaski, Tennessee in 1866. The name was apparently derived from the Greek *Kykos*, meaning approximately "circle." Indeed, the English word "circle" is derived from it. The "suffix" *Klan* was added for alliterative reasons.

KKK became a vehicle for Southern White underground resistance to Radical Reconstruction. The KKK struggled to restore White supremacy in the South by whipping and killing freed Blacks and their White supporters. They wore white robes and sheets to maximize the terror to their Black victims.

In night raids they did not cry out "Allāh Akbar" (God is great), but they often used the burning cross for further intimidation. White supremacy in Tennessee, North Carolina and Georgia was indeed restored partly as a result of Klan action.

In response to continuing violence among local KKK branches, the US Congress started legislating in ways that threatened the civil liberties of White folk. Congress passed the Force Act of 1870 and Ku Klux Klan Act of 1871 authorizing the President to suspend the writ of *habeas corpus*, suppress KKK disturbances by force, and impose heavy fines on such terrorist organizations.

President Ulysses S. Grant sent federal troops to some areas, suspended *habeas corpus* for some counties in South Carolina, and detained hundreds of Southerners for conspiracy. Such strong measures against White people was something new.

However, in 1882 the U.S. Supreme Court declared the KKK Act unconstitutional—and the KKK subsided to rise another day. The Supreme Court's decision legitimizing the KKK was made in the case *the United States versus Harris* of 1882.

In the nineteenth century civil liberties were curtailed by an act of Congress. Since September 11, 2001, civil liberties are curtailed at the initiative of Attorney General, John Ashcroft.[8]

President Bush described the attacks of September 11 as "an act of war" and responded with war in Afghanistan. Yet prisoners of Al-Qaeda and Taliban fighters are denied the rights of prisoners of war according to the Geneva convention. Even U.S. allies in Europe are disturbed that the U.S. is slipping away from civilized standards and from obeying international law. What kind of legal advice is Attorney General Ashcroft giving President Bush?

Yet in most of the twentieth century the terrorism of the KKK encountered few of such tough preventive measures from the Federal Government. In the 20th century the new KKK rose near Atlanta, Georgia, in 1915. This was before Martin Luther King was born. But at its peak this terrorist organization in the United States had four million members nation-wide. Its agenda of prejudice had widened. In addition to being anti-Black it became anti-Catholic, especially in 1928 when Alfred E. Smith, a Catholic, won the nomination of the Democratic Party for President. The new KKK was also anti-Jewish, anti-immigrant, and against organized labour.

For actual lynching by KKK, the victims were overwhelmingly black.[9] Lynchings continued into the second half of the twentieth century, though their numbers had drastically declined. Some of the lynchings were perpetrated by supporters of KKK who were not necessarily members. NAACP organizers were killed in Mississippi while trying to register Black voters in the 1950s. These included Reverend George W. Lee and Lamar Smith. Martin Luther King was killed the following decade.

The most shocking lynching of the 1950s was the 1955 murder of a fourteen-year old Black boy Emmett Till, who was visiting Mississippi from Chicago, and was dared by other Black boys to say something courageous to a White woman in a shop. Emmett Till gathered enough courage to say to the White woman "Bye, Baby"! As a Northern boy from Chicago he was showing off he could do something daring to a White woman.

Those two words not only cost the boy's life. He was picked up, tortured, had an eye pulled out, shot in the head, chained to a seventy-five pound cotton gin and thrown into a river to sink. The body surfaced a few days later and was identified. An all-White jury returned a verdict of "Not guilty" on people who had kidnapped Emmett Till and must have been the ones who killed him. They were even acquitted of kidnapping.

But for the first time in the history of Mississippi, a Black man testified against an accused White man. Mose Wright, Emmett's uncle, found the courage to identify the White folks who had picked up his nephew. Courage is different from fearlessness. Courage is to be afraid and still be able to do what needs to be done. Mose Wright was courageous in that court as he pointed out the kidnappers of his nephew.

It took the murder of a White woman ten years later in Alabama before the President of the United States would go on television to publicly denounce the Ku Klux Klan. President Lyndon Johnson at last condemned the organization in March 1965 in a nationwide television broadcast. He also announced the arrest of four Klansmen for the murder of the civil rights worker—a White woman in Alabama.

Yet even the 1990s it was still possible for a Black man to be tied at the back of White man's truck and dragged on the ground until his head rolled off his body. Individualized racial terrorism was still alive and well in the United States when in 1998 James Byrd Jr. was chained behind a pick-up truck in Jasper, Texas, and mutilated in this manner by a couple of White racists As for racially inspired police brutality in the 1990s, this included the forty-one shots fired by the police, which killed an unarmed West African immigrant standing outside his home in New York—a Muslim casualty of New York police brutality.[10] The policemen were acquitted. There was also the brutal sodomization of the Haitian Louima also by New York police officers.[11]

Nevertheless, September 11, 2001, took terrorism to entirely new levels of destructiveness. It was not the terrorism of the powerful against the vulnerable, as in the case of the KKK violence against underprivileged Blacks. September 11, 2001 was terrorism against the most powerful in the world. The Pentagon was a symbol of America's military might. The World Trade Center was a symbol of America's economic might. If Al-Qaeda were the terrorists of September 11, 2001, this was action by cave dwellers against the super-rich and the super-powerful. It was criminal and cruel, but it was David fighting Goliath, and in this case David came to pay a heavy price.

While the KKK picked on vulnerable minorities to terrorise, Al-Qaeda has picked on the mightiest power to challenge. If the KKK was racially inspired, Al-Qaeda was religiously motivated. The result has been catastrophic for both sides.

COUNTER-TERRORISM: MARTIAL AND MORAL

Let us now turn to two forms of counter-terrorism. Martial counter-terrorism involves use of weapons and confrontational politics. Moral counter-terrorism involves passive resistance and ethical struggle. In the United States George W. Bush symbolizes martial counter-terrorism especially against religiously inspired terror. Martin Luther King Jr. represented moral counter-terrorism, especially against racial terror.

Let us also remember the link between terrorism and assassination (as with the deaths of Anwar Sadat and Indira Gandhi). I was privileged to meet Dr. Martin Luther King Jr. when I was a graduate student at Columbia University in New York. King was already sensitive to issues beyond the American shores. The period was 1960-1.

African Davids were fighting European imperial Goliaths. Let me repeat that Dr. King and I talked about the Kenyan leader called Tom Mboya, at that time the second best known East African politician after Jomo Kenyatta. Mboya and King were about the same age. Of course, we had no idea that the lives of both King and Mboya would be cut short by an assassin's bullet before the decade of the 1960s was out. They were victims of individualized terrorism. Although Martin Luther King was so sensitized quite early to issues beyond these shores, was his dream too parochial? Was his dream too U.S.-based? Perhaps King never became as Pan African as Malcolm X did. Nevertheless, King did respond quite early to intellectual influences from beyond the American shores. He particularly emphasized his moral debt to Mahatma Mohandas Gandhi, the Indian leader of resistance against British rule in India. King once observed: "It is ironic that the greatest Christian of the modern age was a man who never embraced Christianity"—that is, Mahatma Gandhi.

As the author Keith D. Miller has reminded us, Gandhi's protest against British repression was done in such a way that it was "a collective expression of Christ-like love." Martin Luther King's life was transformed by that one single and particular Indian. King learnt moral counter-terrorism from Mohandas Ghandi. Did King first get interested in Gandhi when he heard Mordecai Johnson of Howard University preach about Gandhi's achievements? The presentation was to King "so profound and electrifying" that King "bought a half-dozen books on Gandhi's life works." But was King inadequately attentive to the larger questions of the world? Did King have the wrong dream? Should he have gone global—and dreamt about the end of the Cold War—East and West, Socialist and Capitalist, reconciled at last? Was he inadequately attentive to the North-South divide?

"Free at last! Free at last! Thank God, Almighty, we are free at last!" Was King less internationalist than Malcolm? The great reconciliation of the last decade of the 20th century was not racial, but ideological. Martin King did start agitating against the war in Vietnam before he died—was he getting internationalized? The ideological Cold War seems to have given way to what Samuel Huntington has called "a Clash of Civilizations."

Let us take a closer look at Martin Luther King's dream as articulated in his famous "I have a Dream" speech, and ask about gains and losses.

> I have a dream that one day on the red hills of Georgia, sons of former slaves and the sons of former slave owners will be able to sit down together at the table of brotherhood. [What about sons of churchgoers and sons of mosque goers?]
>
> I have a dream that one day even the state of Mississippi, a state sweltering with the heat of injustice, sweltering with the heat of oppression, will be transformed into an oasis of freedom and justice. [But will the Department of Justice in Washington D.C. be an oasis of justice?]
>
> I have a dream that my four little children will one day live in a nation where they will not be judged by the color of their skin, but by the content of their character. [What about being judged by a new racial profile as Arab Americans are?]
>
> I have a dream today! I have a dream that ... one day right there in Alabama, little black boys and black girls will be able to join hands with little white boys and white girls as sister and brothers ... [What about Arab American boys and girls?]
>
> And when this happens, and when we allow freedom to ring, when we let it ring from every village and every hamlet, from every state and every city, we will be able to speed up that day when all God's children, black men and white men, Jews and Gentiles, Protestants and Catholics, will be able to join hands and sing in the words of the old Negro spiritual: "Free at last. Free at last. Thank God Almighty, we are free at last."

Was that dream too parochial, too US-based? And even within the U.S.A., what is the balance sheet today? How much of that dream has been realized? There have in fact been gains and losses since the

1960s.

King said "We can never be satisfied as long as the Negro is the victim of the unspeakable horrors of police brutality." We have made progress. And yet in the 1990s it took the video tape involving a man called Rodney King to shock the world into the full realization that police brutality against Blacks is alive and well, at least in some parts of the country. There was yet another tape in July 2002 of police brutality in Los Angeles.[12] That part of King's dream still poses problems. And as we pointed out, an unarmed Black man, Amadu Diallo, a West African in New York City, was shot 41 times by the police—and the policemen were acquitted.

Reverend Martin King said "We can never be satisfied as long as our bodies, heavy with the fatigue of travel, cannot gain lodging in the motels of the highways and the hotels of the cities." At least hotels no longer have to keep racially mixed couples out, as they used to before the Supreme Court struck down in 1967 the Anti-Miscegenation laws of many states. (Loving vs. the State of Virginia). Here there is some gain. Overt discrimination in hotels, restaurants, and other public places has almost disappeared, though *de facto* discrimination in some Christian churches persists, as President Carter once reminded us. As for the Ku Klux Klan it is down to a few thousand regular members nation-wide. Discrimination in private clubs is still rampant, but less so than in the 1960s.

Dr. King said "We cannot be satisfied as long as the Negro's basic mobility is from a smaller ghetto to a larger one." For many U.S. Blacks, this condition still persists—the Black underclass is larger than ever. Some old concerns persist; some new concerns like HIV have arisen. Poverty, crime, infant mortality, drugs and now AIDS have been decimating large sections of ghetto populations.[13] Even teen homicides are much higher today. King's worry about the ghetto-isation of the Black experience is still serious.

Dr. King said: "We can never be satisfied as long as our children are stripped of their self-hood and robbed of their dignity by signs stating "For Whites Only." The actual visible signs have all but disappeared—but there are still obstinate psychological signs which say to many African Americans "For Whites Only." We have indeed made real progress. But the color-bar has gone invisible in large areas of life. Is that invisibility a gain or a loss? There are controversial arguments which say that better open prejudice than subversive undercurrents of racism. But other people would strongly disagree and say that open prejudice is worse. In any case, has "driving while Black" been replaced by "flying while Muslim?"

Reverend King said: "We cannot be satisfied as long as the Negro in Mississippi cannot vote and a Negro in New York believes there is nothing for which to vote." There has been a change in Mississippi—the so-called "Negro" now can vote. But there has been no change in New York—the so-called "Negro" still believes there is nothing for which to vote. But at least the Ku Klux Klan is no longer able to terrorize Blacks against voting. Nor are the lives of NAACP workers at risk when they register voters. But we should worry about the likes of Steven Emerson, a religious bigot dangerous to Muslims.

Reverend King proclaimed loudly "No! No, we are not satisfied, and we will not be until justice rolls down like waters and righteousness like a mighty stream." But we do need a Department of Justice in Washington which cares enough about justice. Justice in the legal sense is certainly not rolling down like waters—the U.S. Supreme Court has moved further to the right than ever. When we add the war on terrorism we see many civil rights gains in the United States in jeopardy. The Attorney General is worried more about security than about justice.

Hotels in the United States are no longer restrictive racially, but police brutality continues—e.g., the beating of Rodney King, the anal torture of a Black suspect, and the killing of Diallo. Segregation by law has ended, but segregation in fact persists. *De facto* segregation in housing, in clubs, in churches has not disappeared. The United States has taken two steps forward, one step backward.

The Congress has become more Republican and the Supreme Court has become more conservative. The judicial and penal system continues to be hard on Blacks—40% of those on death row are Blacks and there are more Blacks in jail than in colleges.[14] The laws against drug abuse and narcotics hit Blacks particularly hard and unfairly.

Who walked with Martin Luther King Jr.? An Indian assassinated in the 1940s walked with King in the 1950s and 60s. King said: "It is ironic, yet inescapably true that the greatest Christian of the modern world was a man who never embraced Christianity"— Mahatma Gandhi. To King, Gandhi's protests amounted to a collective expression of Christ-like love.

The Black predicament in the U.S.A. is full of contradictions. Martin Luther King preached non-violence but saw Blacks disproportionately represented in the U.S. Army. Was Muhammad Ali a better Gandhian when he refused to fight in Vietnam? Is violence in uniform less violent than violence in the streets? With the end of the ideological war, is there an intensification of the racial war worldwide?

There is the possible birth of global apartheid. In the aftermath of September 11, the white world is closing ranks. There is now greater Pan-Europeanism than anything since the Holy Roman Empire. The European Union is admitting new members.[15] The Cold War has ended a deep ideological split which once existed within the white world. Is the shadow of global apartheid looming over us— a new racial hierarchy on a global scale? Is there a new clash of civilizations between the darker races and the fairer ones? Is this clash of civilizations more imminent after September 11 and George Bush's martial counter-terrorism?

TOWARDS GLOBALIZING KING'S DREAM

Yes, Martin Luther King Jr. was politically molded by two personal forces external to the Black experience. In the case of King the two external personalities were Jesus Christ and Mahatma Gandhi. Many people believe that Lenin operationalized Marx from the world of ideas to the world of policy. King believed that Gandhi operationalized the love-ethic of Jesus from the world of ethics to the world of action. Both of Martin Luther King's ultimate mentors were, in a sense, assassinated. The Jesus of Christianity was assassinated through the crucifixion. Mahatma Gandhi was assassinated by a bullet from a fellow Hindu. Was the crucifixion of Jesus an act of state terrorism? The assassination of Gandhi was privatized terrorism.

King used the legacy of soul-force from Jesus and Gandhi as a means to an end. The end was the liberation and dignification of Black people. For Martin Luther King Jr., the union between Jesus Christ and Mohandas Gandhi was indissoluble. If Christianity had been—like Hinduism—a religion based on reincarnation, Reverend King would have wondered whether Mohandas Gandhi was a reincarnation of Jesus Christ. At least so far the union between Jesus and Gandhi has turned out to be more truly indissoluble than the union between Marx and Lenin.

Martin Luther King's dream remains relevant, but it needs to be globalized. It needs to reconcile not just different races, but different civilizations. This is particularly urgent since September 11, 2001. So, let freedom ring from the shores of Somalia and the high plateaus of Ethiopia, let freedom ring from the deep valley of the Brahmaputra and Euphrates, let freedom ring from the isles of the Caribbean and the deep recesses of the Amazon, let freedom ring from Hungary to Harlem, from Palestine to Chechnya, from the snows of Kilimanjaro to the winds of Chicago. As we continue to paraphrase Reverend King, let freedom ring from Kashmir to Capetown. We need a global coalition for moral counter terrorism, and not merely a global alliance of martial terrorism.

And when this happens, and when we have allowed freedom to ring in every village and every city, in every country and every continent, we will speed up the day when all God's children—Indo-Guyanese and Afro-Guyanese, indigenous and immigrant, men and women, White and Black, Jew and Gentile, Afghan and American, Hutu and Tutsi, Palestinian and Israeli, Sharonites and Arafites, Muslim and Christian, Ashcroft and the legacy of Malcolm X, Hindu and Buddhist, Saint and Sinner, will be able to join hands and globalize both Martin Luther King and Malcolm X—"Free at last, Free at last, Thank God Almighty! We are free at last!"

Yet even that powerful line needs cultural globalization—a world beyond either heroic or horrific terror; a universe beyond revolutionary, racial, state and religious violence.

Thank God Ruhanga, Almighty, we are free at last;
Thank Jehovah, Almighty, we are free at last;
Thank Bhagwan, Almighty, we are free at last;
Thank Omuchwezi, Almighty, we are free at last;
Thank Ogun, Almighty, we are free at last;
Thank Mwenye ezi Mungu, we are free at last;
Thank Allahu Akbar, we are free at last;
Thank the heavens, thank the stars, we are free at last.
Āmīn to One, Āmīn to all.

A CONCEPTUAL CONCLUSION

We have sought to demonstrate in this chapter that terrorism has a variety of doctrinal stimuli—the most common of which are racial, religious, statist and revolutionary stimuli. Racially inspired terrorism has ranged from the Ku Klux Klan in America to apartheid in South Africa. Religiously-stimulated terrorism has included Sikh terrorism in India, Al-Qaeda from the Muslim world, the Irish Republican Army's role in the "Troubles" of Northern Ireland, and Zionist terrorism before and after the creation of the state of Israel. Revolutionary terror in its modern guise probably started in the French revolution in the late eighteenth century. In Africa Shaka Zulu unleashed revolutionary terror in a bid to create a new Zulu political order. Terror by the State has included the right-wing variety of the Nazis and the left-wing variety by Stalinists and Maoists. Less drastic have been terrorizing techniques by the Israeli state especially under Ariel Sharon—targeted killings, use of missiles on civilian neighborhoods, collective punishment through demolition of homes, and cruel general repression by an occupying power.

All these four categories (race, religion, revolution and the state) are sources of doctrinal stimulation to terrorism. But terrorism can also be distinguished by pervasiveness. Supporters of the African

National Congress in South Africa resorted to "necklace lynching" as a method of executing those accused of treason to the cause of liberation. Such incidents constituted episodic terrorism. On the other hand, the racial order of apartheid and its police-machinery were eventually founded on systemic terrorism. Apartheid had evolved from racial tyranny to racial terror.

The third area of differentiation in terrorism is ethical in judgment rather than doctrinal in-inspiration. Heroic terrorism has noble goals but ignoble means. Horrific terrorism, on the other hand, is illegitimate at the level of both ends and means. Palestinian suicide bombers may be engaged in heroic terrorism. Palestinians are an oppressed people whose dreams of liberation are legitimate, though their means are sometimes ignoble. On the other hand, there is almost universal consensus that the destruction of the World Trade Center in New York on September 11, 2001, was a case of horrific terrorism.

A fourth distinction to be borne in mind is between individualized terrorism, perpetrated by one person or two, and terrorism by a movement. The unibomber in recent American history was the supreme case of individualized terrorism. The anthrax scare in 2001-2002 might also turn out to be a case of individualized terrorism. The destruction of the Federal Building in Oklahoma City in 1995 was probably half-way between individualized terror and a movement. On the other hand, Al-Qaeda in the new millennium and the Mau Mau in Kenya in the 1950s have been cases of movement-terrorism.

Finally, this chapter has also drawn a distinction between martial counter-terrorism and moral counter-terrorism. The martial variety invokes military power and emphasizes the use of physical force. George W. Bush and his team have led an alliance of martial counter-terrorism against Al-Qaeda, the Taliban and others.

Moral counter-terrorism, on the other hand, is what Mahatma Gandhi called *satyagraha* (soul force) in the face of violence verging on terror. Among Gandhi's most distinguished non-Indian disciples was, of course, Martin Luther King Jr., who mobilized "soul force" against the legacy of the Ku Klux Klan and against officially sanctioned segregation in the southern states of the United States. Moral counter-terrorism has often relied on passive resistance and appeal to a higher moral order.

In this chapter, we also described the crucifixion of Jesus Christ as a case of state terrorism. Why was the crucifixion "terrorism" instead of just an act of state violence? Because the Roman policy of crucifying offenders and letting them hang until they died was indeed intended to create terror as a form of judicial deterrent. Although Jesus Christ was the most famous victim of crucifixion of all history, crucifixion itself was a relatively common form of judicial terror in parts of the Roman Empire. (For purposes of analysis we are accepting the Christian tradition about the crucifixion.)

Although the phenomena of terror and terrorism go back to ancient times, their study is a relatively recent area of investigation. State terrorism especially goes back to the earliest days of the state and of empires. On the other hand, revolutionary terrorism is more modern in orientation, probably emerging out of the French revolution.

What is much more recent is what might be called *terrorsmology*—not the study of terror but the study of terrorism as a strategy of combat in an ideological context. This chapter has been part of the quest for a paradigm of terrorsmology, a quest for exploring the doctrines, methods, ethics, and causes of an emerging system of warfare. The science of terrorsmology is still in its infancy.

NOTES

1. This chapter first appeared as a monograph with the title *Comparative terror from Shaka to Sharon: Revolutionary, Racial, Religious and State Violence* (University of South Africa, 2002).
2. Reporting for the *British Broadcasting Corporation* (BBC) about the Lebanon disaster, Gerald Butt writes that: "As defence minister, and without explicitly telling Prime Minister Menachem Begin, he sent the Israeli army all the way to Beirut, a strike which ended in the expulsion of Yasser Arafat's Palestine Liberation Organisation (PLO) from Lebanon. The move stopped

the PLO using Lebanon to launch attacks against Israel, but also resulted in the massacre of hundreds of Palestinians by Lebanese Christian militiamen in two Beirut refugee camps under Israeli control." See Gerald Butt, "Ariel Sharon: Controversial hardliner." *BBC News,* Tuesday, December 4, 2001.

3.   *CNN.com* reports that Israeli Prime Minister Ariel Sharon has described an attack on a residential area of Gaza City that killed at least 15 people, including seven children, as "a great success" because it killed its target—a Hamas military leader." See "Sharon Praises airstrike 'success.'" *CNN.com* July 23, 2002.

4.   Leopold Senghor, "Shaka" in *Senghor: Prose and Poetry.* edited and translated by John Reed and Clive Wake (London: Oxford University Press, 1965), pp. 143-145.

5.   Leopold Senghor, *Ibid.*

6.   From a French-language work which was translated by Christopher Fry as *Tiger at the Gates* (1945).

7.   Eugene Victor Walter, *Terror and Resistance: A Study of Political Violence with Case Studies of Some Primitive African Communities* (London and New York: Oxford University Press, 1959 and 1972), pp. 109-10.

8.   For more discussion in more details about what John Ashcroft's initiative has done to civil liberties, see the chapter on "The Global Hostage Crisis" in this book.

9.   Writing about the lynching of blacks in the United States John Hope Franklin and Alfred A. Moss, Jr., pointed out that, "The new century [1900] opened tragically with 214 lynchings in the first two years." See John Hope Franklin and Alfred A. Moss, Jr., *From Slavery to Freedom: A History of African Americans,* seventh edition (McGraw-Hill, Inc. 1994), p. 263.

10. See "Activists call for national police brutality summit." *CNN.com,* February 25, 1999.

11. See "Abner Louima testifies at retrial of ex-officer." *CNN.com,* June 25, 2002.

12. See "Protests seek officer's arrest in taped beating." *CNN.com,* July 12, 2002.

13. According to the United States Census Bureau, in 2000, the national poverty rate was 11.3%, but 22.1% for blacks. See "Nation's Household Income Stable in 2000, Poverty Rate Vir-

tually Equals Record Low, Census Bureau Reports." *U.S. Census Bureau.* Tuesday, September 25, 2001. CB01-158.

The U.S. Department of Health and Human Services reports the following: (1) Infant Mortality. According to Health, United States 2000, infant mortality rates are more than twice as high for African-Americans (14.6 infant deaths per 1,000 live births in 1999) than for whites (5.8 infant deaths per 1,000 live births). There were 8,822 infant deaths in 1999; (2) Substance Abuse. In 2000, approximately one-third of new AIDS cases among African-American women were due to injection drug use or sex with an injection drug user. Recent illicit drug use was more common among African-American adults (8 percent) than among white adults (5.7 percent) in 1998. However, African-American teenagers ages 12-17 years were less likely to use alcohol, marijuana or cocaine than white teenagers in 1999; (3) HIV/AIDS. In 1999, 7,893 African-Americans died of HIV/AIDS, the sixth leading cause of death for African-American males, and the 10th leading cause of death for African-American females. In 2000, 47 percent of all cases reported in the U.S. were among African-Americans, and the rate of new AIDS cases among African-Americans was almost 10 times higher than among non-Hispanic whites. In AIDS cases among all African-American females, 55 percent were due to injection drug use or sex with an injecting drug user; (4) Homicide. In 1999, 7,648 African-Americans died from homicide, the eighth leading cause of death for this population. African-Americans were 5.4 times as likely as whites to die of homicide in 1999, even when differences in age distributions were taken into account. Homicide was the leading cause of death for black males ages 15-34. See "Closing The Health Gap." HHS Fact Sheet. *U.S. Department of Health and Human Services.* November 15, 2001; and (5) Crime. According to a *PBS* online NewsHour program, Professor David Cole of Georgetown University points out: "Look at African-Americans. They're 13 percent of the general population; they're 14 percent of illegal drug users. Yet if you look at drug possession, they're 35 percent of those arrested for drug possession; they're 55 percent of those convicted for drug possession; and they're 74 percent of those sentenced to serve time for drug possession.

So a crime that they commit at a rate that's equal to their representation in the population, they're serving sentences at a rate six times their representation in the population." See "IN THE SYSTEM." Online NewsHour, *PBS,* August 28, 2001.

14. According to a *PBS* online NewsHour program: "The incarcerated population under state and federal jurisdiction [in 2000, excluding 620,000 in local jails] includes: Over 1.2 million men and over 83,000 women. Male prisoners are 35 percent white, 46 percent black, 16 percent Hispanic. Nearly 10 percent of black males, aged 25 to 29, were in prison in 2000." See "IN THE SYSTEM," Online NewsHour, *PBS* August 28, 2001. According to the National Center for Education Statistics (NCES), in 1999, there were a total of 1,640,700 black students enrolled in degree-granting postsecondary institutions in the United States. Out of that total, black males comprised 603,000 (36.75%) and black females comprised 1,037,700 (63.25%). See U.S. Department of Education, National Center for Education Statistics, Higher Education General Information (HEGIS), "Fall Enrollment in Colleges and Universities" surveys; and Integrated Postsecondary Education Data System (IPEDS), April 2001.

15. The following nations: Slovenia, Hungary, Poland, Slovakia, Cyprus, Czech Republic, Estonia, Latvia, Lithuania and Malta have been invited to join the European Union in 2004. See T. Fuller, "The Next Europe at What Price a Bigger EU?" *International Herald Tribune,* June 13, 2002.

CHAPTER TEN

THE NUCLEAR OPTION
AND INTERNATIONAL JUSTICE
ISLAMIC PERSPECTIVES[1]

Two partitions of the twentieth century have profoundly affected the Muslim world. One was the partition of India—which gave the Muslim world the miracle of a new member. The other was the partition of Palestine, which gave the Muslim world the challenge of a new adversary. Those two momentous events occurred within two consecutive years. In 1947 we saw the birth of the Muslim state of Pakistan. In 1948 we witnessed the birth of the Jewish state of Israel. Islam in the twentieth century was never to be the same again.

This chapter is comparative. 1948 was significant for Africa as well as for the Muslim world—though the reasons were initially entirely different. While in that year the Middle East witnessed the triumph of Zionism as the Israeli flag was raised over Palestine, Africa in the same year witnessed the prospective triumph of a full-fledged apartheid as the National Party was swept into power in South Africa. And yet only a prophet of Biblical proportions could have told that Zionism in the Middle East and apartheid in South Africa would later become political allies. Only such a prophet could possibly have foreseen military collaboration between the two forces.

But where does the nuclear factor fit into this complex equation? The Muslims of South Asia lived to witness the nuclearization of their much larger and powerful neighbor, India. The Muslims of the Middle East lived to witness the nuclearization of their small but powerful neighbor, Israel. Over time the question even arose whether India and Israel would conspire to prevent the nuclearization of Pakistan. In the Middle East, meanwhile, Israel on her own was exercising a veto over the nuclearization of Iraq and the rest of the Arab world—while simultaneously facilitating the nuclearization of the apartheid regime in South Africa.

What all this means is that the coming of the nuclear age has been bad news for both the Muslim world and Africa, at least for the time being. This has been compounded by the attitude of the United States. Washington turned the other way, if not actually helped, the nuclearization of Israel and the Republic of South Africa. Yet Washington has been strongly opposed to "nuclear proliferation" in either the Muslim world or Africa. This was well before Saddam Hussein became America's new bogey man. As for the nuclearization of India, Washington was ambivalent. On the one hand, a nuclear India could reduce the arms race with Pakistan. On the other hand, a nuclear India could counterbalance a nuclear China in the regional politics of Asia.

But the nuclear shadow over the Muslim world probably began in the Middle East rather than in South Asia. The two partitions of 1947 and 1948 created conditions of military rivalry and technological competition in both South Asia and the Middle East respectively. But technological change occurred much faster in Israel than in any other country in the two regions. To that extent the nuclear specter began in Israel—with consequences not only for the Muslim world but also for Africa. Let us now examine this nuclear saga in greater detail.

THE NUCLEARIZATION OF ZIONISM

In 1957 Israeli Prime Minister David Ben-Gurion proposed to his cabinet that a nuclear reactor be established at Dimona in the Negev Desert. Secretly the French government agreed, if not offered, to help Israel in designing and building that Dimona reactor.

In that same year a company was formed in Pennsylvania. The company was called the Nuclear Materials and Equipment Corporation (NUMEC). It was established by Dr. Zalman Shapiro, who had previously worked on nuclear research programs of the US Navy. Dr. Shapiro was an ardent supporter of Israel. The company took on contracts from the federal government, including contracts to transform highly enriched uranium into fuel for US Navy reactors.

About seven years later it was discovered by the Atomic Energy Commission (AEC) that at least two-hundred pounds of highly enriched uranium were unaccounted for at Dr. Shapiro's corporation. The Atomic Energy Commission was also startled by NUMEC's cooperation with the state of Israel in which the company served as "the technical consultant and training procurement agency for Israel in the United States." Dr. Shapiro denied that he had diverted any enriched uranium to Israel, but he did pay the 1.1 million dollars in fines for the nuclear materials unaccounted for.

Carl Duckett, Deputy Director for Science and Technology of the Central Intelligence Agency (CIA) from 1967 to 1976, later reported that by 1968 the CIA already believed that Israel had developed nuclear weapons, and had noted that this development coincided in time with the disappearance of the enriched materials from Dr. Shapiro's company. When Duckett reported this to his boss, CIA Director Richard Helmes, Duckett was ordered to keep the findings secret. And when Helmes reported this to President Lyndon Johnson, the President preferred to keep it secret even from his own Secretary of State, Dean Rusk and Secretary of Defense, Robert McNamara.

The US therefore represents a second partner for Israel in the history of its nuclear adventure. The first major partner was France—then an adversary to Muslim North Africa. Israel and France had just emerged out of the Suez fiasco of 1956. The joint attack on Nasser's Egypt had, from all evidence, been initially a Franco-Israeli conspiracy, which was then joined by Great Britain under Anthony Eden. The United States was kept in the dark until the plans were ready for an Israeli invasion of the Sinai, followed by an invasion of Egypt by Britain and France ostensibly to protect the Suez Canal.

Mainly because of American, Soviet and UN opposition to the tripartite invasion of Egypt by the three powers, the adventure failed in its aims. But the period was one of substantial political intimacy between the French government and the Israeli's. It was also a period of considerable anti-Arab and even anti-Islamic sentiment in official circles in France, mainly because of Arab and Muslim support for the ongoing Algerian revolution. French collaboration with Israel on a nuclear reactor was in part an extension of their collaboration in the Suez adventure of 1956, and was politically related to the Algerian war of liberation and Nasser's support for it.

So far we may certainly conclude that the French collaboration was at the official and governmental level. But what about American collaboration with regard to the disappearance of enriched uranium from NUMEC? Was this American collaboration purely unofficial, involving private sympathizers of Israel, or did it implicate the Government of the United States? There are a number of theories within intelligence circles in the United States, as well as among commentators. Perhaps the most conspiratorial of the theories is the one that alleges actual CIA involvement in the disappearance of enriched materials and its diversion to Israel. According to this theory, Johnson's eagerness to cover up the issue was partly because a major agency of the United States was involved. Another theory attributes the alleged diversion of the enriched material to Israel's own secret service, the MOSSAD, which subsequently also worked out strategies of diverting French uranium, as well as American.

Based on evidence elsewhere, Senator Robert Kennedy is re-

ported to have given warning as early as 1965 that Israel had stock-
piled "weapon-grade fissionable material" and that she could "fabri-
cate an atomic device within a few months." But at that time
Kennedy's conclusion was very tentative. Nor was he aware of the
"cover-up" which was later attributed to President Lyndon Johnson.

The third country after France and the United States to have
featured prominently in the nuclear history of Israel is the Republic
of South Africa. This is basically a phenomenon of the 1970s and
early 1980s. The relations between Israel and South Africa in the
economic field began to improve before the October War of 1973.
Trade between the two countries took a dramatic turn for the better
from 1971 onwards. And the level of Israel's diplomatic representation in Pretoria, which had been lowered following the Sharpeville
massacre of 1960, rose when Ambassador Dr. Michael Michaels was
appointed to head the Israeli mission in Pretoria in 1972. What all
this means is that the Israeli-South African axis was not born out of
Black Africa's diplomatic break with Israel following the 1973 war
in the Middle East, but had already started before that October War.

Two areas of military relevance became important in the evolving collaboration between Israel and South Africa. One was the area
of counter-insurgency, techniques of combating guerrilla movements
and terrorist tactics. Before the outbreak of the Palestinian *Intifādah*,
Israel had been relatively successful in containing the operations of
Palestine Liberation Organization (PLO) fighters. The Republic of
South Africa recognized with humility Israel's triumph in this field,
and sought to learn Israel's expertise in counter-insurgency.

The other area of military collaboration between these two countries (both increasingly isolated internationally in the 1970s and
1980s) was the area of nuclear cooperation. Apartheid South Africa
had the uranium and some expertise bequeathed to it by more than a
decade of collaboration in the nuclear field with the United States
and other Western countries. Israel in turn had additional technological expertise that could help to enhance South Africa's military ef-
fectiveness. There is a widespread belief in both Africa and the Middle
East that substantial progress in weapon development has occurred

149

as a result of this collaboration between Israel and South Africa.

These suspicions rose to a new level with the "mystery flash" somewhere in the south Atlantic or Indian Ocean area—a flash which was detected by a U.S. Vela spy satellite in September 1979. The characteristics of the flash were strongly those normally associated with a nuclear explosion but the Carter Administration kept the news secret for a few weeks until it leaked. Initial announcements attributed the flash to a South African device. But in February 1980 the Colombia Broadcasting System (CBS) network of the United States carried a report by its Israeli correspondent, Dan Raviv, attributing the explosion to Israel. In other words, at first the inference was that the blast in the South Atlantic or Indian Ocean was a South African bomb probably aided by Israel. But the CBS Report in February 1980 converted it into an Israeli bomb, probably aided by South Africa.

Since then alternative theories have been advanced, including formal reports by investigative committees. The alternative theories about the mystery flash range from stories about a meteorite to South Africa's own theory that a small nuclear accident had occurred on a Soviet vessel in the area concerned. Those governments that are eager to minimize the chances of a nuclear arms race either in Africa or in the Middle East would in any case have been inevitably tempted to opt for a scenario which would not portray either South Africa or Israel as nuclear powers.

But the bulk of the evidence available justifies the suspicion that 22 September 1979 was an ominous day for both the Arab world and Africa. An unholy alliance between Zionism and apartheid had got nuclearized. The whole of the Muslim world and the whole of the Black world were bound to feel the reverberations for many years to come. The 22nd of September 1979 helped to emphasize that the nuclear age was for the time being bad news for both Islam and the African people.

In 1990, on the eve of the beginning of negotiations for sharing power with Blacks, the white government of South Africa at last agreed to sign the Nuclear Weapons Non-Proliferation Treaty (NPT)— making sure that what had been sauce for the white goose would not become sauce for the Black gander. Prior to that Egypt had been persuaded or coopted into the NPT regime also—while Israel still refused to sign.

ISLAM VERSUS THE NUCLEAR AGE

But more specifically why has the nuclear age been such bad news for Islam? The new science arrived at a time when Islam had been pushed to the periphery of technological civilization and the margins of scientific know-how. Gone were the days when Muslims were so advanced in mathematics that the very numbers of calculation bore the name "Arabic numerals." Gone were the days when the Arabs led in pushing the frontiers of the metric principle. Who even remembers that words like average, algebra, amalgam, atlas, cypher, chemistry and zenith were originally Arabic?

The arrival of the nuclear age in the twentieth century also coincided with the disappearance of the Islamic Caliphate in the world system for the first time in centuries. The Ottoman Empire had disintegrated after World War I. Almost the entire Muslim world came under Euro-Christian domination—from Egypt to Indonesia, from Senegal to Malaya, from the Gulf states to Northern India. Never was the Muslim world more convincingly humbled. Ataturk's Turkey and Iran were barely semi-independent. The rest of Islam was well and truly under Euro-Christian subjugation.

The world did not realize it at the time, but there were two super-powers about to establish a divided hegemony upon humanity following World War II. The Semitic factor was once again linked. One superpower was the United States—with a Jewish enclave that was destined to become one of the most important (if indirect) factors in the history of the Middle East in the twentieth century. The other superpower was of course the Soviet Union—with a Muslim enclave seemingly as unimportant in influencing Middle Eastern trends as the Jewish enclave in America was decisive in the same role.

By the 1980s the Soviet Union had a Muslim population of

well over fifty million in a total Soviet population of two hundred and fifty million. The United States had a Jewish population of less than seven million in an American population of two hundred and twenty million. And yet the less than seven million Jews of the Western super-power had more relevance for Islamic history than did the nearly fifty million Muslims in the Soviet Union. One reason was simply the fact that the Soviet Union was not a liberal democracy—and therefore electoral numbers counted less than they did in the United States. There is little doubt that had there been fifty million Muslims in the United States instead of the same number in the Soviet Union, the history of the whole world would have been more discernibly different. The Muslims in the United States would have begun to outweigh in some matters the influence of American Jews on American foreign policy towards the Middle East—for better or worse.

Of course this did not happen. The superpower that emerged as the nuclear leader in world politics was in any case the one with a seven million Jewish enclave rather than the one with a forty to fifty million Muslim enclave. The Islamic factor in the nuclear history of the world was doubly marginalized—not least because Western Jews were among the innovative giants of the nuclear age while Muslim scholars were scientifically peripheral in the twentieth century. The era of the atom was also the era of Albert Einstein, the most towering scientist of the twentieth century and one of the most famous Jews of all time. The stage was set for a future Jewish involvement (Einstein, Oppenheimer, Teller) in the nuclear age, against a background of global Muslim marginality, as we have indicated.

In a sense we are back to that issue of a nuclearized Jewish state. No collective re-incarnation in history has been more dramatic than the re-creation of the Jewish state. The last Jewish state died two thousand years previously—only to be re-born in the full scientific glare of the nuclear age. The new state of Israel was born within three years of the dropping of the atomic bombs on Hiroshima and Nagasaki by the United States. A Jewish political entity that had died two millennia ago in Biblical times was suddenly re-born and started blinking at the brightness of a "nuclear dawn."

Within a single generation the Jewish state itself became a nuclear power. That was bad news for the Arabs and for their supporters in the rest of the Muslim world. Without nuclear power, Israel's conventional superiority could one day have been neutralized by Arab numerical preponderance—as the skill and organizational differential between Arabs and Israelis narrowed. But the acquisition of nuclear weapons by Israel has helped to create a potentially permanent military stalemate. Even when the Arabs become one day the equals of the Israelis in conventional weapons, and match the Israelis in nuclear capacity, the principle of the nuclear deterrent may work in the context of the Arab-Israeli conflict with greater certainty than it will necessarily continue to work in the East/West conflict. Israel just happens to have been created at a time when a nuclear stalemate could conceivably ensure its survival. That may be good for world Jewry—but it is not necessarily good news for the Muslim world if Jerusalem is forever lost to Muslim sovereignty. The old Cold War between East and West has now ended. Some conflicts between Israel and Palestinians are in the process of being resolved. But if the USA and the USSR nearly went to war over Cuba in 1962, will Israel and the Arabs in the future still go to war over Jerusalem?

Even in the realm of the peaceful uses of atomic energy, the nuclear age is potentially a disservice to Islam. It is oil rather than uranium ore which has recently given Islam new economic leverage in the world system. The Organization of Petroleum Exporting Countries (OPEC) is primarily a Muslim organization in composition and is Arab-led.

THE CRESCENT OVER THE MUSHROOM CLOUD

If Islam gets nuclearized, two regional rivalries are likely to have played an important part in it. One is the rivalry between India and Pakistan; the other is the aforementioned rivalry between Israel and the Arabs. Saddam Hussein's aspirations in Iraq were part of a wider story of ambition and frustration.

153

India may have decided to speed up its nuclear program more because of China than because of Pakistan; but Pakistan's decision to speed up its own program was almost certainly influenced if not inspired by India's explosion of a nuclear device in 1974.

The cultural rivalry of Muslims versus Hindus is also more relevant in Pakistani attitudes than in India's policies. Basically the attitude of the Indian government towards Pakistan has relatively little to do with the fact that Pakistan is a Muslim country. The Indian government deals with a variety of other Muslim countries on an entirely different basis. In contrast, the attitude of the Pakistani government towards India is presumably often clouded by a historical rivalry with Hindus. India itself is of course a secular state; Pakistan is an Islamic Republic. Perceptions of the state within Pakistan are conditioned by a cultural and religious self-consciousness. The pursuit of a new form of power like nuclear energy, and the quest for the new form of status as a member of the nuclear club, almost inevitably carries in Pakistan a sense of Muslim pride and cultural ambition. The basic dialectic in the Pakistani psyche between Islam as a religion in its own right and Islam as an antithesis of Hinduism is bound to have conditioned Pakistan's nuclear program, as it has conditioned many other major directions of national, regional and global policies adopted in Pakistan.

Pakistan's nuclear ambitions go back to the late Prime Minister Zulkifar Ali Bhutto. In Bhutto's case, as in the minds of subsequent leaders, nuclear capability was seen as part of cultural and religious vindication. Prime Minister Bhutto was quoted as saying: There was a Christian bomb, a Jewish bomb, and now a Hindu bomb. Why not an Islamic bomb?[2]

Pakistan's effort to match India's nuclear capability seems to have been considerably aided by the work of Dr. Abdel Qader Khan. Dr. Khan worked for a while in a laboratory in Amsterdam and had access to a wide range of classified documents and scientific processes relevant to "sensitive" nuclear research. According to reports he was even able to spend some time at the Urenco consortium's secret Uranium Enrichment Plant at Almelo near the border between the Federal Republic of Germany and the Netherlands. Dr. Khan could thus closely observe the centrifuge process.

It would seem that Khan originally accepted the job in the Netherlands purely as a means of livelihood prior to becoming a Dutch citizen (he was himself partly educated in Holland and was married to a Dutch woman) but reports imply that some time in 1974, presumably after India's explosion of its nuclear device and the impact this had on many Pakistanis still reeling from their defeat in the Indo-Pakistani War of 1971, Khan was apparently persuaded to become a nuclear spy for Pakistan. Later on, he left Holland to go back to his native country—and became in absentia the most controversial Third World scientist in recent international history. Holland was taken to task by its Urenco partners, Britain and West Germany. The Israelis also lodged a vigorous protest to the Netherlands. The United States temporarily suspended most forms of aid to Pakistan; and much of the world speculated whether Libyan money and Pakistani know-how were together on their way towards nuclearizing Islam.

Was Dr. Khan on a crusade not only to nuclearize Islam, but also to break the nuclear monopoly of the Northern hemisphere more widely? For both self-regarding and global reasons, was Khan prepared to share nuclear expertise with relevant developing countries at large?

Under pressure from the United States the President of Pakistan had Dr. Khan arrested in 2003. The scientist confessed to selling nuclear expertise and materiel to third parties, but insisted that Pakistani authorities had not been involved in these acts of proliferation. Khan asked President Musharraf for forgiveness. Since Musharraf was now regarded as an ally of the United States, Washington decided to look the other way when Musharraf pardoned Dr. Khan.

While Pakistan's nuclear ambitions have been conditioned by rivalry with India, Libya's military ambitions were connected with its bid for leadership in the Arab world and its hostility towards Israel. A more likely Arab nuclear innovator than Libya turned out to be Iraq in spite of the setback of the destruction of its original reactor by Israel (or perhaps because of that destruction). International controversy erupted in the summer of 1980 concerning a French nuclear deal with the government of Iraq. Reports had it that a hundred technicians of the French government company Technitome, an arm of France's Atomic Energy Commission, were already in Iraq to install a powerful Osiris resurge reactor and a smaller Isis reactor under a contract which included supplying enriched uranium. The technicians were also scheduled to train six-hundred Iraqis to run the reactors. Voices of protest were heard, especially from Israel, Britain and the United States.

It was reported that the first shipment of approximately thirty-three pounds of highly enriched uranium (out of a total of some one-hundred and fifty-eight pounds over three years) had left for Iraq in June 1980. Western scientists calculated that one-hundred and fifty-eight pounds of the 93% enriched uranium could enable Iraq to make between three and six nuclear bombs. It was estimated that it would take Iraq approximately five years to acquire this modest military nuclear capability.[3]

There was suspicion from quite early that the Israelis would attempt to abort the French-Iraqi deal even to the extent of committing murder and attempting sabotage. Important parts of one of the reactors were blown up in 1979 in a commando-style operation. And an Egyptian nuclear expert working for Iraq was murdered in Paris in June 1979. The French authorities and others strongly suspected Israeli involvement. And in the course of the controversy of the summer of 1980 western diplomats expressed fears about possible Israeli preemptive military action if and when intelligence revealed that Iraq was about to build nuclear weapons. As it turned out, Israel did not wait for such evidence before destroying Iraq's reactor in June 1981. Did the Israeli aggression in Iraq in 1981 contribute towards inflating rather than reducing Iraq's military ambitions? Did Israel create a self-fulfilling prophecy—an Iraq newly converted to acquiring dangerous weapons?

The anxieties expressed by the Israelis carried a certain historical cynicism. After all, France had sold Israel a reactor without any inspection safeguards in the 1960s. While Iraq has signed the Nuclear

Nonproliferation Treaty (NPT) of the UN, Israel still has not done so. It has been reported that in the 1950s Israeli scientists at the Weizmann Institute perfected a new and economical way of making the heavy water that moderates the chain reaction in the nuclear reactor. Speculation has it that the Israelis sold their secrets to France in exchange for a reactor. That reactor, situated at the secret Dimona Nuclear Plant, featured in a report of the United States' CIA to the effect that Israel may already have between ten and twenty nuclear weapons.[4]

Whatever may be the extent of Israel's nuclear capability there is little doubt that the arms race in the Middle East, like the arms race between India and Pakistan, is a fundamental part of the background to the forthcoming nuclearization of Islam. Even the peaceful uses of nuclear energy of the kind cautiously envisaged for Egypt by President Richard Nixon would, quite probably, be only a few years away from potential military uses accessible to a future government in Cairo, especially if political radicalism returns to Egypt.

How does all this relate to issues of leadership and politics at the global level? We should first note that the danger of nuclear war does come from two primary sources—vertical nuclear proliferation among the great powers and horizontal nuclear proliferation in the Third World. Vertical proliferation involves greater sophistication and diversification of nuclear options and nuclear technology in the arsenals of the great powers. The same nuclear powers increase and diversify their destructive capabilities.

Horizontal proliferation, on the other hand, involves entirely new members of the Nuclear Club. The NPT was in fact intended to deal with both the risk of vertical proliferation among the great powers and horizontal addition of new nuclear powers. The great powers were supposed to embark on effective steps toward disarmament, while at the same time helping to reduce the risk of more and more countries acquiring nuclear weapons. In reality, since 1968 when the NPT struggled to be born, both vertical and horizontal proliferations have taken place. And the vertical variety among the great powers has escalated faster than the horizontal addition of new members to the nuclear club.

But what could effectively motivate the great powers not only to decelerate the arms race but also generally to declare nuclear weapons illegitimate and subsequently to start the process of conventional disarmament? It would seem that vertical proliferation has sometimes motivated the great powers to seek ways of containing the arms race. The Strategic Arms Limitation Treaties (SALT) were in part a response to the stresses of vertical nuclear proliferation, a search for ways of containing the competition. And yet for the time being vertical nuclear proliferation has not been adequate for the bigger goal of motivating the great powers to give up nuclear weapons altogether.

The question that arises is what sort of concern is likely to be effective enough to lead to the military denuclearization of the world. One type of shock could be a somewhat limited accidental nuclear catastrophe of a military kind. The civilian accident at the Three Mile Island in Pennsylvania did more for the anti-nuclear movement in the western world than almost anything else before the Soviet accident at Chernobyl. Had the accident gone out of hand, and a bigger catastrophe resulted, the revulsion against nuclear energy would have been even more dramatic.

Similarly, had the periodic computer errors in the United States about a Russian "attack" resulted in a really precipitate American response, the disaster might have provided enough of a shock to create an irresistible anti-nuclear movement among the populations of the great powers themselves.

But one should not pray for disasters, however accidental. An alternative approach to shocking the world into nuclear renunciation is to take a risk with horizontal proliferation. In this scenario the possibility, if not the certainty, of a disaster remains. The logic here is that a certain degree of nuclear proliferation in the world is bound to increase nuclear anxieties within the population of the great powers themselves, and strengthen pressures for the total abandonment of nuclear weapons by everyone. The great powers do not trust Third World countries with those weapons. That distrust could become an asset if the threat of nuclearization of the Third World creates enough consternation in the Northern hemisphere to result in a massive international movement to declare nuclear weapons illegitimate for all, and to put an end to nuclear arsenals in every country that has them. What this means is that although the greatest risks of nuclear war come from vertical proliferation in the Northern hemisphere and, only secondarily from horizontal proliferation in the Third World, the vertical variety in itself has not been enough to end this dangerous nuclear order. The "vaccination" of horizontal nuclear proliferation might be needed to cure the world of this nuclear malaise—a dose of the disease becomes part of the necessary cure.

Here the Muslim world comes into relevance again. The most dangerous part of the Third World from the point of view of global war is the Middle East. Modest horizontal proliferation in the Middle East would be more dangerous in global terms than a slightly higher level of proliferation in, say, Latin America or Black Africa. This is partly because a regional war in the Middle East carries a greater risk of escalating into a world war than a regional war in Latin America or Black Africa.

If then horizontal nuclear proliferation is a necessary vaccine against the existing nuclear order itself, proliferation in the heartland of the Muslim world should work faster than proliferation elsewhere. Although Brazil is much larger than either Iran or Iraq, Brazil's nuclear capability would be less of a global shock than Iranian or Iraqi nuclear bombs. Pakistan's explosion of a nuclear device would carry with it greater fears than a successful explosion by Argentina. Three nuclear powers in the Islamic world could be perceived as a greater threat to world peace than five nuclear powers in some other parts of the Third World. In the total struggle against nuclear weapons in the world as a whole the Muslim world might well play a decisive role in the years ahead.

In this instance Islam might at first be playing a Russian nuclear roulette with two other civilizations—with Hinduism in South Asia and with Zionism and politicized Judaism in the Middle East. But out of the dangerous regional game might emerge an impetus for global reform; out of limited horizontal proliferation there might ultimately evolve global denuclearization.

Where does Africa fit into these nuclear calculations? How have cultural and racial inequalities affected Africa in the nuclear age? It is to this theme that we must now turn.

Africa and the Traditions of Combat

The possibility of weapons of mass destruction in Africa has been explored either in the extreme north of the continent (especially regarding Libya) or the extreme south (especially regarding the Republic of South Africa). For a while, Africa itself was ambivalent about militarism and rearmament. This was partly because of earlier conceptions of the whole doctrine of non-alignment. As one African country after another became independent, a duty envisaged for each one of them was that of helping to moderate the tensions among the Great Powers. The first conference of independent African states held in Accra, Ghana, in April 1958, appealed to the Great Powers to discontinue the production of atomic and thermo-nuclear weapons and to suspend all such tests "not only in the interests of world peace but as a symbol of their avowed devotion to the rights of man." The meeting reaffirmed the view that the reduction of conventional armament was "essential in the interests of international peace and security"—though the conference went on to condemn "the policy of using the sale of arms as a means of exerting pressure on Governments and interfering in the internal affairs of other countries."[5] Libya was represented at the Accra conference, but South Africa was not because it was still under a white apartheid government.

Non-alignment in those early days was still seduced by the ideals of disarmament. This was partly because of India's ambivalence on the precise relationship between non-violence and non-alignment. The two most important Indian contributions to African political thought were the doctrines of non-violence and non-alignment. Gandhi contributed passive resistance to one school of African thought; Nehru contributed non-alignment to almost all African countries. As Uganda's Milton Obote put it in his tribute to Nehru when the Indian leader died:

> Nehru will be remembered as the founder of non-alignment
> ... The new nations of the world owe him a debt of grati-
> tude in this respect.[6]

But how related were the two doctrines of non-alignment and
non-violence? For India itself Gandhi's non-violence was a method
of seeking freedom, while Nehru's non-alignment came to be a method
of seeking peace. And yet non-alignment was in some ways a translation into foreign policy of some of the moral assumptions that un-
derlay passive resistance in the domestic struggle for India's independence. Gandhi himself once said:

> Free India can have no enemy ... For India to enter into the
> race for armament is to court suicide ... The world is look-
> ing for something new and unique from India ... With the
> loss of India to non-violence the last hope of the world will
> be gone...[7]

In spite of Gandhi's vision, independent India did not practice
abstinence. Gandhian non-violence was not fully translated into foreign policy. Suspicion of Pakistan in particular was too strong to
permit that. And yet of all the countries in the world, and in spite of
its wars with Pakistan, India under Nehru came nearest to symboliz-
ing the search for peace. For a crucial decade in the history of Africa
and Asia, India was the diplomatic leader of both continents. In the
doctrine of non-alignment India bequeathed to many of the new states
a provisional foreign policy for the first few experimental years of
their sovereign statehood.

With that policy the wheel of global pacification had come full
circle. Asia and Africa had once been colonized partly with the view
to "imposing peace" upon them. But now non-alignment had turned
the tables on old concepts like Pax Britannica. It was now those who
were once colonized who were preaching peace to their former im-

perial tutors.

And yet India's non-alignment was destined to go nuclear. India was indeed the first non-aligned country to explode a nuclear device. This happened in 1974. India was also the first country without a permanent seat in the Security Council of the United Nations to explode a nuclear device. The first five nuclear powers were precisely the war-lords with the veto in the Security Council—the United States, the Soviet Union, Great Britain, France and the People's Republic of China. India at last had broken this neat equation, and put the issue of nuclear proliferation onto a new footing.

But is nuclear non-alignment a contradiction in itself? Should Africa and the other Third World countries continue in their older tradition of distrusting militarism? If one of the ambitions of non-alignment continues to be the effort to moderate tensions in the world, then two Third World legacies had to go nuclear. One is the legacy of Nehru in India and the other is the legacy of the warrior tradition in Africa. The nuclearization of non-alignment would mean not merely using nuclear power for peaceful purposes, but using that power to reduce the danger of East-West convulsion.

The nuclearization of the warrior tradition, on the other hand, would imply a reassertion of adulthood in the Third World, a rejection of the imperial monopoly of warfare. Non-alignment would seek to reduce tensions; the warrior tradition would seek to reduce dependency.

India has already moved into the nuclear field. For the time being, India has assured the world that it will use its nuclear capacity for peaceful purposes, though at the same time, India has warned that such a non-military commitment would partly depend upon Pakistan's nuclear policy in the years ahead. But how far is Africa from a comparable nuclear role? And in what way would proliferation of nuclear weapons beyond India into Africa be a contribution to global pacification?

Militarily, Africa is still a dependent continent in terms of weaponry. Apart from the white-dominated countries in the south, and to some extent apart from Egypt, the technology of making sophisticated weapons is for the time being a distant aspiration for African countries except on an extremely modest scale.

And yet seven traditions of combat have been particularly pertinent in Africa. In Muslim Africa there may be a resurrection of the *jihād* tradition—a commitment to defend Islam with the sword if need be.

Passive resistance, on the other hand, could be described as being—in part—a Christo-Gandhian tradition. This combines a commitment to social transformation with renunciation of violence. Passive resistance often tends to include the crucifixion syndrome, the pursuit of martyrdom as a strategy of protest.

Curiously enough, the Iranian revolution in its strategy against the Shah was "Christo-Gandhian" in appearance but basically derived from the *jihād* tradition. Thousands of unarmed people poured out into the streets of Tehran in what was the most impressive people's revolution of the second half of the twentieth century. It was also the most impressive case of passive resistance since Mahatma Gandhi inspired the masses of India to rebel against the British Raj.

To that extent Ayatollah Khomeini was strikingly similar to Mohandas Gandhi in terms of a historic role. Both leaders mobilized cultural and religious symbols to move the hearts of their compatriots against what they regarded as unjust. Libya after its own 1969 revolution included a *jihād* factor in its foreign policy under Muammar Qaddafy.

The third tradition of combat in the modern world (after the *jihād* and passive resistance) is the wider one of warrior tradition. It survives in a variety of forms in different cultures—from the Samurai code in Japan to the residual "Deer Hunter" image in the United States. The warrior tradition is based on the hard virtues of individual masculinity—toughness, courage, endurance, and even purposeful ruthlessness. The warrior tradition also survives in a variety of forms in Africa—sometimes disguised behind the uniform of a modern army.

The fourth combat culture operating in Africa and elsewhere, especially in the Third World, is the guerrilla tradition. It has been particularly important in struggles for national liberation and for social revolutions. Increasingly, this mode of combat is becoming androgynous—rallying both men and women to the struggle. The wars in Southern Africa belong to this category.

A closely related tradition is the one of terrorism. This includes skyjacking, hostage holding, blowing up bars and the like. But unlike a guerrilla movement, terrorism need not include a literal organized army, though it often does require "operators" and "agents."

Normal usage of the term "terrorism" is conditioned by the values of the power structure with a vested interest in "law and order" rather than in fundamental social reform. The word therefore tends to have negative connotations. But my use here attempts to be normatively neutral. Terrorism is a form of warfare rather than a form of deviancy. Just as there can be a just war and an unjust one, so there can be just and unjust terrorist movements. Like guerrilla movements, revolutionary terrorism now tries to be androgynous—recruiting both men and women.

On the whole, other forms of warfare destroy in order to incapacitate the enemy. Terrorism destroys in order to frighten the population. To incapacitate the war machine of the enemy is harder to accomplish than to erode the self-confidence of the population.

Terrorism is often the ultimate weapon of the weak, a strategy of last resort. Lord Acton was perhaps right in his suspicion that "power corrupts; absolute power corrupts absolutely." But since then we have indeed come to recognize in the twentieth century that powerlessness also corrupts—and absolute powerlessness can lead to acts of desperation. Terrorism is often born out of the agonies of frustration. That is what the bombs in the markets of Jerusalem and the pubs of Ulster are all about.

What should also be remembered is that the power structure of a state can also become terroristic. The record of the British forces in Northern Ireland has had its moments of moral degeneracy—as the European Commission on Human Rights has at times been compelled to note. But far guiltier of counter-terrorism is the state of Israel—which has insisted on killing dozens of Arabs (no matter how innocent) for every Jew that has fallen in a terrorist act.

Marxist debates have long agonized over the concept of "state capitalism." Liberal debaters should also recognize "state terrorism" as an aberration with a logic of its own even in liberal societies. The state of Israel is a classic case of a domestic liberal democracy that has produced a terrorist foreign policy. The periodic bombing of Lebanese villages by the Israelis has been a feature of this policy. The terrorist is not always the sly, disguised individual about to plant a bomb in a market place. The terrorist could be the ruthless state official who plans comparable acts on others, and gives orders that the acts be carried out under governmental auspices. Of course, Israel has also plotted individual assassinations and kidnapping over the years.

But "state terrorism" can sometimes be an aspect of the sixth tradition of combat. This is what is sometimes called conventional war—a confrontation between two organized armies, representing different societies, or different states, or different regions of the same society or state. This combat tradition also tends to be de facto masculine, though not always because of any conscious cultural logic.

If the guerrilla is symbolized by the sten gun, the terrorist by the time-bomb, the more collective effort of conventional warfare is symbolized by the modern tank.

Towards the Nuclearization of Africa

As for the seventh tradition of combat, this is what nuclear power is all about. Africa was in attendance at the birth of the nuclear age. It was in part Africa's uranium from Zaire that helped to set in motion the first nuclear reactor in North America. And, for better or for worse, Africa's uranium may have facilitated those dreadful atomic bombs, which were dropped on Hiroshima and Nagasaki in August 1945. But of course Africa had no say in the matter. It was not an exercise in Africa's warrior tradition at all. An African resource had simply been pirated by others—and once again played a major role in a significant shift in Western industrialism.

Not that uranium was all that scarce even in the 1940s. What was significant was that outside the Soviet Bloc and North America, uranium seemed to be substantially available only in Black Africa. As Caryl P. Haskins put it way back in 1946:

> [Uranium] stands next to copper in abundance, is more abundant than zinc, and is about four times as plentiful as lead ... However, the outstanding deposits are narrowly distributed, being confined to the United States, Canada, the Belgian Congo, Czechoslovakia and possibly Russia. The fact that the richest deposits of uranium ore occur in a fairly limited number of places makes international control feasible; but it also foreshadows violent competitive struggles for ownership of the richest deposits (the struggle for oil greatly intensified).[8]

Since 1946 other reserves of uranium ore have been discovered in the world, including in different parts of Africa. African uranium has continued to fill many a reactor in the Western world, and to help create many a nuclear device.

The second service (after uranium supply) that Africa rendered to the nuclear age was also symbolic. Africa provided the desert for nuclear tests in the early 1960s. In this case Africa's nuclear involvement had slightly shifted from a purely indigenous resource (uranium) to a partially Islamic context of sovereignty (the Sahara). The transition was from providing indigenous nuclear material to furnishing a neo-Islamic laboratory in the desert for a Western bomb. At least two of the legacies of Africa's triple heritage were inadvertently involved—from the mines of Zaire to the sands of Algeria. North Africa was the first African soil to be violated by somebody else's nuclear tests—the French tests in Algeria before 1962.

The third African point of entry into the nuclear age has been through the Republic of South Africa. For better or worse, South Africa before F.W. De Klerk had probably become a nuclear power or was close to it. This provided the third leg of Africa's triple heritage. Indigenous resources (Africa's uranium), a semi-Islamic testing laboratory (the dunes of the Sahara) and an actual Western productive capability (South Africa's expertise).

A circle of influence developed. The progress of the French nuclear programme and its tests in the Sahara probably helped Israeli's nuclear programme. This was a period when France was quite close to Israel in terms of economic, diplomatic, military, and technological collaboration. The French helped the Israelis build a nuclear reactor at Dimona and seemed at times to be closer to the Israelis in sharing nuclear secrets than even the Americans were. The evidence is abundant and clear—the French nuclear programme in the late 1950s and 1960s served as a midwife to the Israeli nuclear programme. And France's tests in the Sahara were part and parcel of France's nuclear process and infrastructure in that period.

By a curious twist of destiny, the Israeli nuclear programme in turn came to serve as a midwife to the nuclear efforts of the Republic of South Africa in the 1970s and 1980s. When a nuclear explosion occurred in the South Atlantic in September 1979, the question that arose was (as we indicated) whether it was primarily a South African nuclear experiment undertaken with Israeli technical aid, or primarily an Israeli explosive experiment carried out with South Africa's logistical support. The cyclical nuclear equation was about to be completed. The Sahara had aided France's nuclear programme, France had aided Israeli's nuclear design, and Israel had in turn aided South Africa's nuclear ambitions. Kwame Nkrumah's fear of a linkage between nuclear tests in the Sahara and racism in South Africa had found astonishing vindication nearly two decades later. It was in April 1960 that Nkrumah addressed an international meeting in Accra in the following terms:

> Fellow Africans and friends: there are two threatening swords of Damocles hanging over the continent, and we must remove them. These are nuclear tests in the Sahara by the French Government and the apartheid policy of the Government of the Union of South Africa. It would be a

great mistake to imagine that the achievement of political independence by certain areas in Africa will automatically mean the end of the struggle. It is merely the beginning of the struggle.[9]

It has turned out that Nkrumah's thesis of "two swords of Damocles," one nuclear, the other racist, was in fact prophetic. Until the 1990s the Republic of South Africa was using nuclear power as a potentially stabilizing factor in defense of apartheid. The old nuclear fall-out in the Sahara in the 1960s involved a linkage between racism and nuclear weapons, which is only just beginning to reveal itself.

Cultural and technological inequalities between white and black in Southern Africa have affected other areas of security—conventional areas as well as nuclear domains. The Republic of South Africa has in the past used its technological superiority to bully its Black neighbors into submission and into "non-aggression" pacts. The sovereignty of Mozambique, Angola, Botswana, Swaziland, Lesotho, and perhaps even independent Zimbabwe has been violated from time to time, sometimes with utter impunity. European technological leadership in the last three centuries of world history has been inherited by people of European extraction operating in Africa—and has been used as a decisive military resource against Black Africans. South Africa's neighbors began to appreciate what it must feel like to be Israel's neighbor—for both Apartheid South Africa and Israel seldom hesitated to use blatant military muscle at the expense of the sovereignty of their neighbors.

Again cultural and technological inequalities have played a part in these politics of intervention. Israelis have enjoyed military preeminence for so long not because they are Jews but because a large part of their population is Western and European. Had the population of Israel consisted overwhelmingly of Middle Eastern Jews, the Arabs would have won every single war they have fought with their Jewish neighbor. Numbers would have counted. Middle Eastern Jews in Israel are often the most hawkish and eager to fight the Arabs, but the military capability for assuring Israeli victory has come more from their European compatriots. Again culture has played a decisive role in deciding victory and defeat in military equations.

The danger both in the Middle East and Southern Africa lies in pushing the weak too far. We have witnessed how desperate conditions in the two sub-regions can easily become fertile ground for different forms of terrorism. For the time being that terrorism in the two geographical areas has not yet gone nuclear. But if the cultural imbalances between Israeli and Arab, between white and black, continue to deepen the sense of desperation among the disadvantaged, we cannot rule out the possibility of their acquiring those nuclear devices one day from radical friends elsewhere. Powerlessness also corrupts—and absolute powerlessness can corrupt absolutely.

In South Africa, political apartheid has come to an end. But economic apartheid seems entrenched. The wealth of the country (from fertile land to lucrative gold and diamond mines) is still in white hands—while Blacks tear each other's limbs in desperation and poverty. Yes, powerlessness also corrupts.

Should African countries stop thinking in terms of making Africa a nuclear-free zone? This was a position which made sense at one time. President Kwame Nkrumah organized a "ban the bomb" international conference in Accra in the early the 1960s, and considered an international march towards the Sahara in protest against French nuclear tests in colonial Algeria. Nkrumah regarded Africa at the time as a continent under the aforementioned threat of two swords of Democles—racism and apartheid in southern African and the nuclear threat France's Sahara tests represented. Nkrumah froze French assets in Ghana as part of the strategy against the nuclear desecration of African soil. Nigeria broke off diplomatic relations with France over the Sahara tests.

All this made sense at the time it was happening in the early 1960s. But in the 1980s Libya under Qaddafy considered going nuclear. It also considered other weapons of mass destruction, but the Western world kept a close eye on Libya, ready to bomb its facilities. By the year 2003, following the Iraqi war, Qaddafy decided to abandon his ambitious pursuit of weapons of mass destruction.

What about Nigeria as a future nuclear power? The development of a nuclear capacity by Africa's largest country is probably a necessary precondition for transcending Africa's diplomatic marginality. Nigeria should follow the example of its fellow giants—Brazil in Latin America and China and India in Asia—and pursue the goal of a modest nuclear capability early in the 21st century. My own reasons for such a capability have nothing to do with making Nigeria militarily stronger. The ultimate purpose is to make the world as a whole militarily safer.

In the long run the alliance between the legacy of Islam and the traditions of Africa might contribute to the right equilibrium in world affairs. For Nigeria, Libya, and Black-ruled South Africa, going nuclear would be a new initiation, an important rite de passage, a recovery of adulthood. No longer will the Great Powers be permitted to say that such and such as weapon is "not for Africans and children under 16."

As for the gap between the militarily powerful and the militarily weak, this will ultimately have to be narrowed first by making the militarily weak more powerful and then by persuading the militarily powerful to weaken themselves. The road to military equality is first through nuclear proliferation in Third World countries, and later in global de-nuclearization for all. African countries will not rise militarily fast enough to catch up with even the middle range northern countries; but African countries could rise sufficiently fast to create conditions for substantial disarmament in the world as a whole.

Africa is still on the periphery of the game of proliferation. To move from periphery to the mainstream of action in the nuclear field in the 21st century, Africa would have to get out of its technological shyness and nuclear inhibitions. When little white children misbehave in some western societies, the mother may sometimes say, "Behave yourself—or a big black man will come and take you away." Today we are dealing not with little white children about to be threatened with the danger of a big black man, but with white adults who must be threatened with the danger of big black men wielding nuclear devices.

Sometimes the threat of a black danger addressed to a little white girl did have the desired effect—the child would behave herself. The question which arises is whether the same threat addressed to the white grown-ups of Washington, Moscow, London and Paris—the ominous threat of nuclearized black power—will in time create enough consternation among the dangerous naughty white war planners of the Northern Hemisphere to induce nuclear sanity at long last.

The struggle itself may have two major historical areas of importance. For Africa the gap between global centrality and political and military marginality will be narrowed. Africa under its triumvirate of diplomatic leaders, partly endowed with nuclear credentials, will have begun to enter the mainstream of global affairs. And the world as a whole, once it discovers the lunacy of its nuclear ways, will have learned an old lesson in a new context—the lesson that wild mushrooms are dangerous.

TOWARDS THE FUTURE

But for the time being the effects of both military disparities and cultural inequalities continue to condition the texture of world arrangements. In fact for much of the 20th century the two most revolutionary normative forces in the world have been Marxism on the one side and Islam on the other. Marxism continued to be a revolution of rising aspirations outside Europe; Islam is a revolution of wounded memory. Marxism is an ideology of how the lowly have risen. Twentieth century Islam is a lament of how the mighty have fallen. At best Marxism is a cry for innovation; at its most obscurantist Islam is a whimper for restoration and revivalism.

The driving force of revolutionary Marxism is, in ideal conditions, class struggle. The driving force of revolutionary Islam is, in ideal conditions, the *jihād*. At least between 1945 and 1985 Marxist (or Soviet) military power globally became a close second to the power of the first world of the West, whereas Islamic military power in the same period receded to global marginality.

Of the two most revolutionary forces of the last quarter of the twentieth century—Marxism and Islam—Marxism became increasingly in favor of the global status quo. Soviet leadership especially virtually became one of the leading apologists of the existing state-system. Its main criticism of the United States was that Washington had become a destabilizing force in the global equation, a threat to the military modus vivendi. In many ways Islam is the more frustrated of the two global revolutionary forces, and Islam in the days ahead is the more likely to take risks against the sanctity of the existing social order.

Islam, in desperation, may be forced to seek its own nuclearization. One possibility would be to marry the financial resources of one part of the Muslim world with the scientific resources of another. Allah in His wisdom has made Egypt and Pakistan the scientific leaders of the Muslim world. Equally in His wisdom, Allah has made Saudi Arabia and other Gulf states the financial leaders of the Muslim world. A marriage of these two Islamic resources (science and money) could help narrow the gap between Islam as part of the Third World, on one side, and the privileged credentials of a capitalist northern hemisphere, on the other side.

All this is quite apart from the danger of pushing Islam not only to desperation, but to despair. Pushing Islam against the wall may arouse the ultimate martyrdom complex, the Kerbala syndrome in the case of the Shī'ites in emulation of the martyrdom of the Prophet's grandson, Hussein.

Islam in despair could be pushed to a nuclear terrorism as a version of the *jihād*. As we indicated, whatever Lord Acton may have meant, it is not only power which corrupts. It is also the frustrated powerlessness. When powerlessness is frustrated absolutely, it can indeed corrupt absolutely. And a future case of Islamic nuclear terrorism—aimed probably against Western interests—may well be the outcome of the present Western and Israeli insensitivity to the sense of fairness and justice of Islamic civilization. The humiliation of Bosnia Herzegovina and the cruel Western abandonment of Bosnian

Muslims in the 1990s was just the latest wound in the collective psyche of the Muslim *ummah*.

A nuclearized Islam or a nuclearized Africa can have another positive effect. Can such "horizontal proliferation" be a cure to vertical proliferation? Again the underlying hope lies in creating the necessary culture shock for a serious international commitment to universal nuclear disarmament. The racial prejudices and cultural distrust of the white members of the nuclear club may well serve the positive function of disbanding the larger club—and dismantling the nuclear arsenals in the cellars which had constituted credentials for membership.

However, nuclear disarmament is not enough. There is need to reduce the risk of war. After all, since the genie of nuclear know-how is already out of the bottle, it can be re-utilized if war broke out—and a new nuclear arms race be inaugurated. The ultimate evil is man's proclivity towards war—and not merely the weapons with which he has fought it. Islam and Africa will have to join forces in the search for a more viable world order. One day the warriors of Africa and the *mujāhidīn* (fighters for Islamic justice) of Islam will put away their swords and spears, as they jointly celebrate with their former adversaries the liberation of Planet Earth from the specter of chemical weapons, nuclear war and the excesses of injustice in human affairs.

NOTES

1. This chapter is indebted to Mazrui's previous works on issues of war and peace in the Third World. See, for example, Mazrui, *Cultural Forces in World Politics* (London: James Currey and Portsmouth, N.H.: Heinemann, 1990) and "The Nuclear Option and International Justice: Islamic Perspectives," in Nimat Hafez Barazangi, et al., *Islamic Identity and the Struggle for Justice* (Gainesville, FL: University Press of Florida, 1996), pp. 95-116.

2. Cited by C. Smith and Shyam Bhatia, "How Dr. Khan Stole the bomb for Islam," *The Observer* (London), December 9, 1979.

3. A United Press International (UPI) report datelined Paris on some aspects of the French-Iraqi atomic deal was carried by many newspapers, including the *Ann Arbor News* (Ann Arbor, Michigan) August 9, 1980.

4. UPI report, *ibid*, and Smith and Bhatia, *op. cit.* Consult also Ryukichi Imai and Robert Press, *Nuclear Nonproliferation: Failures and Prospects*, A Report of the International Consultative Group on Nuclear Energy (New York and London: The Rockefeller Foundation and the Royal Institute of International Affairs, 1980).

5. Consult the declaration of the First Conference of Independent African States (April 15-22, 1958), Appendix; C. Legum, *Pan-Africanism* (London: Pall Mall, 1962 edition) Appendix 4, pp. 147-148.

6. *Uganda Argus*, (Kampala), May 29, 1964.

7. *Harijan*, October 14, 1939.

8. Caryl P. Haskins, "Atomic Energy and American Foreign Policy," *Foreign Affairs* (New York), vol. 24, no. 4, (July 1946), pp. 595-6. Consult also A. Boserup, L. Christensen and O. Nathan (editors), *The Challenge of Nuclear Armaments* (Copenhagen: University of Copenhagen, Rhodos International Publishers, 1986).

9. Kwame Nkrumah, *I Speak of Freedom: A Statement of African Ideology* (London: Heinemann, 1961), p. 213. Consult also Ali A. Mazrui (ed.), *The Africans: A Triple Heritage* (London: BBC Publications and Boston: Little Brown and Company, 1986), Chapter 8 on "Tools of Exploitation;" and Sadruddin Aga Khan (ed.) *Nuclear War, Nuclear Proliferation and their Consequences* (Oxford: Claredon Press, 1985).

SECTION THREE

DOMESTIC-INTERNATIONAL: THE "GLOBAL" DIVIDE

CHAPTER ELEVEN

THE BLACK EXPERIENCE
AND THE AMERICAN EMPIRE
BETWEEN GLOBALIZATION AND COUNTER-TERRORISM

Two trends relevant for Black people have been under way since the second half of the 20th century. One trend is the globalization of Africa and the other is the hegemonization of the United States. Africa and people of African descent are becoming more and more of a global presence. And the United States is becoming more and more of a hegemonic empire seeking to control the world.

The concept of globalization is new but the processes of globalization have been going on for centuries. At its most comprehensive globalization are all the forces that are pushing the world towards becoming a global village. These forces include the spread of universalistic religions and universalistic ideologies; the expansion of new technologies; the emergence of a world economy and the dispersal and migration of peoples across continents.

Recent stages of globalization have emphasized global economic interdependencies and new technologies of information and communication. Economic globalization includes the tightening of economic interdependence across vast distances. Informational globalization includes the rise of the Internet, the computer revolution and the consolidation of the Information Superhighway.

Africa's globalization is partly the penetration of these wider forces into the African world. But Africa's globalization also encompasses the participation of Africans and people of African descent in those wider global forces external to the African continent. We are dealing with how the world has been changing Africa; but we are also dealing with how people of African descent have been changing the world.

While people of Africa and the Diaspora have been getting globalized, the United States has been growing into more and more of an unprecedented hegemonic force in world history. America has been evolving into a new form of empire, controlling millions of people through a variety of inducements and intimidations. The United States extends the carrot of security and a billion dollars per year for Kuwait and Egypt respectively. While the United States wields Saddam Hussein the stick of military might, it gives North Korea the carrot and the stick. For most of the world the United States declares a doctrine of perpetual American supremacy. It has never happened in history that a nation is so far ahead of its nearest rival in economic, military, technological and political power. In military might, the United States is stronger than the next ten countries added together.

If Japan is the next industrial power in the world, it is a very distant second. If Germany is the next technological power in the world, it is also way behind the United States. If Russia is still supposed to be second militarily, Russia is now a limping and damaged war machine—with a fraction of the resources and combat-effectiveness of the United States.

There was a time when Great Britain, France and Spain were far bigger cultural forces in the world than any other Western powers. This is no longer so. American media, Hollywood films, American pop-culture and television programs, American fast-food, the jeans and T-shirt cultures, have all added up to the *coca-colanization* of the world. Culturally much of the world is getting Americanized.

The Roman Empire was once the model of one-power controlling much of the world. Then the British Empire equaled the Romans in scale and outperformed Rome in changing the human race. But during the days of Rome technologies of control were weak and the geographical area answerable to Rome was only a fraction of Planet Earth. The British ruled a much bigger part of the human race than the Romans had done. But Britain—though ahead of its rivals—nevertheless had close competitors. Spain, France and later Germany were among serious rivals to British power at different stages of history.

What is different about the new American empire is that it is truly without a peer—the first among unequals. The United States has become the Gulliver of the Globe, reducing much of the rest of the world into a Lilliput.

In the first half of the twentieth century the United States was one major power among several. Indeed, that is how five countries became permanent members of the Security Council with a veto power for each—the United States, the Soviet Union, the United Kingdom, France and China. In 1945 it looked as if global power was a pentagon with a small p—global power was five-sided.

In reality the United Nations was recognizing a reality that was about to end. Before the end of that decade of the 1940s it was becoming clearer that world power was not penta-polar (with five poles) but bi-polar. A system of only two superpowers unfolded soon after World War II—the United States and the Soviet Union. This was the reality of the second half of the twentieth century. But the Soviet Union disintegrated in the final years of the twentieth century. We unexpectedly had a world with only one superpower by the beginning of the twenty-first century. A stage was being set for a unique hegemonic presence in human affairs. The United States was in the process of transition from a mere superpower into a super-empire. A superpower may have mighty capabilities but may choose not to use them. A super-empire seeks to control and manipulate. The Administration of George W. Bush has even articulated the right of pre-emptive war whenever it feels that a country may one day become a threat to the United States even if that threat is a quarter century away.

BLACKS ON GLOBAL STAGE

While America has been developing into an empire, Africa and the Diaspora are getting globalized. Indeed, African Americans are in the middle of those two processes. African Americans are themselves becoming not only more of a global presence; they are also inevitably part of the American machinery of empire. On the one hand African American soldiers, airmen and women, and sailors in the United States Navy are part of the country's military might and the country's instruments of force and control. African Americans are part of the empire of America. Moreover, African Americans are also part of the dispersal of the African peoples and their demographic globalization. African Americans are a factor in the imperialization of America and a factor in the globalization of Africa. Under the administration of George W. Bush the African American factor has become even more visible both as part of the American empire and as part of Africa's globalization. The appointment of Colin Powell to be Secretary of State and Condeleeza Rice to be National Security Advisor have propelled African Americans to the highest levels of the Empire in policy-making.

There have been occasions in recent months when these two African Americans especially have been at the center stage of America's role as a global machine of manipulation. On the other hand, Colin Powell at his best has tried to be a dove among militant Bush hawks. For much of the year 2002 Powell was a voice of restraint in the Bush administration. Has Powell now lost his battle with the hawks? An elaborate discussion about the rise of Africans to positions of leadership in global organizations is to be found in our chapter on "Globalization between the Market and the Military."

BETWEEN THE GLOBAL *UMMAH* AND GLOBAL AFRICA

Globalization has also forged new links between Islam and Global Africa, and provided opportunities for African Muslims to play a bigger role in both the global *ummah* and among countries in Global Africa. When Mahtar M'Bow was the Director-General of UNESCO he was the highest ranking Muslim of any race in the United Nations system. Professor M'Bow was an African of the blood from Senegal. Ismael Serageldin, as one of the Vice Presidents of the World Bank in the 1990s, has been the highest-ranking Muslim in this International Bank for Reconstruction and Development. Serageldin is an African of the soil from Egypt. Another African Muslim of the soil became head of the World Court at the Hague when Justice Mohammed Bejaouni of Algeria was elected President of the International Court of Justice in 1994. The Organization of Petroleum Exporting Countries (OPEC)—with its headquarters in Vienna, Austria—has four African members. These are Nigeria and Gabon (Africans of the blood) and Algeria and Libya (Africans of the soil). From time to time these African countries have provided Secretaries-General and other OPEC leaders, often Muslim. And of course the Organization of African Unity (now African Union), the most important continent-wide organization in Africa, had a Muslim Secretary-General throughout the 1990s. Salim Ahmed Salim is an African of the blood from Tanzania.

There are 1.2 billion Muslims in the world—but the only continent that has a Muslim majority is Africa. The total population of Africa is over 700 million of whom over half are now Muslim. Nigeria has more Muslims than any Arab country. When Nigeria is combined with Ethiopia, Egypt and Congo (Kinshasa)—the four most populous African countries—the Muslim population is over 160 million. There is now a significant amount of Muslims in the United States.[1] The population of Muslims in the United States has begun to outstrip the population of Jews.[2] Of the 6 to 7 million Muslims in the USA 42% are black.[3] The Nation of Islam under Louis Farrakhan is part of that 42% but only a fraction of it.

Why has there been a Black fascination with Islam? Why is the Muslim population in Global Africa still expanding? Among African Americans there have been push-out factors in the mainstream culture, and pull-in factors in the cultural and ethical attraction of Islam. The push-out factors in the wider American society have made African Americans feel excluded or rejected at some levels. The pull-in factors in Islam and Islamic culture have made some African Americans feel welcome and intrigued. The push-out factors in the wider American society are rooted in centuries of racial experience and the sociology of racial exclusion. The pull-in factors in Islamic culture offer a paradoxical alternative—both cultural autonomy and religious universalism for African Americans. Sobriety and prohibition of alcohol in the Islamic ethos have also fascinated sections of the Black Diaspora that have been decimated by drug abuse and alcoholism.

Africa is not only the first continent to have a majority of Muslims; it is also witness to the largest continuing expansion of Islam. Conversions to Islam are faster in the Black world than in other sections of humanity. Natural population growth among Muslims in Africa and in the world is faster than among non-Muslims. Indeed, the Muslim world as a whole is expected to become 25% of the human race in the course of the 21st century. The largest country in population in Africa is Nigeria—which probably has a majority of Muslims. The second largest country on the African continent is Egypt—which is of course an Islamic leader. The largest African country in territory is Sudan—which is about two-thirds Muslim. Almost half the members of the Organization of the Islamic Conference (a world-wide 53 member inter-governmental Islamic fraternity) are African. Its Secretaries-General have ranged from the African of the blood Hamid Algabid (Niger) to the African of the soil Azzedine Larak (Morocco).

Should African Muslims establish links with Global Africa as a whole? African Americans are of course a large descended population lodged in the most powerful nation on earth. Perhaps Muslims of all races in the United States should join forces with African Americans of all faiths in a joint struggle for both racial justice and cultural dignity. The Nation of Islam and other Muslim groups in the country have sometimes adopted that principle as a cornerstone of their national agenda.

There are now at least as many Muslims as Jews in the USA and probably more—though the Muslims are more subdued and far less powerful than the Jews. And yet, numerically there are more African Americans than there are Jews in the whole world added together. What Black and Muslim people can learn from the Jews include the following:

1. Solidarity in a common cause;
2. Organization and mobilization;
3. Purposeful Manipulation of the political process;
4. Creative Tapping of the guilt complexes of former oppressors;
5. Turning martyrdom into a political resource.

This is where the crusade for Black reparations looms into relevance.[4] Jews have received partial compensation for the horrors of the Holocaust under the Nazis in Europe (1933-1945).[5] In the 1990s Swiss Banks have been held accountable for illegitimate gains they might have made from Jewish victims of genocide during World War II. Also in the 1990s German manufacturing corporations are being forced to set aside billions of dollars to compensate those who had worked under slave-labor conditions during the Third Reich. A relatively few Jewish activist organizations have been able to hold powerful economic giants in Europe liable for compensation for exploited and victimized Jews. What about compensation for hundreds of years of Black enslavement? Or is that a joke?

IN SEARCH OF HISTORIC REPARATIONS

Globalization has reawakened the crusade for Jewish reparations. Also getting globalized is the reparations movement to com-

183

pensate Black people for hundreds of years of enslavement and exploitation.[6] The fighters for the abolition of slavery became known as "abolitionists;" the new crusaders for Black compensation are the "reparationists."

In 1992, I and eleven others were sworn in before the Presidents of Africa. We were to constitute the Group of Eminent Persons to pursue and to explore the modalities and logistics of campaigning for such reparations. The "swearing in" occurred in Dakar, Senegal. Reverend Jesse Jackson came to meet with our Committee to give us moral support. So did Nelson Mandela, who was at the time newly liberated, but not yet elected President of South Africa.

We elected Chief Moshood Abiola as Chairman of our group of 12 Eminent Persons. Abiola was a Nigerian philanthropist and publisher. He ran for the Presidency of Nigeria—and won in June 1993. However, he was not allowed to take office. The army in Nigeria aborted the electoral process. When he called a rally and declared himself President of Nigeria, he was arrested and charged with treason.

In 1996, I saw General Sani Abacha, the Military Head of State of Nigeria at the time. I asked him to continue Nigeria's support for the reparations movement and to release our Chairman of the Reparations Group, Chief Abiola. President Abacha was gracious to me, but unbending on the issue of Abiola.

Chief Abiola was still in prison when General Abacha died suddenly in June 1998. Prospects for Abiola's release improved. Unfortunately, Abiola too was suddenly taken ill and died unexpectedly on the eve of his being released from prison. The reparations movement received a severe blow because Abiola had been a man of means committed to the cause. Nigeria lost a gifted leader and—for some of us—a dear friend.

There is a distinct reparations movement in the United States—including a brave attempt in Congress by Representative John Conyers to get a bill passed to appoint a commission to go into the feasibility of reparations.[7] There is also a reparations movement in the United Kingdom with one champion in the House of Commons

(Bernie Grant) and one champion in the House of Lords. Reparations has also been a topic on talk-shows in the Caribbean. Globalization has given reparations a new momentum, but just as the abolitionist movement took generations, so will the reparationist crusade.

Also relevant was President Bill Clinton's tour of African in 1998—the first U.S. President to go to so many African countries, meet so many African leaders, and come so near to apologizing for the wrongs that American had done to the Africans across the centuries. Of course Clinton did not offer compensation—nor was he asked for it. But the next best thing to compensation is an apology for the sins of one's forbears. Clinton in Africa came close to expressing deep regret—though not an apology.[8]

Black demands for reparations are one response to wrongs perpetrated by the West. Militant Arab demands for revenge are an alternative response to injustice committed by the West.

COUNTER-PENETRATING THE AMERICAN CITADEL

If one phase of clash of civilizations is the hegemony of a world with one Superpower, how is the might of the United States to be moderated? Firstly, through greater self-reliance by other societies abroad, asserting their autonomy of the United States. Secondly, by making Americans pay a price for any abuse of power abroad. The price could be by making Americans feel disliked by others, or even making Americans feel unsafe. The extreme and least legitimate form of this strategy is anti-American political violence. And thirdly, through counter-penetrating the citadels of U.S. power. The United States may be an empire abroad, but it is still a democracy at home. Different nationalities within the United States should learn from Cuban Americans and Jewish Americans—minorities who have shaped American policies.

In an article in the Saudi Arabian English language online newspaper, *arabnews.com,* Mark Weber, Director of the Institute for Historical Review, examines the achievements and political influence of Jewish Americans in the United States, and points out the following:

> As Jewish author and political science professor Benjamin Ginsberg has pointed out:
> "Since the 1960s, Jews have come to wield considerable influence in American economic, cultural, intellectual and political life. Jews played a central role in American finance during the 1980s, and they were among the chief beneficiaries of that decade's corporate mergers and reorganizations.
> Today, though barely two percent of the nation's population is Jewish, close to half its billionaires are Jews. The chief executive officers of the three major television networks and the four largest film studios are Jews, as are the owners of the nation's largest newspaper chain and the most influential single newspaper, *The New York Times* ... The role and influence of Jews in American politics is equally marked ...
> Jews are less than three percent of the nation's population and comprise eleven percent of what this study defines as the nation's elite. However, Jews constitute more than 25 percent of the elite journalists and publishers, more than 17 percent of the leaders of important voluntary and public interest organizations, and more than 15 percent of the top ranking civil servants."

Two well-known Jewish writers, Seymour Lipset and Earl Raab, pointed out in their 1995 book, *Jews and the New American Scene:*

> During the last three decades Jews [in the United States] have made up 50 percent of the top two hundred intellectuals ... 20 percent of professors at the leading universities ... 40 percent of partners in the leading law firms in New York and Washington ... 59 percent of the directors, writers, and producers of the 50 top-grossing motion pictures from 1965 to 1982, and 58 percent of directors, writers, and producers in two or more primetime television series.[9]

186

The influence of American Jewry in Washington, notes the Israeli daily *Jerusalem Post*, is "far disproportionate to the size of the community, Jewish leaders and U.S. officials acknowledge. But so is the amount of money they contribute to [election] campaigns." One member of the influential Conference of Presidents of Major American Jewish Organizations "estimated Jews alone had contributed 50 percent of the funds for [President Bill] Clinton's 1996 re-election campaign ..."[10] The most important reason for Jewish power in the United States is the successful counter-penetration by Jews into the citadels of American power.

African Americans are twice the population of world Jewry but African Americans have not counter-penetrated the citadels of power. Americans from South Asia and the Orient are counter-penetrating the Silicone Valley of Technology. Muslim Americans are outstripping Jews in numbers, but cannot hold a candle to Jewish power.

The United States as an Empire can only be checked by the United States as a democracy. African Americans, Latinos and Muslim Americans have a lot to learn from Jews about how to be empowered Americans.

CONCLUSION

Samuel P. Huntington may be in the process of being partially vindicated for his controversial 1993 prediction. A new clash of civilizations may be unfolding between the United States and some of its allies, on one side, and, on the other side, a substantial body of Muslim opinion across the world. Under the U.S. administration of George W. Bush this clash of civilizations may even be drifting towards increasing militarization. However, Huntington was wrong in suggesting that a clash of civilizations involving the West was something new. On the contrary, the West has been declaring war on other civilizations for the last four hundred years. In the Americas and (Australasia) there was the First Phase of Genocidal Clash of Civilizations when new European conquerors and settlers annihilated native civilizations and destroyed millions of indigenous lives.

There followed the Second Phase of Enslaving Clash of Civilizations when millions of Africans were captured and exported as slaves to the plantations of the Americas and the Caribbean. This period overlapped with the Third Phase of the Imperial Clash of Civilizations when the West conquered and colonized much of the rest of the world, flying European flags of conquest from Jakarta to Jamaica, from Lahore to Lusaka and from Malta to Mozambique.

The Fourth Phase of Clash of Civilizations is the age of the United States as an Empire, especially since the country became the sole superpower. The United States is an informal empire, controlling millions of people abroad through economic inducements and economic threats, diplomatic pressure and state manipulation, the power of trade and the lure of aid, promises of military security and threats of destabilization, the pervasive use of the technology of espionage and control, and the domination of such global institutions as the United Nations, the World Bank, the International Monetary Fund and the World Trade Organization. As an Empire, the United States also exempts itself from global rules that it does not like— such as the Kyoto Protocols on the environment and the new International Court for war crimes and crimes against humanity.

Bridging the genocidal phase: the first genocidal phase of civilizational conflict (mainly against ancient native civilizations of the Americas) was not formally ended. It just petered out. In some parts of the Americas it may still be continuing in the form of the brutalization of rural Indians. Bridging the enslaving phase: the second slavery phase of civilizational conflict (mainly at the expense of enslaved Africans) was gradually ended as a result of abolitionist movements in Europe and the Americas, and following a civil war in the United States. Bridging the colonial phase: the third imperial and colonial phase of civilizational conflict (at the expense of much of Latin America, Africa, Asia and many islands of the sea) took centuries to bring to a close. The last of the great European empires came to an end in the twentieth century except for such small pockets as the Falklands, Gibraltar, some British West Indian dependencies, and Portuguese Macao on the China Coast. Bridging the American Empire: how do we end the fourth hegemonic phase of clash of civilizations—the phase of the United States as an informal Empire, especially since it became the sole Superpower?

Here there are three vital strategies. One is the promotion of greater autonomy from the United States and greater self-reliance in those countries which have come to lean too heavily on America as a market, or as a source of foreign aid, or as an umbrella of military security, or as a customer for their goods. For example, Egypt needs to be weaned away from too much reliance on annual foreign aid from the United States; and Saudi Arabia and Kuwait should learn to lean less heavily on Washington for military security. Another strategy against excessive American imperialism is to make the United States pay a price for its abuse of power. The extreme case of this is trying to make Americans feel unsafe anywhere in the world. The third solution to the imperial role of the United States as the sole superpower may have to lie within the United States itself. Although the country has indeed become an Empire, it is still a democracy. The ultimate check upon America as an empire is America as a democracy. It is to be hoped that the internal demographic changes will eventually be reflected on the political process and in policy choices. The population of the United States is on its way towards becoming more clearly multi-racial, multi-religious, multi-ethnic and to a limited extent multi-lingual. Other parts of the world have—through patterns of immigration—been counter-penetrating America as a society, but many have not yet counter-penetrated America as a citadel power. The supreme examples of minorities successful in shaping of the policies of the United States are Cuban Americans, on one side, and Jewish Americans, on the other. Cuban Americans have tended to be a lobby for a single-issue—American policy towards Cuba. The Cuban immigrants have held that policy hostage for more than forty years.

The achievement of Jewish Americans is more wide-ranging and more pervasive. Although Jewish Americans have indeed been crucial in determining the United States' policy towards the Israeli-Palestinian conflict, American Jews have been major participants in other sectors of American life as well. As we have indicated, Jews have been staggeringly successful not only politically in America, but also economically, educationally and culturally. Jews are the supreme example and ideal model of an American minority that has successfully used the American system to its full advantage.

If African Americans, Muslim Americans, Arab Americans, Latinos and women of all races became half as successful as the Jews in influencing directions of American policy, their effect would probably be towards liberalizing the foreign policy of the United States. At the moment America is torn between a domestic philosophy based on rights and a foreign policy based on might. Demographic changes in the United States may tilt the balance towards a better and more humane equilibrium.

It is true that a fourth clash of civilizations has indeed begun, with the United States at the center of it. However, the seeds of redemption may also lie in America. Those seeds are carried by emerging populations potentially more responsive to other cultures and civilizations than the contemporary U.S. power-elites seem to be. The imperial tunnel is still dark—but the light of a more inclusive Americana democracy can be seen at the end of this tunnel.

The last fifty years have witnessed the globalization of Africa. Those years have also experienced the hegemonization of America. Africa as a global presence has coincided with America as a global force. It is partly up to globalized Africa to help tame and pacify hegemonized America. The African Diaspora will continue to be critical in bridging the divide between America as an Empire and America as a democracy in the coming decades.

NOTES

1. An overview of Muslims in America may be found in Yvonne Y. Haddad, *The Muslims of America* (New York: Oxford University Press, 1991).
2. See Mary H. Cooper, "Muslims in America," *Congressional Quarterly Researcher* 33 (30 April 1993).
3. Ibid.

4. See Ali A. Mazrui, "Global Africa: From Abolitionists to Reparationists," *African Studies Review* 37, 3 (December 1994), pp. 1-18.

5. Discussions on some of the early reparations to Israel and the Jews may be found in Ronald H. Zweig, *German Reparations and the Jewish World: A History of the Claims Conference* (Boulder, CO: Westview Press, 1987) and Nana Sagi, *German Reparations: A History of the Negotiations* (Jerusalem, Hebrew University: Magna Press, 1980).

6. There has also been economic and political studies done on black reparations; see, for example, Clarence J. Mumford, *Race and Reparations: A Black Perspective for the 21st Century* (Trenton, NJ: Africa World Press, 1996), and Robert S. Browne, "The Economic Basis for Reparations to Black America," *The Review of Black Political Economy* 21 (Winter 1993), pp. 99-110.

7. See the report in the *New York Times* (July 21, 1994), Section B, p. 10. Of course, in the current conservative majority in Congress, it is understandable that Conyers' Reparations Study Bill has been stalled in the House Judiciary Committee; see *The Tri-State Defender*, 45, 48 (December 4, 1996), p. 7A.

8. For one report on Clinton's trip to Africa, see *New African* 363 (May 1998), pp. 8-9.

9. See Seymour Lipset and Earl Raab, *Jews and the New American Scene* (Cambridge, Massachusetts: Harvard University Press, 1995), pp. 26-27.

10. Mark Weber, "A Look at The Powerful Jewish Lobby." *www.arabnews.com.* July 14, 2002. Richard Cohen, columnist for the *Washington Post* also notes in an article that, "At the elite Ivy League schools, Jews make up 23 percent of the student body. They are a measly 2 percent of the U.S. population." See Richard Cohen, "A Study in differences," *Washington Post* (May 28, 2002).

CHAPTER TWELVE

BLACK *INTIFĀḌAH*
THE MAU MAU UPRISING AND THE PALESTINIAN RESISTANCE IN COMPARATIVE PERSPECTIVE[1]

The Palestinian tragedy had two illegitimate parents—one parent consisted of the pro-Jewish policies of the British Mandate and the second parent were the anti-Jewish policies of the Nazis. The aftermath of two political texts have led to the heavy burden of the Palestinian people—the pro-Jewish text of the Balfour Declaration of 1917 and the anti-Jewish text of Hitler's *Mein Kempf* of 1938. The Jewish friendly legacy of the Balfour Declaration led to the disempowerment of Palestinians. Hitler's atrocities against the Jewish people enhanced the case for a separate home for the Jews. The Nazi Holocaust made the world more receptive to the aspirations of the Zionists. Lord Balfour and Adolf Hitler were the historic architects of the 1948 creation of Israel. Balfour was the Dr. Jekyll and Hitler the Mr. Hyde of the Palestinian calamity.

Our story in this chapter goes back further than either Hitler or Lord Balfour. It goes back to the time when the British were ready to offer parts of Africa to the Zionist movement for Jewish settlement and occupation. However, the British later attempted to turn Kenya into a white man's country instead of a Jewish homeland. However, this chapter is also about the contradictions in the attitudes of post-colonial countries towards the Palestinian tragedy. Some of these post-colonial states see their history in the present predicament of the Palestinians. But other post-colonial states including some Arab countries, collaborate with Western powers, with Pax Americana and with the Zionist global lobby.

Kenya has included both aspects of post-coloniality—solidarity with Palestinians as fellow victims of occupation and dependent solidarity with Israel as an extension of Western hegemony. The dialectic is still unfolding. One of the questions hanging over the post-KANU Kenya is whether the new regime under President Mwai Kibaki in Nairobi will be less Pro-Israel in its Middle Eastern policies than the governments of Daniel arap Moi and Jomo Kenyatta had been when the Kenya African National Union (KANU) was the ruling party. It is one of the ironies of Kenya that the land which had virtually invented African versions of the anti-colonial guerrilla war had for so long been out of step with the Palestinian struggle against Israeli occupation. Why was Kenya's Jomo Kenyatta so different from South Africa's Nelson Mandela on the issue of sympathizing with the Palestinians?

Palestine and East Africa have been historically linked in at least four distinct additional ways. Firstly, both Palestine and East Africa experienced European colonial rule and racial betrayal. Tanganyika, like Palestine, was even declared a Mandate of the League of Nations and later a trusteeship of the United Nations.

Secondly, both Palestine and parts of East Africa had historically been considered for Jewish settlements. The British Colonial Secretary at the beginning of the twentieth century had offered parts of Uganda and Kenya to the Zionist movement as a basis of a new

Jewish state. Joseph Chamberlain's life spanned from 1836 to 1914. He nearly created an Israel in Africa.

Thirdly, both Palestine and parts of East Africa had subsequently engaged in armed resistance and liberation struggle. The Mau Mau movement in Kenya in the 1950s turned to armed struggle and even terrorism in order to end White settlements on African lands and terminate British occupation of Kenya as a whole.

The Palestinians *intifādah* in the last quarter of the twentieth century and the first decade of the twenty first century had also sought to end with armed struggle foreign settlements (Jewish) in Arab lands and terminate Israeli occupation of what remained of Palestine. The Mau Mau movement in Kenya had exploded in 1951-1952 only three or four years after Israel was created. Mau Mau was a Black Intifadah against white settler rule in Kenya—a struggle which lasted nearly a decade.

The fourth link between Palestine and East Africa concerned the extension of the Palestinian struggle to include East Africa as a battlefield. Has the Palestinian struggle exploded beyond its own borders and encompassed some of the former battlefields of Kenya's own Mau Mau movement—from the streets of Nairobi to the beaches of Mombasa? In terms of a macro-comparison across history, the Mau Mau struggle in Kenya was a national uprising in the context of North-South relations. The Palestinian *intifādah* has been an international struggle in the context of global relations. Let us look more closely at these four or five links between the tragedy of Palestine and the experience of East Africa.

THE ZIONISTS AND THE ZINJI?

The offer of fertile parts of Uganda and Kenya was made to the Zionist movement by Joseph Chamberlain as British Colonial Secretary in the first decade of the twentieth century. Theodor Herzel presented the offer to the Zionist movement. At that time the Jewish dream was to find for a people without land (the Jews) some land without people. The British authorities regarded Eastern Africa at the time as "land without people"—partly because they did not recognize the "natives" as real "people." Since Palestine was still under Ottoman Muslim rule, moreover, it seemed easier to settle Jews in fertile East Africa, distant form Ottoman complications. And so, on December 21, 1902, Joseph Chamberlain made the following entry into his diary: "If Dr. Herzel were at all inclined to transfer his efforts to East Africa, there would be no difficulty in finding suitable land for Jewish settlers."[2] Theodor Herzel, the founding father of Zionism, subsequently recorded in his own diary that Chamberlain had indeed offered him "Uganda." After consideration and debate among Zionists, it was concluded that "Uganda" was a possible extension of a future Jewish homeland rather than the core. Herzel wrote: "Our starting point must be in or near Palestine. Later on we could also colonize Uganda; for we have vast numbers of human beings who are prepared to emigrate."[3]

Julian Amery, a distinguished British public intellectual, later wrote a biography of Joseph Chamberlain. In the biography Avery insists that what Chamberlain offered to the Zionists was not really what today we regard as "Uganda." It was the cool and fertile highlands of Kenya. According to Avery, "there is no better white man's country anywhere in the tropics."[4] God had offered the followers of Moses a promised land across the Red Sea from West to East. Great Britain in 1902 offered the followers of Moses a new promised land across the Red Sea in the reverse direction of East to West. The ancient Jews had sought escape from enslavement in North Africa and followed Moses into the unknown. At the beginning of the twentieth century the modern Jews were invited to seek security and asylum in Eastern Africa under the umbrella of Pax Britannica.

Some Zionists were tempted by Joseph Chamberlain's offer. The Zionist "figuratists" believed that the new Israel could figuratively be anywhere on God's earth which afforded safety to God's Chosen People. But the Zionist "literalists" insisted that the new Israel had to be literally close to where ancient Israel once flourished. The Zionist literalists were often less secular and more nationalistic than the figuratists.

In the end the Zionist movement turned down the British offer of what was then regarded as "Uganda." The boundaries of Uganda at that time included what is today's Kenya. The British colonial authorities later reserved the best of that land in Kenya for European settlement rather than Jewish settlement. The land became the so-called "White Highlands of Kenya" instead of "Jewish Homeland." It was precisely this reservation of the best land in Kenya for whites only which helped to precipitate the Mau Mau *intifadah*. Like the Palestinian uprising, the Mau Mau war was unequal in military weaponry. While the Israelis have used tanks and rockets, the British in Kenya in the 1950s used airplanes and aerial bombardment of the Abedaire Mountains.

While Mau Mau did not produce suicide-bombers, the fighters did resort from time to time to other forms of terrorism—such as targeting a white farming family in the White Highlands for total elimination. Almost all armed liberation movements of the twentieth century all over the world included terrorist actions from time to time. The absence of suicide bombers among the Mau Mau fighters was partly because Mau Mau was not in possession of the kind of explosives that would have made suicide a viable method of targeting the enemy. In any case, indigenous Kikuyu culture does not lend itself as readily to suicidal martyrdom as Semitic cultures (both Arab and Jewish) have done in history. However, Mau Mau did demonstrate that those who made the most sacrifices in a liberation movement were not necessarily those who benefit the most from the fruit of liberation. The Mau Mau fighters were militarily defeated, but their goals of ending white settlements and terminating British occupation of Kenya were triumphant. Other Kenyans benefited from Mau Mau sacrifices—although Mau Mau warriors remained unsung heroes for fifty years.

The fertile soil in East Africa, which Joseph Chamberlain had once offered to the Zionist movement and which subsequent British Colonial Secretaries had reserved for European farmers, was finally returned in the 1960s to indigenous ownership and control. Had Theodor Herzel and the Zionist movement accepted the British offer of East Africa for Jewish settlements, apartheid as a system would have started earlier in African history than it did. The creation of a Jewish state in East Africa would have been the equivalent of dividing a country into separate homelands according to ethnicity. East Africa would have had a religio-cultural apartheid, separating Jews from Black gentiles (so called Zinj) long before South Africa had a racial apartheid, separating white skin from black skin. The difference is that the racial apartheid of South Africa had proven easier to dissolve than the creation of a Jewish state in East Africa would have been. "Zionist versus the Zinj": This would have been a more deadly racist confrontation.

Yet, the creation of Israel from Mandated Palestine has not completely protected East Africa from the consequences of Zionist triumphalism. In the 1970s a Jewish-owned hotel in Nairobi, the Norfolk, was partially damaged by a bomb planted by an Arab nationalist who had stayed there. Was Kenya being punished for being pro-Israel? Could the reason have been that the people who inherited power in Kenya from the British Raj were not the same people who militarily fought the British rulers and white settlements in central Kenya?

In South Africa, power passed from the architects of apartheid to those who had picked up arms against apartheid. In post-colonial Kenya power by-passed the Mau Mau fighters and was given instead to those who had denounced or disowned the Mau Mau liberation fighters when the war was being fought. In August 1998, the American Embassies in Nairobi and Dar es Salaam were destroyed seemingly by Middle Eastern terrorists—killing hundreds of East Africans and fewer than two dozen Americans. Had Kenya been targeted because it was perceived as an ally of Pax Americana?

FROM THE TORAH TO THE TERROR

The problem was compounded by the pro-Zionist tendencies of postcolonial Kenyan governments. Had independence in Kenya been handed over to those Kenyans who had directly fought against British rule and while settlements, post-colonial Kenyan governments would probably have been as sympathetic to the Palestinian struggle as most Black fighters against apartheid in South Africa had been. But the beneficiaries of the Mau Mau war were not the fighters themselves but were sometimes even the collaborators with the British rulers.

Kenya collaborated with the Israelis in the Entebbe raid by Israeli troops against Idi Amin's Uganda and against pro-Palestinian hijackers in July 1976. Nairobi was used as a re-fuelling stop for Israeli planes after the raid and as a stop for medical treatment for any Israelis wounded from Entebbe. Because the rulers of postcolonial Kenya were not the Mau Mau fighters themselves, the Kenyan government was not even minimally neutral when the Kurds of Turkey were engaged in their own liberation movement. The Kenyan authorities helped to capture and hand over to Turkey the leading PKK Kurdish leader Abdullah Ocalan who was at the time hiding in Nairobi. The capture dealt a death blow to the Kurdish resistance in Turkey.

Postcolonial Kenya's continuing collaboration with Pax Americana, Pax Britannica and Zionism continued to make Kenya a target for Middle Eastern resistance movements. In November 2002 Kenya was once again a battleground for Middle Eastern conflicts. A suicide bomber targeted the Israeli owned and Israeli occupied Paradise Hotel in Mombasa, killing nearly twenty people. Twice as many Kenyans as Israelis were killed in the attack. Once again a country that had been spared the fate of becoming an African Israel was not spared the consequences of the equally unjust creation of Israel in Palestine. Jews as children of the ancient Torah became parents of the modern terror in the Middle East. Postcolonial Kenya was caught in the crossfire. Also in November 2002 there was a failed attempt in Mombasa to shoot down an Israeli plane with tourists on board. In the 1950s the Mau Mau never attempted to shoot down a British plane. Although Mau Mau were themselves bombed by British planes, they did not have the technology to shoot them down.

On the other hand, a liberation movement in Rhodesia (later

Zimbabwe) twenty years later did have the technology to shoot down an airplane with whites on board. Joshua Nkomo's ZAPU party did have surface to air missiles. In 1978 they did shoot down a civilian airline with white folks on board. Nkomos's liberation fighters even attempted to kill the survivors after the crash. Outside Africa, the Israelis did shoot down in 1973 a civilian Libyan airline with 108 passengers, ostensibly because the Israelis thought the plane was a military threat. In 1988 the Americans shot down an Iranian civilian aircraft in the Gulf area, again pleading an honest and regrettable mistake. There were 292 civilians on board. The Russians were less hypocritical when in 1982 they shot down a South Korean airplane over Soviet territory because they were convinced that the plane (though civilian) was nevertheless engaged in espionage on behalf of the United States. Some 290 people were killed including a member of the U.S. Congress. There is also the debate about Pan-American flight 103 over Lockerbie in Scotland in 1988. In spite of the verdict by a Scottish Court on a Libyan suspect, confusion has persisted whether the real culprits were Iranians (avenging the shooting down of their own civilian craft) or pro-Palestinian Arab saboteurs. The 2002 attempt to shoot down a civilian passenger plane in Mombasa was unprecedented in Kenya, the land of Mau Mau, but it was not unprecedented in either Africa as a whole or within the global aviation history.

The events in Mombasa in the last week of November 2002 did once again illustrate that the land of Mau Mau and the politics of the Palestinian *intifāḍah* continued to be interlocked. The ghosts of Joseph Chamberlain and Theodor Herzel continue to haunt the land that nearly became a tropical Israel in the shadow of Mount Kenya; an Israel along the shores of Lake Victoria.

THE GLOBAL CONTEXT

By a strange twist of destiny, Kenya in 2001 was coming to terms with its Mau Mau history at about the same time as the United States was engaged in its war on terrorism. The Mau Mau movement against white settler rule in Kenya in the 1950s had been widely denounced by its critics as a terrorist movement. African loyalists to the British colonial regime were sometimes assassinated by Mau Mau, and from time to time a European farming family would be wiped out in a midnight raid by Mau Mau. By October 1952 the British Governor of Kenya, Sir Evelyn Baring, was forced to declare a state of emergency in the colony.

As the fiftieth anniversary of the outbreak of Mau Mau war was approaching, the Kenyan authorities started contemplating in the year 2001 major gestures to honor Mau Mau as a movement of patriotic heroism and nationalist sacrifice. The British had arrested and executed Dedan Kimathi, a Mau Mau "commander" in the forest. In the year 2001 Kenya was considering turning into national monuments the place where Kimathi was arrested and perhaps the place where many Mau Mau fighters were once detained. There is also a movement to seek out Dedan Kimathi's remains, give him a hero's funeral and build a special Mausoleum. Certain Kimathi enthusiasts are even demanding a Kimathi Day annually as a day to honour those who gave their lives in the liberation war for Kenya's independence in the 1950s.

Almost exactly fifty years later the atrocities of September 11, 2001, occurred at the World Trade Center in New York (a symbol of American economic might) and at the Pentagon (Department of Defense, a symbol of American military might) in Washington, D.C. A third plane, probably intended by the terrorists for either the White House or the Congressional building (the Capitol), was aborted and crashed in a field in Pennsylvania.

International terrorism is one more area of intermingling between the policies of the Middle East and the politics of Africa. Before the end of colonialism and the end of apartheid in Africa, what was described as "terrorism" was as common in Africa as in the Middle East. Since the collapse of political apartheid in the 1990s, the term "terrorism" has more narrowly been focused on the politics of the Middle East. This is unfair to Middle Eastern liberation fighters.

Both the Middle East and Africa have been paying a price for

Israeli repression and the anti-American terrorism. The violent price which the Middle East is paying is obvious, especially in Palestine, Iraq and in neighboring Afghanistan. What is the price which Africa is paying for terrorism against the United States?

Firstly, there is the issue of being caught in the crossfire. Africa has been the victim of violent action intended by the terrorists for the United States; Africa has also been a victim of violent action taken by the United States and intended for the terrorists. In order to kill twelve Americans, Middle Eastern terrorists killed, as we indicated, about two hundred Kenyans in the streets of Nairobi a few years ago. This was the attack on the US Embassy in Nairobi in August 1998. There were also Tanzanian casualties when the US Embassy in Dar es Salaam was targeted at the same time.

On the other hand, Sudan was caught in the crossfire soon after when U.S. President Bill Clinton ordered the bombing of an apparently harmless pharmacy near Khartoum. President Ronald Reagan before Clinton had ordered the bombing of Tripoli and Benghazi in Libya because Reagan thought the Libyans were responsible for a bomb in a German bar that had killed Americans. Violence between Americans and Middle Easterners had been spilling over into Africa for decades.

Since the destruction of the Israeli Paradise Hotel in Mombasa in November 2002, matters have continued to move from bad to worse in Palestine. However, there is a chance that matters are moving from bad to better in Kenya following the ouster of the Kenyan African National Union and the end of the legacy of Daniel arap Moi. Jomo Kenyatta had had a better influence on the history of Kenya than Moi had but Kenyatta's legacy was also of collaboration with the West and with the Zionist lobby in Nairobi. Both Kenyatta and Mandela had been imprisoned by their respective white adversaries—but Mandela had never disowned the armed struggle against apartheid, while Jomo Kenyatta had persistently denied any connection with Mau Mau even after he became President of Kenya. Had the real Mau Mau fighters inherited postcolonial power in Kenya, the history of Kenya's relations with the Palestinian movement would probably have been dramatically different. The land that nearly became Africa's Israel might well have become a land more truly sympathetic to the Palestinian cause.

Yet it is not too late. Kenya after KANU may learn to be more independent of both the West and the Zionists. Kenya may become another African ally to the Palestinians. Countries like Kenya were spared the fate of an African Israel on their soil, but have not been spared the global repercussions of the unholy alliance between the legacy of Lord Balfour and the aftermath of Adolf Hitler. The pro-Zionist policies of the British Mandate, and the anti-Jewish policies of the Nazis were the two forces that together created a world more receptive to the creation of a Jewish state. The aftermath has been disastrous for Palestinians, for Israelis and for the world. Humanity needs to find a way out of this monumental tragedy.

AFRICA AND THE MID-EAST: DIVERGENT RESPONSES

Why has terrorism continued to escalate in the Middle East while it has declined in Africa? Why is Africa talking about "Truth and Reconciliation" with the White man and Reparations from the Western World—while the Arabs and much of the rest of the Muslim world are angrier than ever against the West? Why do Arab militants regard "Pay Back Time" in terms of retribution against the West—while so many African nationalists regard "Pay Back Time" in terms of reparation from the West? Let us now look much more closely at the dynamics of politics in Africa and the Middle East from the point of view of reparation versus retribution.

The 2001 conference in Durban against racism and xenophobia took the issues of reparations forward. But the terrorist events in New York on September 11 might have caused a setback to the cause of reparations. Both Durban and September 11 have demonstrated once again a link between Africa and the Middle East, and the link has been affected by the forces of globalization.

I would like to explore the issue of reparations, on one side, and terrorist retribution, on the other, as alternative methods of "PAY

BACK." I would like to place Africa alongside the Middle East in comparative perspective. Africa and the Middle East are in any case overlapping regions. Comparing them in this way is particularly appropriate when discussing globalization. Imperialism in the Middle East created conditions in which "PAY BACK" time threatened to be revenge. Imperialism in Africa, on the other hand, created conditions in which reparations appeared to be a more appropriate form of "PAY BACK."

Imperialism in the Middle East provoked the worst levels of anti-Western terrorism after formal liberation from European colonial rule. The British had been in power in Egypt, Iraq, Jordan, Sudan and elsewhere. The French had been in power in Syria, Lebanon, Algeria, Morocco, Tunisia and elsewhere. Palestine had been a United Nations trusteeship under British rule. Imperialism in Africa provoked the worst levels of anti-Western terrorism before formal liberation from European colonial rule: that is to say, before Independence Day. Let us also relate the comparison to comparative rage. Imperialism in Africa triggered the most explosive anti-Western anger before European colonialism left Africa. Imperialism in the Middle East triggered off the most explosive anti-Western anger after European colonialism had left the Arab world.

What the colonial powers and white minority governments had condemned as "terrorism" in Africa included the Mau Mau war in Kenya, and the liberation wars in Algeria, Angola, Zimbabwe, Mozambique, and South Africa. What the Western world has condemned as "terrorism" in the Middle East has included hostage taking in Lebanon, hijacking of planes in the 1970s, as well as suicide bombs in the streets of Israel. The most spectacular was the destruction of the World Trade Center and the attack on the Pentagon on September 11, 2001.

In what sense are we to conclude that while the impact of Imperialism in the Middle East created conditions for violent "PAY BACK" against the West, the impact of imperialism on Africa has been to create conditions which are ideal for "PAY BACK" in terms of reparations from the West?

PAY BACK AND SITUATIONAL DIFFERENCES

Some of the differences between Africa and the Middle East are situational, while other differences are primarily cultural. The postcolonial situation in the Middle East included a permanent loss of territory imposed by outsiders. The postcolonial situation in Africa involved recovery of territory—including recovery of land previously parceled out by apartheid in South Africa. This was won back to Africa.

Africa had also been spared the forceful creation of a Jewish state in Uganda and Kenya earlier in the twentieth century. Joseph Chamberlain, the Colonial Secretary at the time, had offered Theodor Herzl, the leader of the Zionist movement, a piece of Uganda and a piece of Kenya at the beginning of the twentieth century for the creation of a new Jewish state. (The boundaries of Uganda early in the twentieth century included parts of present-day Kenya.) Had the Zionist movement accepted the offer, and a permanent Jewish state been established in East Africa, it is conceivable that African anger against the West today would be comparable to anti-Western rage in the Middle East. But the Zionist movement in 1903 could not reach consensus about creating "Israel" in East Africa—and therefore the postcolonial situation in Africa today involves no permanent loss of territory.

A related situational difference is that while the postcolonial conditions in Africa meant a clear end of foreign occupation, the postcolonial situation in the Middle East carried new forms of foreign occupation. It involved not just the creation of the state of Israel but also the occupation by Israel of the West Bank of the Jordan, the occupation of Gaza, the annexation of the Golan Heights of Syria, the annexation of the whole of Jerusalem and the occupation for a while of a piece of Southern Lebanon. While the postcolonial period in Africa is truly post-occupation, the postcolonial period in the Middle East has entailed new forms of territorial annexations.

Where does the United States fit into this equation? When European powers occupied Africa and parts of Asia, the image of America was that of an anti-colonial force in world affairs. The United States put a lot of pressure on its European allies to speed up the process of giving independence to the colonies. Even as late as 1956—when Britain, France and Israel invaded Egypt in response to Egypt's nationalization of the Suez Canal—the Eisenhower Administration turned against its allies. The United States forced Israel to withdraw from the Sinai, and forced Britain and France to give up Port Said in Egypt. The British Prime Minister had a nervous breakdown—Anthony Eden gave way to Harold McMillan.

Egypt's Nasser emerged as a world figure—partly because the United States would not support the Anglo-Franco-Israeli invasion of Egypt. Nasser had been militarily defeated, but emerged politically triumphant. The Eisenhower administration—wittingly or unwittingly—had helped the Egyptian president rise to global stature.

John F. Kennedy as President dismissed the concerns of the white settlers elsewhere in Africa when they objected to the phrase "Africa for the Africans." Kennedy insisted: "Who else would Africa be for if not for Africans?" The United States was on the side of the aspirations of African nationalists. However, two things were happening which future historians would later have to disentangle. The United States was moving towards greater globalization and expanding the role of interventionism in other parts of the world. In the second half of the 20th century the United States began to be seen more and more as an imperial power, and a supporter of Israeli policies of occupation and repression.

PAY BACK AND CULTURAL DIFFERENCES

The differences between Africa and the Middle East in relation to political rage are not only due to divergent post-colonial situations. There are also basic differences in culture between the Arabo-Hebrew Semitic peoples (both Arabs and Jews) on one side, and the majority of Black people in sub-Saharan Africa.

One major difference is the martyrdom complex, which is much more developed among Middle Eastern peoples than among the Bantu and other peoples of sub-Saharan Africa. The Jews have developed memories of the Holocaust into a major doctrine of Jewish martyrdom in history. As for readiness to commit collective suicide, the Israeli nuclear program is partly based on the premise of the Samson option—a readiness to defend Israel even if it means destroying it and much of the rest of the region.

Among Muslims of the Middle East (both Arab and Iranian) there is also the martyrdom complex in varying degrees. Historically it has been more developed among Shī'ite Muslims than among Sunni. Suicide bombers against Israel and American troops in Lebanon started among Shī'ite Lebanese. But anger against Israel and the United States has now resulted in the extension of the martyrdom complex to the Sunni population of the Middle East. It is probable (though not yet proven) that the daredevils who destroyed the World Trade Center and the Pentagon were indeed Middle Easterners. Because culturally the Middle East has a martyrdom complex, which is much more highly developed than among any groups in sub-Saharan Africa, it is the Middle East that has been readier than Africa to commit suicidal political violence against the West. In the postcolonial period it is the Middle East, more than Africa, which has been ready to engage in acts of suicidal terrorism against the West.

Another major cultural difference between the Middle East and Africa concerns comparative hate retention. Cultures differ in hate-retention. Some cultures preserve a grudge across centuries. The Irish of Northern Ireland quarrel every year about a Protestant victory of the Orange Order against Catholics four centuries ago. The Irish have a high hate-retentive capacity. The Armenian massacres of 1915 by the Ottoman Empire are still remembered bitterly by Armenians—and from time to time this memory results in the assassination of a Turkish diplomat somewhere in the world. The Jews also have high hate-retentiveness, but they have sublimated it through the martyrdom complex. The Holocaust is given a sacred meaning rather than merely remembered as hate. Because the Arabs have a vastly different history from Jews in the last fourteen centuries, the Arabs' experience as a persecuted people is relatively recent. Their hate-retention and their martyrdom complex is not as well developed or as sophisticated as that of the Jews. But Arabs and Jews do both share a fascination with the martyrdom complex.

Now contrast this culturally with Black Africa. A major reason why Black Africa has not produced postcolonial political violence against the West is Africa's short memory of hate. Mahatma Gandhi used to prophesy that it would probably be through Black people that the unadulterated message of soul force *(satyagraha)* and passive resistance might be realized. If Gandhi was indeed right, this could be one more illustration of comparative hate-retention.

Yet "Pay Back" as an African demand is a claim for reparations—contrasting sharply with "Pay Back" as political retribution against the West by other damaged regions of the world. The West should respond positively to this softer, gentler version of "Pay Back Time" between the West and the Rest. Better the music of reparations than the drums of terror.

Finally, I will have a word about terrorism and germ warfare. How does bio-terrorism relate to the African condition and Pax-Americana? Let us now explore this dimension.

BETWEEN AIDS AND ANTHRAX

Those who are campaigning against AIDS and HIV are jealous of the attention and publicity anthrax is getting. Bill Clinton tried to make AIDS a national security issue. George W. Bush has had more success with mobilization against anthrax.

There is a widespread belief among Black people that HIV and AIDS are part of a racial bacteriological or viral war. Since AIDS has hit Black people so disproportionately, especially on the African continent, there is a strong temptation to conclude that HIV is viral or bacteriological ethnic cleansing. Is somebody trying to shrink the population of Black people?

In the middle of this inconclusive debate as to whether AIDS is part of a racial war there has now surfaced the question as to whether anthrax and other bacteria are part of a war between civilizations. Is

208

the recent scare of anthrax connected with the horrendous atrocities of September 11th in New York, Washington, and Pennsylvania? And are those atrocities part of a clash of civilizations? Or are they home-grown aberrations?

Thabo Mbeki, the President of South Africa, has attributed AIDS not to viral or bacteriological ethnic cleansing but to a class war between the Haves and the Have-nots. Mbeki has argued that the collapse of immune systems in Africa is at least as likely to be due to poverty and deprivation of nutrition as to HIV. To Mbeki, AIDS could be one of the latest manifestations of the global class struggle between the Haves and the Have-nots.

Westerners opposed to Saddam Hussein in Iraq have long suspected him of developing bacteriological and chemical weapons designed to be used against Israel and the Western world. And yet when Saddam Hussein was being humiliated with a devastating defeat in 1991 and again in 2002 he never resorted to either chemical weapons or germ warfare. Saddam Hussein may have been rational enough to threaten germ warfare, yet not so irrational as to carry out the threat when the chips were down.

The return of germ warfare to the Americas at a time when the United States has the most Hispanic-friendly President (George W. Bush) in a century is replete with ironies. The destruction of the original indigenous American civilizations in North America was as much due to new diseases that the white man had brought with him to the New World as to any gunpowder. Indeed, there is evidence to suggest that just when the Aztecs were about to defeat the Spaniards in Central America a single Spanish soldier with smallpox helped to decimate a third of the Aztec population four centuries ago.

Let us hope the new bacteriological threat to North America through modern day terrorism does not materialize as a new version of Montezuma's revenge. Far from the Western world being a cause of AIDS and ethnic cleansing in Africa, Africa needs the West to help control the AIDS pandemic. The threat of anthrax is a diversion from older and more fundamental problems. These older problems include not only Thabo Mbeki's concern about poverty and health, but also international concern about the festering wound of Palestine and its potential for global instability.

The Kenyan medical authorities claimed in October that Kenya was the second country after the United States to be targeted with anthrax. Kenya was a choice that could not have been made by the same mind that chose the World Trade Center as a symbol of America's economic might and the Pentagon as America's military might. The choice of the American targets was made by a brilliant military tactician, however evil.

Sending anthrax to a developing country like Kenya, and to an ordinary citizen instead of a high profile Kenyan, could only have been done by a much more mediocre tactician, or by a copy-cat. It made no sense whatsoever for Al-Qaeda to have chosen Kenya for a major anthrax attack instead of Great Britain or Israel. Since then almost every Western country has witnessed copycat alarms and false alarms. But why pick Kenya before Britain? Was the whole scare in Kenya a fake?

Yet whoever is experimenting with "germ warfare," whether by a major organization or as a private vendetta, should be hunted down as a criminal of the first order. What we should avoid is mistaking scapegoating for genuine criminal investigation.

Let us now return to relations of war and peace between Africa and the Middle East. In the year of the Prophet Muḥammad's birth (570 C.E.) Mecca was attacked by Abyssinians (Ethiopians) riding elephants. The Qur'ān says that Mecca was saved by a flock of birds from Heaven throwing pebbles at the invaders. The "birds and pebbles" are widely interpreted as an outbreak of pestilence among both elephants and the invaders. (See *Sūrat al-Fīl* or The Elephant, Qur'ān, 30:105). Could the pestilence have been anthrax? The Ethiopian invasion of Mecca was foiled.

Less than fifty years later Ethiopia provided asylum to Muslims on the run from persecution in pre-Islamic Arabia. Thanks to pestilence among their elephants Ethiopians failed to conquer Mecca. Yet two generations later Ethiopians were helping to save nascent Islam. Africa and the Middle East had once again played their convergent roles in the history of civilization.

NOTES

1. This chapter is based on a presentation at the conference on "Britain and the Inalienable Rights of the Palestinian People" sponsored by the Palestinian Return Centre, April 23, 2003, London, England.
2. See Julian Amery, *The Life of Joseph Chamberlain*, vol. 4 (London: Macmillian 1951), especially pp. 262-5.
3. *Ibid.*
4. *Ibid.* Kenya as a separate country had not yet been created in 1902. Much of what is today Kenya was included by the British within the boundaries of what they called "Uganda" at the time.

CHAPTER THIRTEEN

AFRICA AND ISLAM
IN THE AFTERMATH OF SEPTEMBER 11:
BETWEEN HOPE AND PERIL

Has the aftermath of September 11 increased sectarian consciousness in Africa? Have Muslim and non-Muslim Africans become more cautious about each other than they were before? Is Africa's ecumenical spirit being eroded?

Africa entered its postcolonial era with more dialogue and less conflict between civilizations than almost anywhere else in the world. Apart from the special problem of Sudan, relations between African Christians and African Muslims were often remarkably harmonious in the political process. Only in Africa could you have a country that was over 90% Muslim and still have a Roman Catholic President for 20 years—and that was Senegal. Only in Africa could you have a *de facto* rotation of the Presidency between Christians and Muslims—Christian Julius Nyerere, Muslim Ali Hassan Mwinyi, Christian

Benjamin Mkapa and potentially Salim Ahmed Salim or another Muslim to succeed him. Only in Africa could you have a Christian presidential candidate and a Muslim running mate—and have the ticket triumph. And that was Kufuor's Ghana following Jerry Rawlings. Alternatively you could have a Muslim presidential candidate and a Christian running mate—as in Malawi.

Africa has also experimented with a system in which Christians controlled the economy and Muslims controlled political power—as in Nigeria in the 1980s and 1990s. This division of power in Nigeria has been interrupted by the current Obasanjo era in which both political and economic control has been centered in the South. It remains to be seen whether Nigeria would return to a system of politically powerful Muslims and economically triumphant Christians—comparable to politically powerful Malays and economically triumphant ethnic Chinese in Malaysia. Only in Africa could you have a member of a religious minority, the Copts, be allowed to rise to eligibility for election to Secretary-General of the United Nations with the support of the Muslim majority Government. I am of course referring to Christian Boutros Boutros-Ghali sponsored and promoted by the Egyptian government to the top post at the United Nations towards the end of the twentieth century. Only in Africa could you have a country of over 90% Muslim population have different Christian First Ladies (wives of the Head of State) for forty years—Madame Senghor and Madame Diouf of Senegal presiding over an overwhelmingly Muslim society. Only in Africa could you have an experiment in federation of cultures, linking ethnic groups across religious differences. This is Ethiopia's model of cultural engineering and religious ecumenicalism.

Africa has had an impressive record of dialogue of cultures and civilizations. This record is now endangered both by internal tensions in Africa and by new external pressures and stresses. Among the new external pressures are the new forms of terrorism and the new styles of fighting it. I was in Barcelona in January 2003. Consciousness of terrorism is not new in Spain. They have been dealing with the Basque separatist rebellion for decades. This separatism has often resorted to terrorism.

Terrorism is a style of warfare—usually resorted to by those who are at great military disadvantage but have a cause they believe in. The United States is assembling a Combined Task Force for the Horn of Africa. The six African countries being brought together are Ethiopia, Somalia, Sudan, Djibouti, Eritrea, and Kenya, alongside Yemen. Apart form Djibouti each one of those countries has experienced domestic terrorism long before September 11, in pursuit of diverse political causes and missions.

Some people say that one person's terrorist is another's freedom fighter. In reality, it is not an either-or distinction. Dedan Kimathi in Kenya's Mau Mau war against the British was both a terrorist and a freedom fighter. Terrorism is a low-intensity form of warfare which often targets civilians—but in reality kills far fewer civilians than ostensibly more "respectable" conventional warfare. The total casualties of the Gulf War of 1991, ostensibly conventional, has been at least one hundred times greater than all casualties killed by Arab terrorists since the 1960s.

TERRORISM AS A TYPE OF WARFARE

Much of the old anti-colonial and anti-apartheid domestic terrorism in Africa in the second half of the twentieth century was targeted against European minority regimes and the colonial powers. Much of the Middle Eastern terrorism of more recent times has been targeted against the United States and Israel.

In the retrospect of history, Africa gained from its own guerrilla movements and terrorist activities against European powers and white minority regimes. The Mau Mau war in Kenya did result in Kenya's independence in I 963: the Algerian revolution did result in the liberation of Algeria in 1962: the anti-colonial wars in Angola, Mozambique and Guinea-Bissau did destroy the Portuguese empire in 1974: the anti-UDI struggle in Zimbabwe ended Ian Smith's Unilateral Declaration of Independence: and the anti-apartheid struggle in South Africa finally triumphed against the official racial order.

Terrorism and guerilla war by Africans against European powers and minority regimes did yield positive results. Terrorism was a form of warfare, and had to be judged in its total political and moral context, and by its ultimate results. What is more, all forms of modern warfare kill overwhelmingly more civilians than combatants. The American War in Vietnam killed some three million Vietnamese civilians, against less than sixty thousand American combatants. However, if anti-European guerilla war and anti-colonial terrorism in Africa had produced good results in the end for Africa, anti-American and anti-Zionist terrorism in the Middle East has not yet found its moment of triumph. In "The Global Hostage Crisis," I discuss how the Middle east and Africa have been paying for the anti-American terrorism.

There was another remarkable terrorist act in Mombasa in 2002 on the same day as the suicide bombing of the Paradise Hotel. This was the attempted shooting down of an Israeli passenger plane with over two hundred tourists. A surface to air missile seems to have been used in an attempt to blow up the Israeli plane. The global media presented this as a wholly new threat to civilian aviation. In fact this attempt to shoot down a civilian plane was not new even in Africa. Sub-Saharan Africa had a 1978 precedent at the level of national terrorism. North Africa was accused of a similar 1988 destruction of a civilian airline at the level of international terrorism.

The sub-Saharan precedent was the shooting down of a civilian government airliner by Zimbabwe liberation forces in 1978, in which about 50 people died. Among those who survived on the ground Joshua Nkomo's forces killed or attempted to kill several of them. *Newsweek* carried a photograph of Joshua Nkomo and Robert Mugabe raising their glasses. The caption of the photograph was "We shot it down." It was not clear whether the photograph was not an old one dug up by *Newsweek* and taken long before the shooting down of the plane. There is no doubt, however, that Joshua Nkomo accepted "credit" for shooting down the plane, and he caused an uproar when he chuckled over the incident in a BBC interview. This was all part of anti-colonial terrorism at the national level of the politics of Rhodesia/Zimbabwe.

Less clear-cut was whether Libya was really responsible for the bombing of the Pan American flight 103 over Lockerbie, Scotland, in 1988. The fact that one Libyan has been convicted by a Scottish court has still left many doubts about the nature of the evidence. But if Libya was indeed responsible for the bomb that destroyed Pan American flight 103, it was North African participation in terrorism at the international level. Libya itself had been a victim of trigger happy Israelis. A 727 Libyan airline was shot down by Israel in February 1973, killing 108 innocent civilian passengers of all ages— young and old, men and women. A country like Israel was in a position to say "Oop! Sorry! My mistake!" And Israel was bound to get away with it.

Similarly, an American warship in the Persian Gulf shot down a Persian civilian airline with 292 civilian passengers on board. This was in July 1988. Again, like Israel, the United States was in a position to cry out "Oops! I didn't mean that! Would you like some dollars to cheer you up?" Apparently, nobody was court marshaled in the United States. The incident was simply described as a "regrettable defense action" or "an unfortunate and tragic error."

The Soviet Union was less hypocritical in its war games. It deliberately shot down a South Korean civilian airline in 1982 over the Shakhalin Islands—accusing the civilian plane of being used by the United States for spying. Over 290 civilian lives were lost. The powerful have been playing war games with civilian airlines in the past and never got punished. The powerless are resorting to similar games—either to end white rule in Zimbabwe, or to end Israeli occupation of Palestine, or to tame the mighty power of the United States.

The city of Mombasa is over a thousand years old. Because historically it had a superb natural harbor it was fought over many times— by the Arabs, by the Portuguese, by the Zanzibaris, by the Mazrui, by the British and by others. Indeed, there was a time when the city of Mombasa was called *MVITA*—the Isle of War. To the present day the Swahili dialect of Mombasa is called KI-MVITA. In ancient days war in Mombasa was fought with swords, spears and later canon balls. It was against this background that these Coastal people coined the proverb *Ndovu wawili wakipigana, ziumiazo ni nyasi* (When two elephants fight, it is the grass that suffers). In the twentieth century a companion concept evolved, not always suitable for polite society—*Ndovu wawili wakitombana, ziumiazo ni nyasi* (When two elephants copulate, it is still the grass that suffers.

Since the attack on the Israeli hotel, The Paradise, in November 2002, has Mombasa reverted to its ancient identity of MVITA, the Isle of War? Are we also back to the older proverb of "When two elephants fight, the grass suffers"? Or are we really confronting an entirely different phenomenon? Is this really a case of the single elephant, the United States, with its protégé, Israel? Has the singularity of the beast created an entirely different jungle game—*Ndovu mmoja akiteza ngoma ziumiazo ni nyasi* (When a single elephant does a war dance, the grass feels the pain). The anguish of Mombasa economically, as well as in terms of security, may have only just begun. The shadows of September 11, the repercussions of the Arab-Israeli conflict and the reincarnation of Mvita have tragically converged on this historic African seaport on the Indian Ocean. Speedy action is needed to restore the sense of dignity of Coastal and Muslim Kenyans before Kenyan Islam is radicalized into a new Black Intifadah. Even speedier action is needed to solve the Israeli-Palestinian conflict.

TOWARDS THE FUTURE

The best place where the USA can demonstrate that its war on terrorism is not a war against Islam is in Africa. In the mid-East plans to invade Iraq, uncritical support for Israel, United States' inclusion of Iran in its Axis of Evil, and the widely believed suspicion that the Bush Administration wants to control the oil reserves of the Muslim world, all lend credibility to an unfolding clash of civilizations.

In South East Asia there is also concern of an unfolding clash between a *Jihād* culture and a secular Western crusade. General Musharaff in Pakistan may be a friend of the Americans, but anti-American feelings are strong in Pakistan. But in Africa the USA

218

stands a chance of fighting terrorism without appearing to fight Islam. US Embassies in Africa are trying to reassure Muslim civilians accordingly. And the decision of the Bush Administration to combine a war on terror with a war on AIDS is an excellent move if the Congress provides the resources.

Terrorism may be a political military process—but terror is a psychological and emotional disequilibrium. A far greater terror than terrorism is the impact of AIDS and HIV in Africa. Millions more people are terrorized by AIDS than by Al-Qaeda, terrorized by the letter H in HIV than by the letter H in (Saddam) Hussein.

If President Bush's proposed billions of dollars to fight AIDS materialize, the US will have recognized that terror is a much more prevalent condition than terrorism. It would lend a new credibility that America is engaged in a fight for a better human condition. The battle should be against all the forces that terrorize the innocent masses of the world, regardless of race, culture or religion.

Out of the appalling evil of September 11, a genuine spirit of global compassion may indeed dawn upon the human race. Marrying conservatism to compassion is one approach. Marrying compassion to global conscience has to be the ultimate human imperative. Let us reach for that star. Let us reach for that moral galaxy.

SECTION FOUR

TOWARDS A MARRIAGE OF CIVILIZATIONS?

CHAPTER FOURTEEN

ISLAM BETWEEN CHRISTIAN ALLIES AND WESTERN ADVERSARIES
A NEW RE-ALIGNMENT?[1]

How significant is it that the terrorist targets on September 11, 2001, did not include a cathedral in New York or Washington? The terrorists of September 11 aimed for the World Trade Center, a symbol of American economic might. They aimed at the Pentagon, a symbol of American military might.

The fourth airplane that crashed in Pennsylvania was probably intended for either the Congressional buildings or the White House, symbols of American political might. What was apparently missing was the desire to hit a symbol of American religious life.

If there was a *jihād* in the hearts of the terrorists of September 11, 2001, it was *jihād* against the West rather than a *jihād* against Christianity. It was not a return to the Crusades of religions at war. The West was not a religious category. There may be a new realignment which has been unfolding. On the global arena mainstream churches and mainstream mosques are experiencing diminishing rivalry. At the global level Islam's confrontation is not therefore with its sister religion, Christianity. Islam's confrontation is with the imperial might of the Western world.

One can go further and argue that since the end of World War, the global situation is pulling Islam and mainstream Western Christianity closer together as allies in an increasingly irreligious world. But even before World War II, but especially since the creation of the State of Israel in 1948, Islam and the secular Western world are in danger of being pulled further apart.

At the global level there is a convergence of relations between Islam and mainstream Western Christianity as systems of sacred values. There is a divergence of relations between Islam and the secular West as political forces on the world scene.

This convergence between mainstream Western churches and mainstream mosques is clearer at the macro-level of global overview than at the micro-level of relations between Christians and Muslims within individual countries. For example, within Third World Muslim countries local militants may not always know where to draw the line between being anti-Western and being anti-Christian. This may put a strain on Muslim-Christian relations in places like Egypt or Nigeria or Indonesia.

But when we look at global trends at the macro-level over the last hundred years or so, there is no doubt that the trend has been towards greater convergence between Islam and mainstream Christianity, especially in the West. There is still considerable tension, but the direction of change is towards less rivalry and more cooperation.

Let us look more closely at the forces that have contributed to this Muslim-Christian convergence, on the one hand, and the other forces that have propelled the trend towards Muslim-Western divergence, on the other.

THE MILITARIZATION OF WESTERN SECULARISM

The West has done more to preserve human life through science and medicine than any other civilization in history. But the West has also done more to endanger human life through war than any other civilization on record. Non-human enemies of the human race like small pox, malaria, leprosy and one day even AIDS have either been subdued by Western science or are in the process of being eliminated, researched or conquered. However, human enemies of the human race like arrogance, greed, desire for dominating other people, dishonesty have reached a level of militarization in the West unmatched anywhere else. In the last one hundred years Western civilization has killed millions more people than any other way of life in the annals of man in a comparable unit of time.[2] Western secular dictators have killed millions of Western Christians, as well as Jews and Muslims.[3]

Many people were more shocked by the attack on the World Trade Center in New York on September 11, 2001, than by the attack on the Pentagon in Washington. The Pentagon could legitimately have been regarded as a military target—though the weapon should not have been a civilian airline full of innocent non-combatants. This time was it Muslim militants avenging symbols of Western secular power? Yet, it has been the West in the preceding hundred years that had made warfare less and less respectful of civilians in spite of Christian teaching. The nature of conventional Western-style war inevitably inflicts what the West itself cynically calls "collateral damage."[4]

World War I killed millions of people but it was still an era when the ratio of combatants dying in the trenches was at least comparable to the civilian casualties. World War II "civilianized" the casualties on a much higher scale. The ruthless bombing of Dresden towards the end of the war, and the nuclear attack on Hiroshima and Nagasaki, abandoned all pretence at sparing civilian lives. Western secular leaders fundamentally changed the nature of warfare and took it well beyond the frontiers of any formal battlefield.[5]

The same is true of the millions who were killed in the Korean

War and in Vietnam.[6] Western rhetoric about saving civilians has repeatedly been contradicted by Western practice. Unfortunately the vices of the powerful acquire some of the prestige of power. The secular West is a good role model as a democracy but not as warrior.

WESTERN IDEALS AND NON-WESTERN PRACTITIONERS

The Christian ethic of the minimization of violence has repeatedly been honored by secular Westerners more in the breach than the observance. In the last hundred years Westerners claiming to be Christians have killed vastly more people than have followers of any other religion in any single century. Many of the millions of victims of Western violence in the two world wars were themselves fellow Christians—though the Holocaust against the Jews and the Gypsies stand out as special cases of genocide perpetrated by Westerners in otherwise Christian nations.

If minimization of violence is part of Christian ethics, it is a standard that has not only been violated by the secular West. It has also been better implemented by other cultures in history. In the first half of the twentieth century India produced Mohandas Gandhi who led one of the most remarkable non-violent anticolonial movements ever witnessed. Westerners themselves saw Gandhi's message as the nearest approximation of the Christian ethic of the first half of the twentieth century.

Mahatma Gandhi's India gave birth to new principles of passive resistance and *satyagraha*. Yet, Gandhi himself said that it may be through the Black people that the unadulterated message of soul force and passive resistance might be realized. If Gandhi was right, this would be one more illustration when the culture which gives birth to an ethic is not necessarily the culture which fulfills the ethic.

The Nobel Committee for Peace in Oslo seems to have shared some of Gandhi's optimism about the soul force of the Black people. Christians who are not Westerners have often been more peace-loving. Africans and people of African descent who have won the Nobel prize for Peace since the middle of the twentieth century have been

Ralph Bunche (1950), Albert Luthuli (1960), Martin Luther King Jr. (1964), Anwar Sadat (1978) Desmond Tutu (1984) and Nelson Mandela (1993). And now Kofi Annan and his UN leadership have joined the galaxy. Neither Mahatma Gandhi himself nor any of his compatriots in India ever won the Nobel Prize for Peace. Was Mahatma Gandhi vindicated that the so-called "Negro" was going to be the best exemplar of soul force? Was this a case of African culture being empirically more Gandhian than Indian culture? Or was it a case of Christianity sometimes shining brighter outside the West?

In reality Black people have been at least as violent as anything ever perpetrated by Indians. What is distinctive about Africans is their short memory of hate. It is a quality not necessarily inspired by Christianity, but a quality closer to the message of Jesus. Jomo Kenyatta was unjustly imprisoned by the British colonial authorities over charges of founding the Mau Mau movement. A British Governor also denounced him as "a leader into darkness and unto death." And yet when Jomo Kenyatta was released he not only forgave the white settlers, but turned the whole country towards a basic pro-Western orientation to which it has remained committed ever since. Kenyatta even published a book entitled *Suffering Without Bitterness*. The message had echoes of the passion on the Cross.

Ian Smith, the white settler leader of Rhodesia, unilaterally declared independence in 1965 and unleashed a civil war on Rhodesia. Thousands of people, mainly Black, died in the country as a result of policies pursued by Ian Smith. Yet when the war ended in 1980 Ian Smith and his cohorts were not subjected to a Nuremberg-style trial. On the contrary, Ian Smith was himself a member of parliament in a Black-ruled Zimbabwe, busy criticizing the post-Smith Black leaders of Zimbabwe as incompetent and dishonest. They probably were. But where else but in Africa could such tolerance occur?

The Nigerian civil war (1967-1970) was the most highly publicized civil conflict in postcolonial African history. When the war was coming to an end, many people feared that there would be a bloodbath in the defeated eastern region. The Vatican was worried that cities like Enugu and Onitcha, strongholds of Catholicism, would be monuments of devastation and blood-letting.

None of these expectations occurred. Nigerians—seldom among the most disciplined of Africans—discovered in 1970 some remarkable resources of self-restraint. There were no triumphant reprisals against the vanquished Biafrans; there were no vengeful trials of "traitors." African culture was more forgiving than Western culture has often been.

We have also witnessed the phenomenon of Nelson Mandela. He lost twenty-seven of the best years of his life in prison under the laws of the apartheid regime. Yet when he was released he not only emphasized the policy of reconciliation—he often went beyond the call of duty. On one occasion before he became President white men were fasting unto death after being convicted of terrorist offences by their own white government. Nelson Mandela went out of his way to beg them to eat and thus spare their own lives. His Africanity resembled the spirit of Jesus seeking to rescue the deviants and sinners of society.

When Mandela became President in 1994 it was surely enough that his government would leave the architects of apartheid unmolested. Yet Nelson Mandela went out of his way to pay a social call and have tea with the unrepentant widow of Hendrik F. Verwoed, the supreme architect of the worst forms of apartheid, who shaped the whole racist order from 1958 to 1966. Mandela was having tea with the family of Verwoed.

Was Mahatma Gandhi correct, after all, that his torch of soul force *(satyagraha)* might find its brightest manifestations among Black people? Or was it the spirit of Jesus residing in the traditions of Black folk? In the history of civilizations there are occasions when the image in the mirror is more real that the object it reflects. Black Gandhians like Martin Luther King Jr., Desmond Tutu and, in a unique sense, Nelson Mandela have sometimes reflected Gandhaian soul force more brightly than Gandhians in India. Part of the explanation lies in the soul of African culture itself—with all its capacity for rapid forgiveness.

It is a positive modification of *The Picture of Dorian Gray.* In

Oscar Wilde's novel, the picture of Dorian Gray is a truer reflection of the man's decrepit body and lost soul than the man himself. The decomposition of Dorian's body and soul is transferred from Dorian himself to his picture. The picture is more real than the man.

In the case of Gandhism, it is not the decomposition of the soul but its elevation that is transferred from India to the Black experience. In the last one hundred years both Indian culture and African culture have, in any case, been guilty of far less blood-letting than the West. Christian minimization of violence has been observed more by non-Western Christians than by ostensible Western followers of the Cross. Empirical relativism continues its contradictions.

SECULAR DIVERGENCE AND RELIGIOUS CONVERGENCE

The wider economic context encompassed the world of international capitalism. The West virtually controlled the world economy while the Muslim world was vital either because of its location (like the value of the Suez Canal) or because of its resources (like petroleum from the twentieth century onwards). The West used its power to exploit the Muslim world's assets and resources.[7] This also contributed dramatically to the forces of divergence between the West and Islam.

Even on the issue of Western militarism, Muslims have become disproportionate victims from the last quarter of the twentieth century. When the West's war against communism was at its height, Koreans and Vietnamese paid a higher military price than Muslims. But since the end of the war in Vietnam, Muslim countries have been disproportionate targets of Western military power. Excluding Palestine, over a million Muslims have been killed by Western military might in the last quarter century. These include Iraqis, Iranis, Libyans, Lebanese, Sudanese as well as Afghans. The divergence between Islam and the West broadens.

George W. Bush's war on terrorism has already carpet-bombed parts of Afghanistan and Iraq.[8] The United States has also sent military personnel to help fight Muslim rebels in the Philippines and

Muslim militants in former Soviet Republics. The divergence between the Muslim world and the West threatens to widen.

The United States has a list of seven countries that it claims support terrorism. These are Iran, Iraq, Syria, Libya, Sudan, North Korea and Cuba. As can be seen, five of the United States' choice of countries allegedly supporting terrorism are Muslim.[9] The list is quite arbitrary, especially since the United States has itself supported terrorist movements from time to time—including movements in Afghanistan during the Soviet occupation. But these recent American tendencies to "Islamize the face of terrorism" have contributed to the divergence between the West and Islam.

However, the West's contemporary historical role suffers from a deep schizophrenia. In its relations with Islam, Western secularism is increasingly a Mr. Hyde. On the other hand, mainstream Western churches are now a benign Dr. Jekyll towards Muslims.

While Western militarism, imperialism, racism and capitalism have all helped to alienate the West from Islam, the main Christian churches and the main leaders of Islam have been moving closer together. For a long time mainstream Christian leadership preferred to have Jerusalem declared as an international city, rather than continue to be a bitterly contested battleground between Israelis and Palestinians.

Pope John Paul II has gone further than any previous Pope to foster good relations between Catholic and Muslims. In May 2002 he visited Azerbaijan, a country with fewer Christians than those who were on his own plane. He was trying to be fair to the Muslim Azaris after visiting Christian Armenians the year before. When Salman Rushdie published his notorious novel *The Satanic Verses* in 1988-1989, the book was declared blasphemous not only by Muslims but also by the Vatican and by the Archbishop of Canterbury in London.

Prince Charles, the Heir to the British Throne and potentially Head of the Church of England, is the patron of the Oxford Centre for Islamic Studies and author of a widely circulating Islam-friendly pamphlet entitled *Islam and the West*. Prince Charles has also proposed that at his Coronation he should swear to be "Defender of Faith" (meaning all faiths) rather than the traditional "Defender of the Faith" (meaning the Church of England).

However, within Third World countries the picture of relations between Muslims and Christians is more mixed. On the one hand, bloody conflicts have broken out in countries like Indonesia, Nigeria, Sudan and occasionally Egypt between Christians and Muslims. On the other hand, Muslim societies in the Third World have sometimes given Christians remarkable access to influence and power. Saddam Hussein's Iraq had Tareq Aziz, a Chalden Christian, as Deputy Prime Minister. Aziz was previously Foreign Minister of Iraq.

Boutros Boutros-Ghali, a Coptic Christian, would never have become Secretary-General of the United Nations had he not previously risen high in the Foreign Service of Egypt. He had served as Minister of State. There is no Western nation which has permitted a Muslim to rise so high.

Senegal is over ninety percent Muslim. Yet it had a Roman Catholic Executive President for twenty years (1960 to 1980). Catholic President Leopold Senghor was succeeded by a Muslim Head of State, Abdou Diouf. Diouf's First Lady was Roman Catholic. A Muslim First Lady or President of a Western country is at the moment mindboggling.

Muslims and Christians in Nigeria fight each other from time to time. But they also vote for each other at election time. Olusegun Obasanjo (a Christian) would never have become President of Nigeria had he not received half his support from the Muslims of Nigeria in 1998.

Muslims in general are more ecumenical towards other faiths than is often recognized.[10]Westerners in their political behavior are less tolerant of other faiths than Westerners themselves realize.

At the macro-level of the world as a whole, relations between mainstream Christianity and mainstream Islam are more cordial than they were before World War II. But relations between the West and the Muslim world are getting more polarized.

Outside the field of militarism the rising forces of secularism constitute shared threats between Islam and Christianity. Religious life generally has been threatened by the impact of such influences as Western television, Hollywood and the cinema, the impact of the West's magazines, newspapers and radio, and the even more pervasive influence of Western models of secular education worldwide.

Islam and Christianity have also had to confront the shared threat of Western materialism. The triumph of market ideologies, acquisitive individualism, maximization of returns, capitalism and the rat-race of the market-place have all emphasized material satisfaction rather than spiritual salvation. Sacred values generally have been at risk as a result. This is a point of convergence between Christianity and Islam as they confront the rising tide of irreligious culture.

The two religions have also been struggling with the forces of Western hedonism. Christianity has been hit harder than Islam by such social difficulties as alcoholism, drugs and narcotics, prostitution and easy sex. But both religions are up against eroding moral restraints in the face of Western hedonism.

ISLAM, THE WEST AND NON-CHRISTIAN RELIGIONS

Finally, there is the issue of the impact of the secular West on Islam's relations with other religions. We know that the impact of the secular West on Islam's relationship with Judaism has been nothing short of catastrophic.

Political Zionism was originally a secular movement designed to create a nation-state (a secular concept) for Jews as a nation, not as a religious community. Political Zionism has been the biggest blow to relations between Muslims and Jews in a thousand years. When the Zionist movement was gathering momentum, hundreds of thousands of religious Jews were against the creation of the State of Israel.

The allies of Muslims in their opposition to political Zionism were disproportionately religious Jews. Devout Muslims and devout Jews shared deep misgivings about creating the State of Israel.

What tipped the scale was the alliance between secular Westerners and secular Jews—aided by the atrocities committed by secular Nazis against the Jews in the Holocaust. From Belfour Declaration to Harry S. Truman secular Westerners prepared the ground for the triumph of the dreams of such secular Jews or Theodor Herzl and the Rothchilds. Jews and Muslims have been killing each other in their hundreds ever since.

There is now a risk that the nature of Western intervention between India and Pakistan may similarly poison relations between Muslims and Hindus for decades to come. In the struggle for political Zionism, the West finally decided that Palestinians were expendable—and secular Westerners and secular Jews plunged Muslim-Jewish relations into an abyss of rage. In the struggle against terrorism after September 11, 2001, Western leaders and the Indian elite may decide that Kashmiri nationalists are expendable—and they may thus plunge Hindu-Muslim relations into an abyss of mutual recrimination for generations. Jewish-Muslim animosities have already cost thousands of lives directly and indirectly. It would be calamitous in the highest degree if Hindu-Muslim animosities were to cost millions of lives in a nuclear Armageddon.

The secular West cannot be trusted with Islam's relations with other religions. The Muslim world should not leave it to Western dignitaries to appeal to India and Pakistan for restraint. The West has its own agenda. When will Muslim Sultans, Muslim Presidents and Arab Kings go to New Delhi and Islamabad actively to appeal for peace and commonsense? Instead Arab Kings wait in their capitals for Pakistan leaders to go to them. How about Arabs trying to influence New Delhi?

If Islam is a religion of peace, Muslim leaders should be promoting peace instead of leaving the initiative to the Foreign Minister of Great Britain, and Defense Secretary of the United States or the President of Russia. However, while everybody is ready to remind General Musharaff about the risks of cross-border terrorism, not enough people are reminding Prime Minister Vajpayee about the risks of governing an unwilling people.

233

Algeria was once declared by France as being part of France—the way Kashmir was declared by India as being part of India. If Algeria was accepted as part of Post-World War II France, it was the only part of France that had a Muslim majority—the way Kashmir was the only part of India that had a Muslim majority.[11] The issue of Algeria in France became inseparable from the issue of patriotism and the national integrity of France—in the same way in which the issue of Kashmir became inseparable from patriotism in both India and Pakistan, and inseparable from the national integrity of India. When violence broke out in Algeria against French rule in 1954, France concluded that insurrection was in reality cross-border violence instigated by Gamal Abdel Nasser in Egypt through functionaries in Tunisia. India has similarly concluded that there is no such thing as Kashmiri nationalism—and that all acts of violence in Jammu and Kashmir are in reality cross-border terrorism instigated by Pakistan.

An opportunity presented itself to India on September 11, 2001. From then on the issue of Kashmir could be presented to the world as nothing more nor less than part of the global problem of terrorism. An opportunity presented itself for France in 1956 when Gamal Abdel Nasser nationalized the Suez Canal. From then on the insurrection in Algeria could be presented as no more and no less than the general destabilization in the Middle East that was being fostered by Gamel Abdel Nasser in Egypt. France, Israel and Britain united in a joint military action against Egypt in 1956.

The question arises whether the violent confrontation between Muslim Algeria and Christian France, especially from 1954 to 1962, eventually turned out to be a prelude to a different kind of integration between North Africa and France. The old idea of dominant white French settlers controlling Algeria was gradually replaced by Algerian immigrants settling in France and changing the nature of French society.

The old idea of French cathedrals in North Africa was replaced by North African mosques in France. The old idea of Algeria as part of France was not replaced by France as part of North Africa—but

France and North Africa were finding new ways of cultural, economic, demographic and cultural convergence.

The question arises about India and Pakistan whether at the end of periodic saber-rattling and nuclear threats, a different kind of positive relationship awaits them at the other end. Perhaps the two countries should look less at Algeria and Palestine for solutions and more at Quebec in Canada. Perhaps Kashmir is the Quebec of the Indian subcontinent. Is Kashmir a distinct society the way Canadians have sometimes seen Quebec as being? Kashmir as distinct society has a fellow Muslim country next door (Pakistan) to support its cause. Quebec as a distinct society does not have a Francophone United States to support its cause. The Unites States is English-speaking. The contexts of Kashmir and Quebec are therefore not identical.

Nevertheless, the debate about Quebec in Canada has raised enough ideas about asymmetrical federalism to give us pointers about new possible scenarios for consideration about Kashmir. One scenario would be for both Pakistani-controlled Kashmir and Indian-controlled Kashmir to be united as a unique and extra-autonomous state of the Indian union, a distinct society with freedom to have cultural and commercial relations with Pakistan without reference to the Indian Foreign Ministry. Kashmir could even have cultural and commercial attaches in Pakistan separate from Indian's foreign service. Similar privileges have been envisaged and partially implemented in Quebec's relations with France. The other scenario—in my opinion less satisfactory—would be for Indian controlled Kashmir to be an extra-autonomous distinct state of India and Azad Kashmir be an extra-autonomous distinct state of Pakistan, with special links between them similar to those sometimes envisaged between Northern Ireland, the Irish Republic and the United Kingdom.

It remains to be seen whether the improved negotiating atmosphere between India and Pakistan since 2003 would result in readiness to explore all such options about Kashmir.

CONCLUSION

We have noted that on September 11, 2001, it was American secular icons that were targeted by the terrorists. The World Trade Center was a symbol of American economic might, the Pentagon a symbol of military power. The fourth plane, which crashed in Pennsylvania, was probably intended for either the White House or the Capitol building of Congress, symbols of American political pre-eminence.

What was obviously not targeted on September 11, 2001, was a major cathedral in either New York or Washington. We have argued that this religious omission was not accidental. The pre-eminent adversary of militant Islam is no longer Christianity, as it might have been in the days of the Crusades. The contemporary adversary to militant Islam is Western global hegemony. This is definitely true at the macro-level of the world arena. The West combines an aggressive secular Mr. Hyde towards Islam and a more benign Christian Dr. Jekyll. However, within religious plural societies in the Third World, there are two ambiguities that have affected relations between Christians and Muslims. Western exploitation creates a situation where ordinary folks are not always sure where Western hegemony ends and the power of Christendom begins. Secondly, although the Third World has had some of the worst clashes between Christians and Muslims, it has also witnessed the most remarkable instances of power-sharing in the political process, including a Christian President in an overwhelmingly Muslim country.

A third force in the Third World that can be destabilizing is globalization. While globalization is, on one side, the enlargement of economic scale, it is, on the other hand, a trigger for cultural revivalism and sectarian rivalries. Globalization has provoked re-tribalization and ethnic rivalries in countries as diverse as Yugoslavia, the former Soviet Republics, the Ivory Coast, India and Indonesia.

Globalization may itself be one of the forces that are contributing to divergence between the West and Islam. Globalization is currently deepening the trends towards cultural alienation in much of the Third World. The impact of the secular West on Islam's relations with other religions can also be alienating. The West helped to poison relations between Islam and Judaism. Will the West now poison relations between Islam and Hinduism?

When all is said and done, history is moving in the direction of making mainstream Christianity and Islam cultural allies in an increasingly secular and often amoral world. However, contemporary political and strategic issues have yet to stem the trend towards alienation between Islam and the secular West. In the Christian identity of the West there is hope for a new realignment of partnership. But the secular identity of the West is still in the shadows of militarism, imperialism capitalism and race. Christian-Muslim relations offer a beacon of optimism. Western-Muslim relations in the secular arena are in danger of vindicating Samuel Huntington's prophecy of "a clash of civilizations." As Muslims and Christians would say: "The Lord preserve us"!

NOTES

1. "Islam Between Christian Allies and Western Adversaries: A New Re-Alignment?," *Middle East Affairs Journal,* Vol. 8, No. 3-4 (summer/fall, 2002).

2. According to Professor Emeritus, R.J. Rummel, of the University of Hawaii, out of an estimated world total 169,202,000 democide—"democide is any murder by government—by officials acting under the authority of government. That is, they act according to explicit or implicit government policy or with the implicit or explicit approval of the highest officials. Such was the burying alive of Chinese civilians by Japanese soldiers, the shooting of hostages by German soldiers, the starving to death of Ukrainians by communist cadre, or the burning alive of Japanese civilians purposely fire-bombed from the air by American airmen."—from 1900 to 1987, 93,035,000 (54.9%) were committed by the U.S.S.R. (1917-87, 61,911,000), Germany (1933-45, 20,946,000), Japan (1936-45, 5,964,000), Poland (1945-48, 1,585,000), Yugoslavia (Tito) (1944-87, 1,072,000), United King-

dom (1900-87, 816,000) and Portugal (Dictatorship) (1926-82, 741,000) combined. See R. J. Rummel, "20th Century Democide." Chapter 1. Table 1.2. *Death by Government: Genocide and Mass Murder in the Twentieth Century.* New Jersey: Transaction Publishers. 1994. www.hawaii.edu/powerkills/DBG. TAB1.2.GIF. Furthermore, R. J. Rummel estimates American democide in the 20th century by claiming that: "Putting together all the subtotals (lines 333 to 350), in this century the United States probably murdered about 583,000 people (line 350), conceivable even as many as 1,641,000 all told. Virtually all of these were foreigners killed during foreign wars. Domestically, throughout this century the American Federal or state governments were responsible for the murder of about 1 out of every 1,111,000 Americans per year." See R. J. Rummel, "Death by American Bombing and Other Democide Estimates, Calculations, and Sources. Chapter 13. *Statistics of Democide.*1997. http://www.hawaii.edu/powerkills/SOD.CHAP13. HTM).

3. For example, according to R. J. Rummel, from 1942 to 1945, Adolf Hitler's democide of European Jews or the Jewish Holocaust costed 5,291,000 lives. From 1932 to 1933, Joseph Stalin's democide in the U.S.S.R. of peasants of the International Ukraine famine costed 5,000,000 lives, from 1928 to 1935, Stalin's Collectivization cost the lives of 3,133,000 peasants and landords. From 1936 to 1938 Stalin's Great Terror left 1,000,000 Communists dead. From 1900 to 1918, the German Kaiser massacred 132,000 Hereros, Khoisan and other ethnic groups in Africa. See R. J. Rummel, "Some Major Episodes and Cases of Democide." Chapter 1. Table 1.5. *Death by Government: Genocide and Mass Murder in the Twentieth Century.* New Jersey: Transaction Publishers.1994. www.hawaii.edu/powerkills/DBG.TAB1.5.GIF.

4. David Zucchino of the *Los Angeles Times* reports on U.S. collateral damages in Afghanistan writes that: "The Defense Department has said it does not plan to count civilian casualties. Relief officials with the U.S.-backed interim government estimate the total civilian dead at 1,000 to 2,000. The *Times* reviewed more than 2,000 reports of civilian casualties from U.S., British and Pakistani newspapers and international wire services.

After eliminating duplicate accounts, the review identified 194 incidents of civilian casualties from the start of the bombing on Oct. 7 until Feb. 28, when the air campaign was largely completed. The reported death toll, including estimates in some cases, was between 1,067 and 1,201. The *Times* excluded 754 civilian deaths reported by the Taliban but not independently confirmed, as well as 497 deaths that were not identified as either civilian or military." See David Zucchino, "The Americans ... They Just Drop Their Bombs and Leave." *Los Angeles Times.* June 2, 2002.

5.   Matthew White (2002) estimates that World War I (1914-1918) cost 8,500,000 military deaths. According to White, the death toll during World War II (1937-1945) is estimated at 50 million. See Matthew White, "Source List and Detailed Death Tolls for the Twentieth Century Hemoclysm" *Twentieth Century Atlas.* May 2002. http://users.erols.com/mwhite28/warstat1.htm. According to R. J. Rummel, "through indiscriminate urban bombing the American Air Force probably murdered 337,000 Japanese during the war." See R. J. Rummel, "Death by American Bombing and Other Estimates, Calculations, and Statistics." Chapter 13. *Statistics of Democide.* 1997. http://www.hawaii.edu/powerkills/SOD. CHAP13.HTM.

6.   For example, R. J. Rummel (1994) estimates that the total Vietnam war-dead and democide from 1945 to 1987 was 3,768,000. See R. J. Rummel, *Death by Government.* New Brunswick, N.J. Transaction Publishers, 1994. Rummel estimates that the Korean War left close to 2,550,000 dead on all sides. See R. J. Rummel, "Death by American Bombing and Other Democide Estimates, Calculations, and Sources." Chapter 13. *Statistics of Democide.* 1997. http://www.hawaii.edu/powerkills/SOD. CHAP13.HTM.

7.   For example, Rob Nixon of the *New York Times*, reports that, it costs the United States over $250 billion a year to import oil and that "$56 billion is spent on the oil itself and another $25 billion on the military defense of oil-exporting Middle Eastern countries." See Rob Nixon, "A Dangerous Appetite for Oil." *New York Times.* Oct. 29, 2001. In addition, research shows that substantial portions of the total exports of Bahrain, Iraq, Kuwait,

Oman, Qatar, Saudi Arabia, Syria, UAE, Yemen, Iran, Indonesia and Malaysia come from oil. Japan, the European Union and the United States are the recipients of almost all of the oil exports from these countries. See Export data compiled from 2001 *CIA World Factbook.* http://www.odci.gov/cia/publications/factbook.

8. David Zucchino of the *Los Angeles Times,* reports that: "Of the 21,737 bombs dropped by U.S. warplanes in Afghanistan, about 60% were "smart" bombs guided by satellites or lasers, compared with 10% during the 1991 Persian Gulf War, the Pentagon said. A preliminary Pentagon study found that 75% to 80% of them hit their targets in Afghanistan. The Defense Department has said it does not plan to count civilian casualties. Relief officials with the U.S.-backed interim government estimate the total civilian dead at 1,000 to 2,000." See David Zucchino, "The Americans ... They Just Drop Their Bombs and Leave." *Los Angeles Times.* June 2, 2002.

9. The estimated total population of these five nations as of July 2001 is 147,510,730 million. For more details, see *CIA World Factbook,* 2001.www.odci.gov/cia/ publications/factbook.

10. For example, Turkey, one of the most influential Muslim countries in the world, with 99.8% Muslim population out of 66.4 million (Source: *CIA World Factbook,* 2001), has instituted secular laws such as those practiced in the West since the end of the Ottoman Empire in 1923. Muslims in secular Western nations tend to have more religious freedom than Muslims in Turkey. However, even though Turkey is a member of the North Atlantic Treaty Organization (NATO) and has made significant efforts to join the European Union, it will not be among the ten European nations (Slovenia, Hungary, Poland, Slovakia, Cyprus, Czech Republic, Estonia, Latvia, Lithuania and Malta) invited to join the European Union in 2004. See T. Fuller, "The Next Europe at what price a bigger EU?" *International Herald Tribune.* June 13, 2002. In a testimony to the Senate Foreign Relations Committee in the United States Congress, former Secretary of State, George P. Shultz speaking of Indonesia's religious tolerance said: "...a tradition of religious tolerance was fostered [in Indonesia]. Indonesia is the largest Muslim country in the world-90 percent are Muslim-but they had a tradition of toler-

ance of other religions of which they were rather proud." See *Hoover Digest*. 2000 no. 3. "The Secretary Testifies" www.hoover.stanford.edu/publications/digest/003/shultz.htm.

11. As of July 2001, out of India's 1,029,991,145 population, Muslims comprise 12% (123,598,937) (Source: compiled from the 2001 *CIA World Factbook*).

CHAPTER FIFTEEN

ISLAMIC AND WESTERN VALUES[1]

DEMOCRACY AND THE HUMANE LIFE

Westerners tend to think of Islamic societies as backward-looking, oppressed by religion, and inhumanely governed, comparing them to their own enlightened, secular democracies. But measurement of the cultural distance between the West and Islam is a complex undertaking, and that distance is narrower than they assume. Islam is not just a religion, and certainly not just a fundamentalist political movement. It is a civilization and a way of life that varies from one Muslim country to another but is animated by a common spirit far more humane than most Westerners realize. Nor do those in the West always recognize how their own societies have failed to live up to their liberal mythology. Moreover, aspects of

Islamic culture that Westerners regard as medieval may have prevailed in their own culture until fairly recently; in many cases, Islamic societies may be only a few decades behind socially and technologically advanced Western ones. In the end, the question is what path leads to the highest quality of life for the average citizen, while avoiding the worst abuses. The path of the West does not provide all the answers; Islamic values deserve serious consideration.

THE WAY IT RECENTLY WAS

Mores and values have changed rapidly in the West in the last several decades as revolutions in technology and society progressed. Islamic countries, which are now experiencing many of the same changes, may well follow suit. Premarital sex, for example, was strongly disapproved of in the West until after World War II. There were laws against sex outside marriage, some of which are still on the books, if rarely enforced. Today sex before marriage, with parental consent, is common.

Homosexual acts between males were a crime in Great Britain until the 1960s (although lesbianism was not outlawed). Now such acts between consenting adults, male or female, are legal in much of the West, although they remain illegal in most other countries. Half the Western world, in fact, would say that laws against homosexual sex are a violation of gays' and lesbians' human rights.

Even within the West, one sees cultural lag. Although capital punishment has been abolished almost everywhere in the Western world, the United States is currently increasing the number of capital offenses and executing more death row inmates than it has in years. But death penalty opponents, including Human Rights Watch and the Roman Catholic Church, continue to protest the practice in the United States, and one day capital punishment will almost certainly be regarded in America as a violation of human rights.

Westerners regard Muslim societies as unenlightened when it comes to the status of women, and it is true that the gender question is still troublesome in Muslim countries. Islamic rules on sexual modesty have often resulted in excessive segregation of the sexes in public places, sometimes bringing about the marginalization of women in public affairs more generally. British women, however, were granted the right to own property independent of their husbands only in 1870, while Muslim women have always had that right. Indeed, Islam is the only world religion founded by a businessman in commercial partnership with his wife. While in many Western cultures daughters could not inherit anything if there were sons in the family, Islamic law has always allocated shares from every inheritance to both daughters and sons. Primogeniture has been illegal under the *Shari'ah* for 14 centuries.

The historical distance between the West and Islam in the treatment of women may be a matter of decades rather than centuries. Recall that in almost all Western countries except for New Zealand, women did not gain the right to vote until the twentieth century. Great Britain extended the vote to women in two stages, in 1918 and 1928, and the United States enfranchised them by constitutional amendment in 1920. France followed as recently as 1944. Switzerland did not permit women to vote in national elections until 1971— decades after Muslim women in Afghanistan, Iran, Iraq, and Pakistan had been casting ballots.

Furthermore, the United States, the largest and most influential Western nation, has never had a female president. In contrast, two of the most populous Muslim countries, Pakistan and Bangladesh, have had women prime ministers: Benazir Bhutto headed two governments in Pakistan, and Khaleda Zia and Hasina Wajed served consecutively in Bangladesh. Turkey has had Prime Minister Tansu Çiller. Muslim countries are ahead in female empowerment, though still behind in female liberation.

CONCEPTS OF THE SACRED

Censorship is one issue on which the cultural divide between the West and Islam turns out to be less wide than Westerners ordinarily assume. The most celebrated case of the last decade—that of Salman Rushdie's novel *The Satanic Verses*, published in Britain in

1988 but banned in most Muslim countries—brought the Western world and the Muslim world in conflict, but also uncovered some surprising similarities and large helpings of Western hypocrisy. Further scrutiny reveals widespread censorship in the West, if imposed by different forces than in Muslim societies.

As their civilization has become more secular, Westerners have looked for new abodes of the sacred. By the late twentieth century the freedom of the artist—in this case, Salman Rushdie—was more sacred to them than religion. But many Muslims saw Rushdie's novel as holding Islam up to ridicule. The novel suggests that Islam's holy scripture, the Qur'ān, is filled with inventions of the Prophet Muḥammad or is, in fact, the work of the devil rather than communications from Allah, and implies, moreover, that the religion's founder was not very intelligent. Rushdie also puts women characters bearing the names of the Prophet's wives in a whorehouse, where the clients find the blasphemy arousing.

Many devout Muslims felt that Rushdie had no right to poke fun at and twist into obscenity some of the most sacred symbols of Islam. Most Muslim countries banned the novel because officials there considered it morally repugnant. Western intellectuals argued that as an artist, Rushdie had the sacred right and even duty to go wherever his imagination led him in his writing. Yet until the 1960s *Lady Chatterley's Lover* was regarded as morally repugnant[2] under British law for daring to depict an affair between a married member of the gentry and a worker on the estate. For a long time after Oscar Wilde's conviction for homosexual acts, *The Picture of Dorian Gray* was regarded as morally repugnant. Today other Gay writers are up against a wall of prejudice.

The Satanic Verses was banned in some places because of fears that it would cause riots. Indian officials explained that they were banning the novel because it would inflame religious passions in the country, already aroused by Kashmiri separatism. The United States has a legal standard for preventive action when negative consequences are feared—"clear and present danger." But the West was less than sympathetic to India's warnings that the book was inflammatory.

246

Rushdie's London publisher, Jonathan Cape, went ahead, and the book's publication even in far-off Britain resulted in civil disturbances in Bombay, Islamabad, and Karachi in which some 15 people were killed and dozens more injured.

Distinguished Western publishers, however, have been known to reject a manuscript because of fears for the safety of their own. Last year Cambridge University Press turned down *Fields of Wheat, Rivers of Blood* by Anastasia Karakasidou, a sociological study on ethnicity in the Greek province of Macedonia, publicly acknowledging that it did so because of worries about the safety of its employees in Greece. If Jonathan Cape had cared as much about South Asian lives as it said it cared about freedom of expression, or as Cambridge University Press cared about its staff members in Greece, less blood would have been spilled.

Targets, sources, and methods of censorship differ, but censorship is just as much a fact of life in Western societies as in the Muslim world. Censorship in the latter is often crude, imposed by governments, mullahs and imams, and, more recently, militant Islamic movements. Censorship in the West, on the other hand, is more polished and decentralized. Its practitioners are financial backers of cultural activity and entertainment, advertisers who buy time on commercial television, subscribers of the Public Broadcasting System (PBS), influential interest groups including ethnic pressure groups, and editors, publishers, and other controllers of the means of communication.[3] In Europe, governments too sometimes get into the business of censorship.

CENSORING AMERICA

The threat to free speech in the United States comes not from the law and the Constitution but from outside the government. PBS, legally invulnerable on the issue of free speech, capitulated to other forces when faced with the metaphorical description in my 1986 television series "The Africans" of Karl Marx as "the last of the great Jewish prophets." The British version had included the phrase, but the American producing station, WETA, a PBS affiliate in Washington, deleted it without author's permission so as not to risk offending Jewish Americans.

On one issue of censorship WETA did consult me. Station officials were unhappy I had not injected more negativism into the series' three-minute segment on Libya's leader, Muammar Qaddafy. First they asked for extra commentary on allegations that Libya sponsored terrorism. When I refused, they suggested changing the pictures instead—deleting one sequence that humanized Qaddafy by showing him visiting a hospital and substituting a shot of the Rome airport after a terrorist bombing. After much debate I managed to save the hospital scene, but surrendered on the Rome airport addition, on condition that neither I nor the written caption implied that Libya was responsible for the bombing. But, ideally, WETA would have preferred to cut the whole segment.

WETA in those days had more in common with censors in Libya than either side realized. Although the Libyans broadcast an Arabic version and seemed pleased with the series as a whole, they cut the Qaddafy sequence. The segment also offended Lynne Cheney, Chair of the National Endowment for the Humanities, who demanded that the endowment's name be removed from the series credits. After she stepped down from her post, she called for the NEH to be abolished, citing "The Africans" as an example of the objectionable liberal projects that, she said, the endowment had tended to fund.

In another case of decentralized censorship that affected my own work, Westview Press in Boulder, Colorado, was about to go to press with my book *Cultural Forces in World Politics* when editors there announced they wanted to delete three chapters: one discussing *The Satanic Verses* as a case of cultural treason, another comparing the Palestinian *Intifadah* with Chinese students' 1989 rebellion in Tiananmen Square, and a third comparing the South African apartheid doctrine of separate homelands for blacks and whites with the Zionist doctrine of separate states for Jews and Arabs. Suspecting that I would have similar problems with most other major U.S. publishers, I decided that the book would be published exclusively by

James Currey, my British publisher, and Heinemann Educational Books, the American offshoot of another British house, which brought it out in 1990. Not even universities in the United States, supposed bastions of intellectual freedom, have been free from censorship. Until recently the greatest danger to one's chances of getting tenure lay in espousing Marxism or criticizing Israel or Zionism.

The positive aspect of decentralized censorship in the West, at least with regard to books, is that what is unacceptable to one publisher may be acceptable to another; what is almost unpublishable in the United States may be easily publishable in Britain or the Netherlands. With national television, the choices are more restricted. Many points of view are banned from the screen, with the possibility of a hearing only on the public-access stations with the weakest signals.

In Western societies as in Muslim ones, only a few points of view have access to the national broadcast and publishing industry or even to university faculties. In both civilizations, certain points of view are excluded from the center and marginalized. The source of the censorship may be different, but censorship is the result in the West just as surely as in the Islamic world.

LIFE AMONG THE BELIEVERS

Many of the issues above are bound up with religion. Westerners consider many problems or flaws of the Muslim world products of Islam and pride their societies and governments on their purported secularism. But when it comes to separation of church and state, how long and wide is the distance between the two cultures?

A central question is whether a theocracy can ever be democratized. British history since Henry VIII's establishment of the Church of England in 1531 proves that it can be. The English theocracy was democratized first by making democracy stronger and later by making the theocracy weaker. The major democratic changes had to wait until the nineteenth and twentieth centuries, when the vote was extended to new social classes and finally to women.[4] The Islamic Republic of Iran is less than two decades old, but already there seem to be signs of softening theocracy and the beginnings of liberalization.

Nor must we forget Muslim monarchies that have taken initial steps toward liberalization. Jordan has gone further than most others in legalizing opposition groups. But even Saudi Arabia and the smaller Gulf states have begun to use the Islamic concept of *shūrā* (consultative assembly) as a guide to democracy.

The West has sought to protect minority religions through secularism. It has not always worked. The Holocaust in secular Germany was the worst case. And even today, anti-Semitism in Eastern Europe is disturbing, as are anti-Muslim trends in France.

The United States has had separation of church and state under the Constitution for over 200 years, but American politics is hardly completely secular. Only once has the electorate chosen a non-Protestant president—and the Roman Catholic John F. Kennedy won by such a narrow margin, amid such allegations of electoral fraud, that we will never know for certain whether a majority of Americans actually voted for him. Jews have distinguished themselves in many fields, but they have so far avoided competing for the White House, and there is still a fear of unleashing the demon of anti-Semitism among Christian fundamentalists. There are now more Muslims—an estimated six million—than Jews in the United States, yet anti-Muslim feeling and the success of appeals to Christian sentiment among voters make it extremely unlikely that Americans will elect a Muslim head of state anytime in the foreseeable future. Even the appointment of a Muslim secretary of commerce, let alone an attorney general, is no more than a distant conjecture because of the political fallout that all administrations fear. When First Lady Hillary Rodham Clinton entertained Muslim leaders at the White House in 1996 to mark a special Islamic festival, a *Wall Street Journal* article cited that as evidence that friends of Hamas had penetrated the White House. In Western Europe, too, there are now millions of Muslims, but history is still awaiting the appointment of the first to a cabinet position in Britain, France, or Germany.

Islam, on the other hand, has tried to protect minority religions through ecumenicalism throughout its history. Jews and Christians had special status as People of the Book—a fraternity of monotheists. Other religious minorities were later also accorded the status of protected minorities (*dhimmīs*). The approach has had its successes. Jewish scholars rose to high positions in Muslim Spain. During the Ottoman Empire, Christians sometimes attained high political office: Sulaiman I (1520-1566) had Christian ministers in his government, as did Selim III (1789-1807). The Moghul Empire integrated Hindus and Muslims into a consolidated Indian state; Emperor Akbar (1556-1605) carried furthest the Moghul policy of bringing Hindus into the government. In the 1990s Iraq has had a Chaldean Christian deputy prime minister, Tariq Aziz. And Boutros Boutros-Ghali, a Coptic Christian would never have been appointed secretary-general of the United Nations if not for his long and distinguished service in the foreign ministry of an otherwise Muslim government in Egypt.

The Republic of Senegal in West Africa, which is nearly 95 percent Muslim, had a Roman Catholic president for two decades (1960-80). In his years presiding over that relatively open society, Léopold Sédar Senghor never once had to deal with anti-Christian disturbances in the streets of Dakar. His political opponents called him a wide range of derogatory names—hypocrite, stooge of the French, dictator, political prostitute—but virtually never taunted him for being a *kāfir* (infidel).

When Senghor became the first African head of state to retire voluntarily from office, Abou Diouf, a Muslim, succeeded him, and he remains president today. But the ecumenical story of Senegal did not end there; the First Lady is Catholic. Can one imagine an American presidential candidate confessing on *Larry King Live*, "Incidentally, my wife is a Shi'ite Muslim"? That would almost certainly mark the end of his hopes for the White House.

One conclusion to be drawn from all this is that Westerners are far less secular in their political behavior then they think they are. Another is that Muslim societies historically have been more ecumenical, and therefore more humane, than their Western critics have adequately recognized. Islamic ecumenicalism has sometimes protected religious minorities more effectively than Western secularism.

BETWEEN THE DAZZLING AND THE DEPRAVED

Cultures should be judged not merely by the heights of achievement to which they have ascended but by the depths of brutality to which they have descended. The measure of cultures is not only their virtues but also their vices.

In the twentieth century, Islam has not often proved fertile ground for democracy and its virtues. On the other hand, Islamic culture has not been hospitable to Nazism, fascism, or communism, unlike Christian culture (as in Germany, Italy, Russia, Czechoslovakia), Buddhist culture (Japan before and during World War II, Pol Pot's Cambodia, Vietnam, North Korea), or Confucian culture (Mao's China). The Muslim world has never yet given rise to systematic fascism and its organized brutalities. Hafiz al-Assad's Syria and Saddam Hussein's Iraq have been guilty of large-scale violence, but fascism also requires an ideology of repression that has been absent in the two countries. And apart from the dubious case of Albania, communism has never independently taken hold in a Muslim culture.

Muslims are often criticized for not producing the best, but they are seldom congratulated for an ethic that has averted the worst. There are no Muslim equivalents of Nazi extermination camps, nor Muslim conquests by genocide on the scale perpetrated by Europeans in the Americas and Australia, nor Muslim equivalents of Stalinist terror, Pol Pot's killing fields, or the starvation and uprooting of tens of millions in the name of Five Year Plans. Nor are there Muslim versions of apartheid like that once approved by the South African Dutch Reformed Church, or of the ferocious racism of Japan before 1945, or of the racist culture of the Old South in the United States with its lynchings and brutalization of black people.

Islam brings to the calculus of universal justice some protection from the abyss of human depravity. Historically, the religion and the civilization have been resistant to forces that contributed to the worst aspects of the twentieth century's interludes of barbarism: racism, genocide, and violence within society.

First, Islam has been relatively resistant to racism. The Qur'ān confronts the issue of national and ethnic differences head on. The standard of excellence it sets has nothing to do with race, but is instead moral and religious worth—what the Qur'ān calls "piety" and what Martin Luther King, Jr., called "the content of one's character." An oft-quoted verse of the Qur'ān reads:

> O people! We have created you from a male and a female, and have made you nations and tribes so that you may know one another. The noblest among you is the most pious. Allah is all-knowing.[5]

In his farewell address, delivered on his last pilgrimage to Mecca in A.D. 632, Muḥammad declared:

> There is no superiority of an Arab over a non-Arab, and indeed, no superiority of red man over a black man except through piety and fear of God ... Let those who are present convey this message to those who are absent.

Unlike Christian churches, the mosque has never been segregated by race. One of Muḥammad's most beloved companions was an Ethiopian, Bilāl Rabah, a freed slave who rose to great prominence in early Islam. Under Arab lineage systems and kinship traditions, racial intermarriage was not discouraged and the children were considered Arab regardless of who the mother was. These Arab ways influenced Muslim societies elsewhere. Of the four presidents of Egypt since the revolution of 1952, two had black African ancestors— Muhammad Nagib and Anwar al-Sadat.[6]

Islam has a doctrine of Chosen Language (Arabic) but no Chosen People. Since the conversion of the Roman Emperor Constantine I in A.D. 313, Christianity has been led if not dominated by Europeans. But the leadership of the Muslim world has changed hands several times: from the mainly Arab Umayyad Dynasty (661-750) to the multiethnic Abbasid dynasty (750-1258) to the Ottoman Empire (1453-1922), dominated by the Turks. And this history is quite apart from such flourishing Muslim dynasties as the Moghuls of India and the Safavids of Persia or the sub-Saharan empires of Mali and Songhai. The diversification of Muslim leadership—in contrast to the Europeanization of Christian leadership—helped the cause of relative racial equality in Islamic culture.

Partly because of Islam's relatively nonracial nature, Islamic history has been free of systematic efforts to obliterate a people. Islam conquered by co-optation, intermarriage, and conversion rather than by genocide.

Incidents in Muslim history, it is true, have caused large-scale loss of life. During Turkey's attempt in 1915 to deport the entire Armenian population of about 1,750,000 to Syria and Palestine, hundreds of thousands of people, perhaps up to a million, died of starvation or were murdered on the way. But—though this does not exonerate Turkey of its responsibility for the deaths—Armenians had provoked Turkey by organizing volunteer battalions to help Russia fight against it in World War I. Nor is the expulsion of a people from a territory, however disastrous its consequences, equivalent to the Nazi Holocaust, which systematically took the lives of six million Jews and members of other despised groups. Movement of people between India and Pakistan after partition in 1947 also resulted in thousands of deaths en route.

Saddam Hussein's use of poison gas against Kurdish villages in Iraq in March 1988 is more clearly comparable to Nazi behavior. But Saddam's action was the use of an illegitimate weapon used in a civil war rather than a planned program to destroy the Kurdish people; it was an evil incident rather than a program of genocide. Many people feel that President Harry S. Truman's dropping of atomic bombs on Hiroshima and Nagasaki was also an evil episode. There is a difference between massacre and genocide. Massacres have been perpetrated in almost every country on earth, but only a few cultures have been guilty of genocide.

Nor did Islam ever spawn an Inquisition in which the burning of heretics at the stake was sanctioned. Cultures that had condemned human beings to burn and celebrated as they died in the flames, even hundreds of years before, were more likely to tolerate the herding of a whole people of another faith into gas chambers. Islam has been a shield against such excesses of evil.

THE ORDER OF ISLAM

Against Western claims that Islamic "fundamentalism" feeds terrorism, one powerful paradox of the twentieth century is often overlooked. While Islam may generate more political violence than Western culture, Western culture generates more street violence than does Islam. Islam does indeed produce a disproportionate share of *mujāhidīn*, but Western culture produces a disproportionate share of muggers. The largest Muslim city in Africa is Cairo. The largest westernized city in Africa is Johannesburg. Cairo is much more populous than Johannesburg, but street violence is only a fraction of what it is in the South African city. Does Islam help pacify Cairo? I, along with many others, believe that it does. The high premium Islam places on *ummah* (community) and *ijmā'* (consensus) has made for a Pax Islamica in day-to-day life.

In terms of quality of life, is the average citizen better off under the excesses of the Islamic state or the excesses of the liberal state, where political tension may be low but social violence has reached crisis proportions? Tehran, the capital of the Islamic Republic of Iran, is a city of some ten million. Families with small children picnic in public parks at 11 p.m. or midnight. Residents of the capital and other cities stroll late at night, seemingly unafraid of mugging, rape, or murder. This is a society that has known large-scale political violence in war and revolution, but one in which petty interpersonal violence is much rarer than in Washington or New York. Iranians are more subject to their government than Americans, but they are less at risk from the depredations of their fellow citizens. Nor is dictatorial government the explanation for the safe streets of Tehran—otherwise, Lagos would be as peaceful as the Iranian capital.

The Iranian solution is mainly in the moral sphere. As an approach to the problems of modernity, some Muslim societies are attempting a return to pre-modernism, to indigenous traditional disciplines and values. Aside from Iran, countries such as Sudan and Saudi Arabia have revived Islamic legal systems and other features of the Islamic way of life, aspects of which go back 14 centuries. Islamic movements in countries like Algeria, Egypt, and Afghanistan are also seeking revivalist goals. A similar sacred nostalgia is evident in other religions such as the born-again Christian sects in the United States and Africa.

Of all the value systems in the world, Islam has been the most resistant to the leading destructive forces of the twentieth century—including AIDS. Lower levels of prostitution and of hard drug use in conservative Muslim cultures compared to other cultures have, so far, helped contribute to lower-than-average HIV infection rates.[7] If societies closer to the *Shari'ah* are also more distant from the human immunodeficiency virus, should the rest of the world take a closer look?[8]

One can escape modernity by striving to transcend it as well as by retreating from it into the past. Perhaps the Muslim world should explore this path, searching for postmodernist solutions to its political tensions and economic woes, and pursuing the positive aspects of globalization without falling victim to the negative aspects of westernization.

THE DIALECTIC OF CULTURE

Western liberal democracy has enabled societies to enjoy openness, governmental accountability, popular participation, and high economic productivity, but Western pluralism has also been a breeding ground for racism, fascism, exploitation, and genocide. If history is to end in arrival at the ultimate political order, it will require more than the West's message on how to maximize the best in human nature. Humankind must also consult Islam about how to check the worst in human nature—from alcoholism to racism, materialism to Nazism, drug addiction to Marxism as the opiate of the intellectuals.

One must distinguish between democratic principles and humane principles. In some humane principles—including stabilizing the family, security from social violence, and the relatively non-racial nature of religious institutions—the Muslim world may be ahead of the West.

Turkey is a prime example of the dilemma of balancing humane principles with democratic principles. In times of peace, the Ottoman Empire was more humane in its treatment of religious minorities than the Turkish Republic after 1923 under the westernizing influence of Mustafa Kemal Atatürk. The Turkish Republic, on the other hand, gradually moved toward a policy of cultural assimilation. While the Ottoman Empire tolerated the Kurdish language, the Turkish Republic outlawed it for a considerable period. When not at war, the empire was more humane than the Turkish Republic, but less democratic.

At bottom, democracy is a system for selecting one's rulers; humane governance is a system for treating citizens. Ottoman rule at its best was humane governance; the Turkish Republic at its best has been a quest for democratic values. Turkey may now be engaged in reconciling the greater humanness of the Ottoman Empire with the greater democracy of the Republic.

The current Islamic revival in the country may be the beginning of a fundamental review of the Kemalist revolution, which inaugurated Turkish secularism. In England since Henry VIII, a theocracy has been democratized. In Turkey, might a democracy be theocratized? Although the Turkish army is trying to stop it, electoral support for Islamic revivalism is growing in the country. There has been increased speculation that secularism may be pushed back, in spite of the resignation in June 1997, under political pressure from the generals, of Prime Minister Necmettin Erbakan, the leader of the Islamist Welfare Party. Is Erbakan nevertheless destined to play in the Kemalist revolution that Mikhail Gorbachev played in the Leninist revolution? Or is Erbakan a forerunner of change. It is too early to be sure. The dialectic of history continues its conversation with the dialectic of culture within the wider rhythms of relativity in human experience.

NOTES:

1. This chapter first appeared as an article written for the 75th Anniversary edition of *Foreign Affairs* (Journal of the Council on Foreign Relations, New York), Volume 76, no. 5 (September/ October 1997), pp. 118-132.

2. In citing the Rushdie case as evidence of Islamic society's repressive nature, Westerners point to the 1989 *fatwa*, or legal ruling, by the Ayatollah Khomeini of Iran indicting Rushdie for blasphemy and the capital crime of apostasy and sentencing him to death in absentia. Iran, however, was the only Muslim country to decree the death penalty for Rushdie. Bangladesh said that Rushdie's crime, if proved, was a capital offense, but that he would have to be tried in a Muslim country to ascertain his guilt. There is a broad consensus that the book is blasphemous (even the Vatican agrees that it is), but Iran stands alone with the *fatwā*.

3. American writers such as Carl Bernstein, Howard Fast, Erica Jong, and Peter Maas have spoken of both overt and covert censorship; see Midge Decter, "The Rushdiad," *Commentary*, vol. 87, no. 6 (June 1989), pp. 20-21.

4. See Leonard Binder, *Islamic Liberalism: A Critique of Development Ideologies*, Chicago: University of Chicago Press, 1988, especially Chapter 9, "Conclusion: The Prospects for Liberal Government in the Middle East," pp. 336-6-

5. Like most other religions and civilizations, Islam tolerated the ownership and trade of slaves for centuries. But slavery among Muslims was almost race-neutral. In contrast to the racially polarized transatlantic slave system—white masters, black slaves— slaves in the Islamic world could be white, black, brown, or other, and so could masters. Moreover, slavery among Muslims allowed for great upward social mobility. Both Muslim India and Muslim Egypt produced slave dynasties; the former slaves who became Mamluk rulers of Egypt dominated the country from 1250 to 1517.

6. Studies by researchers in Ivory Coast of Muslim countries in Africa have shown that approximately half as many Muslims as non-Muslims are likely to be infected with HIV. See Catherine Tastemain and Peter Coles, "Can a Culture Stop AIDS in its

Tracks?" *New Scientist* (London), vol. 139, no. 1890 (September 11, 1993), p. 13.

7. See Catherine Tastemain and Peter Coles, "Can a Culture Stop AIDS in its Tracks?" *New Scientist*, London (September 11, 1993), volume 139, issue 1890, p.13.

CHAPTER SIXTEEN

GLOBALIZATION, ISLAM, AND THE WEST
BETWEEN HOMOGENIZATION AND HEGEMONIZATION[1]

GLOBALIZATION: ORIGINS AND SCOPE

The southern hemisphere in the twenty first century is likely to be one of the final battlegrounds of the forces of globalization—for better or for worse. This phenomenon called "globalization" has its winners and losers. In the initial phases, Africa for one has been among the losers as it has been increasingly marginalized. There are universities in the United States that have more computers than the computers available in an African country of twenty million people.[2] This has been the great digital divide. The distinction between the Haves and Have-nots has now coincided with the distinction between the Digitized and the "Digiprived."

Let us begin with the challenge of a definition. What is globalization? It consists of processes that lead toward global interdependence and the increasing rapidity of exchange across vast distances. The word globalization is itself quite new, but the actual processes toward global interdependence and exchange started centuries ago.[3]

Four forces have been major engines of globalization across time: religion, technology, economy, and empire. These have not necessarily acted separately, but often have reinforced each other. For example, the globalization of Christianity started with the conversion of Emperor Constantine I of Rome in the year 313. The religious conversion of an emperor started the process under which Christianity became the dominant religion not only of Europe but also of many other societies later ruled or settled by Europeans. The globalization of Islam began not with converting a ready-made empire, but with building an empire almost from scratch. The Umayyads and Abbasids as dynasties put together bits of other people's empires (e.g., former Byzantine Egypt and former Zoroastrian Persia) and created a whole new civilization. The forces of Christianity and Islam sometimes clashed. In Africa the two religions competed for the soul of a continent.[4] Has Africa's role in religious globalization been that of a subject or an object—that of an actor or somebody acted upon? The most globalizing concept in the history of religion has turned out to be monotheism, or belief in one God. It is widely agreed among secular historians that the first thoroughgoing monotheist in recorded history was an African—Pharaoh Akhenaton of Egypt of the 18th Dynasty (1379-1362 BCE).[5]

Voyages of exploration were another major stage in the process of globalization. Vasco da Gama, helped by East African navigators, opened up a whole new chapter in the history of globalization. Economy and empire were the major motives. There followed the migration of people. The Portuguese helped to build Fort Jesus in Mombasa. The migration of the Pilgrim Fathers to America was in part a response to religious and economic imperatives in Europe. Demographic globalization reached its height in the Americas with the influx of millions of people from other hemispheres. In time, the population of the United States became a microcosm of the population of the world, for it contained immigrants from almost every society on earth. The making of America was the making of a globalized society or universal nation. South Africa had Dutch settlers three centuries ago—a potential universal nation on the African continent was initiated.

The Industrial Revolution in Europe represents another major chapter in the history of globalization. This marriage between technology and economics resulted in previously unknown levels of productivity. Europe's prosperity whetted its appetite for new worlds to conquer. The Atlantic slave trade was accelerated, moving millions of Africans from one part of the world to another.[6] Europe's appetite also went imperial on a global scale, and one European people, the British, built the largest and most far-flung empire in human experience, most of which lasted until after World War II.

The two World Wars were themselves manifestations of globalization. The twentieth century is the only century that has witnessed globalized warfare—one from 1914 to 1918 and the other from 1939 to 1945. The Cold War was another manifestation of globalization (1948-1989)—because it was power-rivalry on a global scale between two alliances, the North Atlantic Treaty Organization (NATO) and the Warsaw Pact. While the two World Wars were militarily the most destructive empirically the Cold War was the most dangerous potentially. The Cold War carried the seeds of planetary annihilation in the nuclear field.

For better or for worse, the globalization of labor in world history began with the slave trade, especially the trans-Atlantic variety. African peoples were scattered in at least four continents—Europe, North America, South America, parts of Asia and of the African continent itself.[7] Never in history was one race scattered so widely as physical workers of African descent. Much later Karl Marx was to proclaim, "Workers of the world, unite! You have nothing to lose but your chains!"

In the new millennium the forces of globalization are likely to continue, against the background of the meaning of the twentieth century in world history. As the twentieth century comes to a close, scholars have interpreted globalization in three distinct ways:

1. Forces that are transforming the global market and creating new economic interdependency across vast distances. Africa is affected, but not centrally.
2. Forces that are exploding into the information superhighway—expanding access to data and mobilizing the computer and the Internet into global service. This tendency is marginalizing Africa.
3. All forces that are turning the world into a global village—compressing distance, homogenizing culture, accelerating mobility, and reducing the relevance of political borders. Under this comprehensive definition, globalization is the gradual villagization of the world.[8] These forces have been at work in Africa long before the trans-Atlantic slave trade.

As we have indicated, the twentieth century is the only century that had world wars—1914 to 1918, and 1939 to 1945. This was the only century that created world diplomatic institutions—the League of Nations and the United Nations. It was World War II that gave birth to a more credible world body—the United Nations, almost eerily realizing Alfred Tennyson's vision in his 1842 poem, "Locksley Hall."

> Heard the heavens fill with shouting, and there rained a ghastly dew
> From the Nations' airy navies grappling in the central blue;
> Till the war drums throbbed no longer, and the battle flags were furled
> In the Parliament of man, the Federation of the world.[9]

This was the only century that created a World Bank—the International Bank for Reconstruction and Development (IBRD) with the International Development Association (IDA). The twentieth century also issued a Universal Declaration of Human Rights—adopted by the United Nations in 1948. This was the only century that established a global university—the United Nations University in Tokyo, Japan. Some of these have affected Africa more deeply than others. This was the only century that had a world health institution—the World Health Organization (WHO). The twentieth century also created a global mechanism to moderate trade relations—the World Trade Organization (WTO). The Seattle meeting of WTO at the end of the millennium illustrated the depth of feelings about the organization.[10] This was the only century that had a part-time global policeman— the United States of America. And, of course, this was the only century which developed a genuine world economy—or at least a close approximation to it. All these were indicators of globalization. Although the term "globalization" is indeed new, the forces which have been creating it, as we indicated, have been going on for generations. It is only now that we have realized that the forces at work have had global repercussions and have been sometimes global in scale. The creation of the African Diaspora as a result of the African slave trade turned out to be a manifestation of globalization.[11]

However, it is questionable if a globalized Planet Earth is really a global village. The world may be globalized—but what would make it villagized? There is something missing—the compassion of the village has yet to be globalized. Planet Earth will never really become a global village until the contraction of distance is accompanied by the expansion of empathy. Education worldwide can have a role in that empathy-creation. The rich must learn to be more sensitive to the poor; the better endowed be more concerned about the less; the North must learn to be more just to the South.[12] But for Africa there is no substitute for self-reliance as a long-term struggle. Shakespeare said, "All the world's a stage" *(As You Like It)*. The new millennium asks: "Is all the world a village?" A stage is a conceit; a village is authenticity. Where does the Third World fit in? A global village needs new levels of empathy.

A distinction has to be drawn between globalization and hemispherization. The colonial policies of the imperial powers had created North-South economic relationships rather than global relationships. Africa's earlier involvement had started with the commodification of labor as slaves were captured, sold and bought.[13] Before Africa began exporting primary products, Africa had been forced to export primary producers (enslaved farmers and rural workers).

The abolition of slavery and the substitution of colonialism resulted in African economies that exported primary commodities at last—cotton, coffee, minerals, sisal, tea.[14] But the direction of exchange was still between the North and the South. It was hemispherization rather than full globalization—although hemispherization (North-South exchange) was a stage towards globalization. For the Third World, full globalization would only arrive when, in addition to North-South exchange, there was substantial South-South exchange. The North already has massive North-North exchange (trade between North America, Europe and Japan). The North has also created in its own image a North-South exchange. Globalization will only be complete when South-South exchange becomes substantial, to counter-balance the exploitativeness of North-South relations.

There is also the debate of whether global financial institutions like the World Bank and the International Monetary Fund here used their conditionalities to deepen unequal hemispherization. Structural adjustment, privatization and free trade have so far failed to maximize South-South cooperation. They have only aggravated the dependency of most countries of the South upon the North.[15]

It is to be noted here that the latest historical stage of globalization came when the industrial revolution was mated with the new information revolution. Interdependence and exchange became dramatically computerized. The most powerful single country by this time was the United States. *Pax Americana* mobilized three of the four engines of globalization—technology, economy and empire. *Pax Americana* in the second half of the twentieth century did not directly seek to promote a particular religion—but it did help to promote secularism and the ideology of separating church from state.

On balance, the impact of Americanization has probably been harmful to religious values worldwide—whether intended or not. Americanized Hindu youth, Americanized Buddhist teenagers or Americanized Muslim youngsters are far less likely to be devout to their faiths than non-Americanized ones.

BETWEEN HEGEMONIZATION AND HOMOGENIZATION

This brings us to the twin-concepts of homogenization and hegemonization. One of the consequences of globalization is that we are getting to be more and more alike across the world every decade. Homogenization is increasing similarity. The second accompanying characteristic of globalization is hegemonization—the paradoxical concentration of power in a particular country or in a particular civilization. While homogenization is the process of expanding homogeneity, hegemonization is the emergence and consolidation of the hegemonic center. With globalization there have been increasing similarities between and among the societies of the world. But this trend has been accompanied by disproportionate global power among a few countries.

As the twentieth century comes to a close people dress more alike all over the world than they did at the end of the nineteenth century. A homogenization is happening to dress. But the dress code which is getting globalized is overwhelmingly the Western dress code. Indeed, the man's suit (Western) has become almost universalized in all parts of the world. And the jeans' revolution has captured the youth dress culture of half the globe.

At the end of the twentieth century the human race is closer to having world languages than it was in the nineteenth century if by a world language we mean one which has at least tree-hundred million speakers, has been adopted by at least ten countries as a national language, has spread to at least two continents as a major language, and is widely used in four continents for special purposes, i.e. homogenization. However, when we examine the languages which have been globalized, they are disproportionately European—especially

267

English and French, and to lesser extent, Spanish. This is also another indicator of hegemonization. Arabic is putting forward a strong claim as a world language, but partly because of the globalization of Islam and the role of Arabic as a language of Islamic ritual.

At the end of the twentieth century we are closer to a world economy than we have ever been before in human history. A sneeze in Hong Kong, and certainly a cough in Tokyo can send shock waves around the globe. This is a sign of homogenization. And yet, the powers that control this world economy are disproportionately Western. They are the G-7: The United States, Japan, Germany, Britain, France, Canada and Italy in that order of economic muscle (Hegemonization).

At the end of the twentieth century the Internet has given us instant access to both information and mutual communication across large distances (Homogenization). However, the nerve center of the global Internet system is still located in the United States and has residual links in the United States Federal Government (Hegemonization).

The educational systems at the end of the twentieth century are getting more and more similar across the world—with comparable term-units and semesters, and increasing professorial similarities, and similarity in course content (Homogenization). But the role models behind this dramatic academic convergence have been the educational models of Europe and the United States, which have attracted both emulators and imitators (Hegemonization).

The ideological systems of the world at the end of the twentieth century are also converging as market economies seem to emerge triumphant. Liberalization is being widely embraced, either spontaneously or under duress. Anwar Sadat in Egypt opened the gates of *infitāh*, and even the People's Republic of China has adopted a kind of market Marxism. India is in danger of traversing the distance from Mahatma Gandhi to Mahatma Keynes (Homogenization).

However, the people who are orchestrating and sometimes enforcing marketization, liberalization and privatization are Western economic *gurus*—reinforced by the power of the World Bank, the

International Monetary Fund, the United States and the European Union. Indeed, Europe is the mother of all modern ideologies, good and evil—liberalism, capitalism, socialism, Marxism, fascism, Nazism and others. The most triumphant by the end of the twentieth century has been Euro-liberal capitalism (Hegemonization).

EGYPT IN THE ANNALS OF GLOBALIZATION

Where does Egypt fit into this saga of globalization, homogenization and hegemonization? We mentioned earlier that the four engines of globalization in history have been religion, technology, economy and empire.

Let us first take the engine of religion. The Pharaoh Akhenaton is widely regarded as the father of monotheism—and monotheism later became the most globalizing of all religious principles. Was the Pharaoh Akhenaton a *rasūl* (apostle) or *nabī* (prophet) or neither. The *Qur'ān* tells us that to each *Ummah* God sends a *rasūl* (Sura X. 47; xvi. 36 for example). Was Akhenaton the *rasūl* to ancient Egypt? Egypt was also where Moses was born. So Egypt was, in that sense, also the cradle of Judaism even if one does not accept the thesis that Moses himself was an Egyptian (a thesis made famous in the twentieth century by Sigmund Freud's theories about Jewish identity). Judaism became another monotheistic tradition born in Egypt. If Egypt was the country from which Moses later fled, Egypt subsequently became the country to which the infant Jesus later found asylum from the deadly machinations of King Herod.

> ... the angel of the Lord appeared to Joseph [Mary's husband] and said, "Rise, take the child and his mother to Egypt, and stay there until I tell you. Herod is going to search for the child to destroy him. (Matthew, 2. 13-23.)

The underlying logic of the story is that without the asylum in Egypt, there would have been no Christianity—for the infant Jesus would have been "crucified" in the cradle. Was Egypt therefore the savior of Christianity? If Egypt was the birthplace of historical mono-

269

theism, and the birthplace of Moses, and if Egypt was also the asylum of the infant Jesus, what is Egypt's historic destiny for Islam? Egypt was the first grand clash between Christian power and Muslim power. This was the Arab military conquest of Egypt away from the Byzantine Empire. Some would argue that this was the first blow that set in motion a process that culminated in the fall of Constantinople to the Muslim invaders several centuries later. The conquest of Constantinople (now Istanbul) in 1453 by the Turks inaugurated the Ottoman Empire.

The Arab conquest of Egypt also fertilized the flowering of an Islamic civilization on Egyptian soil, one of whose institutions is Al-Azhar University, a center of learning that has lasted a thousand years. Can we describe Al-Azhar as the first global university—attracting, as it does, students from all corners of the Muslim world?

We earlier referred to technology as another engine of globalization across time. Were ancient Egyptians the first to use technology for grand constructions of eternal durability? Long before the construction of the Aswan Dam by Soviet engineers in the 1950s there was the construction of the great pyramids linking the living with the dead. Ancient Egypt was arguably among the first grand civilizations. Technology and empire were linked in anticipation of new worlds to conquer.

Much closer to our own day was a different kind of construction in Egypt—the building of the Suez Canal in the nineteenth century, led by the French engineer Ferdinand de Lesseps. Hundreds of lives of Egyptian workers were lost in the construction of the canal. The Canal was a product not just of Western expertise and capital, but also of Egyptian sweat and blood. The Canal was a major contribution to globalization since it helped to connect Europe, Africa and Asia in new ways. But the canal was also a monument to technology and economy as engines of globalization.

By the second half of the twentieth century Gamal Abdul Nasser, Egypt's President (1953-1970) saw Egypt as a center of three circles—Arab, Islamic and African (a triad of cultures). Egypt had indeed become a bridge across three continents—Africa, Asia and Europe (a triad of continents). In one way or another Egypt had nursed four different traditions of monotheism (Akhenaton, Judaism, Christianity and Islam—a monotheistic quadrangle).

However, is Egypt a victim of globalization in the later chapters of its history—however great an initiator of the processes of globalization it once was? And, when all is said and done, how is Islam faring between the forces of homogenization and those of hegemonization?

ISLAM: VICTIM OR VICTOR?

At the moment the Muslim world is a net loser from both homogenization and hegemonization. However, will Islam one day gain from homogenization? Only if Muslim values penetrate the global pool. Can people share Muslim values without sharing the Muslim religion? For example many U.S. Muslims find themselves sharing social values with Republicans in the United States:

1. in favor of prayer at school;
2. against easy abortion;
3. against too much homosexual permissiveness;
4. in favor of family values and stable marriages.

One can be in agreement with Islamic values without being a Muslim. Indeed, the US after World War I briefly agreed with the Muslim value against alcohol—and passed a whole Constitutional Amendment outlawing alcohol. However, not enough Americans were convinced. A decade later (after Al Capone's adventures) another Constitutional Amendment was passed allowing alcohol. Will Muslim values in the 21st century once again gain favor?

Islam has contributed to the development of various aspects of Western civilization. However, the counterpenetration of Islam and Muslims into Western civilization will not stand along with Western hegemonization. An Islamic presence in the Western World on a significant scale may begin to reverse at long last the wheels of cultural homogenization. Values will begin to mix, tastes compete, perspectives intermingle, as a new moral calculus evolves on the world scene. Amen.

NOTES

1. This chapter was based on a presentation at the Conference on "Islamic Paradigms of International Relations" sponsored by the School of Islamic and Social Sciences (Leesburg, Virginia) and the Center of Political Research and Studies, Cairo, Egypt on December 2, 1997.
2. A February 2002 report by Mike Jensen on "African Internet Status" (at http://www3.sn.apc.org/africa/afstat.htm) pointed out that Uganda, with a population of about 20 million had only about 10,000 dialup subscriptions to the Internet!
3. Recent discussions on globalization may be found in Mohammed A. Bamyeh, *The Ends of Globalization* (Minneapolis: University of Minnesota Press, 2000); Mark Rupert, *Ideologies of Globalization: Contending Visions of A New World Order* (London and New York: Routledge, 2000); and Colin Hays and David Marsh, eds., *Demystifying Globalization* (New York: St. Martin's Press in association with Polsis, University of Birmingham, 2000).
4. Consult, relatedly, Jeff Haynes, ed., *Religion, Globalization and Political Culture in the Third World* (New York: St. Martin's Press, 2000).
5. On the Egyptian Pharoah, a recent text to consult is Carl N. Reeves, *Akhenaten: Egypt's False Prophet* (London; New York: Thames & Hudson, 2001).
6. Classics on the Atlantic slave trade include John Thornton, *Africa and Africans in the Making of the Atlantic World, 1400-1800* (Cambridge: Cambridge University Press, 1998) and Hugh Thomas, *The Slave Trade: The Story of the Atlantic Slave Trade, 1440-1870* (New York: Simon and Schuster, 1997).
7. On the African diaspora, consult, for example, Alusine Jalloh and Stephen E. Maizlish, *The African Diaspora* (College Station, TX: Texas A & M University Press for University of Texas at Arlington, 1996).
8. Relatedly, see Marshall McLuhan and Bruce R. Powers, *The Global*

Village: Transformations in World Life and Media in the 21st Century (New York: Oxford University Press, 1989).

9. Christopher Ricks, (ed.), *The Poems of Tennyson (2nd ed.),* vol. 2 (Berkeley and Los Angeles: University of California Press, 1987), p. 126.

10. For one analysis of the causes of discontent with the Seattle meeting and WTO, see Nicholas Bayne, "Why Did Seattle Fail? Globalization and the Politics of Trade," *Government and Opposition* 35, 2 (Spring 2000), pp. 131-151.

11. Relatedly, consult John Karefah Marah, *African People in the Global Village: An Introduction to Pan African Studies* (Lanham, MD: University Press of America, 1998).

12. We may recall Gandhi's words, "Wherever I live in a situation where others are in need, whether or not I am responsible for it, I have become a thief." Cited in Denis Goulet, *Cruel Choice* (New York: Atheneum, 1971), p.133.

13. Consult relatedly, Barbara L. Solow, "Capitalism and Slavery in the Exceedingly Long Run," *Journal of Interdisciplinary History* 17 (Spring 1987), pp. 711-737; Joseph E. Inikori and Stanley L. Engerman, eds., *The Atlantic Slave Trade: Effects on Economies and Peoples in Africa, the Americas, and Europe* (Durham, NC: Duke University Press, 1992); and of course, the classic Eric Williams, *Capitalism and Slavery* (London: Andre Deutsch, 1944, 1987).

14. For an early assessment of this dependence, see Henry W. Ord and Ian G. Stewart, eds., *African Primary Products and International Trade,* (Edinburgh: University Press, 1965), and for a view that still points to the dependence of sub-Saharan Africa on primary products trade, see Richard E. Mshomba, *Africa in the Global Economy* (Boulder, CO: Lynne Rienner Publishers, 2000), pp. 139-40.

15. For African views on structural adjustment, consult, for instance, Thandika Mkandawire & Charles C. Soludo, *Our Continent, Our Future: African Perspectives On Structural Adjustment* (Dakar, Senegal: CODESRIA; Ottawa, ON, Canada: International Development Research Centre; and Trenton, NJ: Africa World Press, 1999), and for a specific case of the harm done by these policies, see Pádraig Carmody *Tearing The Social Fabric: Neoliberalism,*

Deindustrialization, and the Crisis of Governance in Zimbabwe (Portsmouth, NH: Heinemann, 2001).

CHAPTER SEVENTEEN

THE UNITED NATIONS
AND THE MUSLIM WORLD
ALLIES OR ADVERSARIES?[1]

Islam and the United Nations were born out of competing concepts of universalism. Islam is a universalistic religion as it seeks to preach to the human race as a whole; the United Nations is a universalist organization as it has sought to represent the human race as a whole. Islam has envisaged a universalism of people, the *ummah;* the United Nations has envisaged the universalism of nation-states, the international community.

The universalism of Islam was to be based on a shared faith; the universalism of the United Nations was based on a joint contract. The faith of Islam consists of its five pillars, the Qur'ān, and the Sunnah. The contract of the United Nations is its Charter and subsequent conventions, declarations and resolutions. A universalism of faith expands by biological reproduction and religious conversion; a universalism of contract expands by signing up new states as members of the world organization.

Since there are fewer than 200 states in the world, and more than five billion people, a universalism of states is achieved more quickly than a universalism of people. At first glance, it might therefore seem that the United Nations has achieved its universalism of states long before Islam has achieved her universalism of people. The UN already has 185 members states.[2]

Today one out of every five human beings is already a Muslim. In the twenty-first century, the Muslim community will reach the mark of a quarter (i.e. 25%) of the human race. It will have become the largest concentration of believers in one religion in history. In terms of population, it is now one of the fastest-growing religions in the world.[3]

However, the United Nations seems to have already achieved a universalism of states. Or is it only pseudo-universalism? Is the UN universalism still a game of smoke and mirrors?

THE UN AND THE CULTURAL COUNTER-REVOLUTION

The UN's universalism represents nation-states and world regions but does not try to represent civilizations. Six out of the last seven secretaries general of the UN have come from Christian traditions.[4] The Christian world is about one-fifth of the population of the world. There has been no Hindu, Muslim, or Confucian Secretary-General although together those populations outnumber Christians by more than two to one. There has been one Buddhist Secretary-General—the Burmese U Thant: one Buddhist and six Christians—although there are probably as many Buddhists as Christians in the world.[5] The ratio raises a question: Should the UN system be more sensitive to proportional representation of cultures?[6]

Should peacekeeping in the future be more sensitive to geo-cultural movements? International geo-cultural organizations like the Organization of the Islamic Conference (OIC) can be relevant in preventative diplomacy or in peacemaking—although the OIC efforts in trying to stop the Iraq-Iran conflict in the 1980s were less than successful.[7] On the other hand, patient efforts by the Economic Community of West African States' Monitoring Group (ECOMOG) in Liberia appear to have been more successful.[8]

Then there are intra-civilizational conflicts with extra-civilizational consequences—like movements of Islamic militancy in places like Algeria and Egypt and potentially Saudi Arabia. Consultations have been taking place between officials of NATO, and some members of the League of Arab States concerning Islamic militancy. Should the UN be involved?

For the time being, the United Nations system is part of the cultural hegemony of the Western world. When Director-General Amadou-Mahtar M'Bow of UNESCO tried to rebel against it, the United States and Great Britain withdrew from UNESCO—and M'Bow was consequently ousted.[9] The UN was formed primarily by the victors of World War II. Those victors belonged to one civilization-and-a-half: Britain, USA, France, USSR. They made themselves permanent members of the UN's powerful Security Council. They made one concession to another civilization—by also making pre-Communist China a permanent member. Of the five original languages of the UN, four were in origin European languages: English, French, Spanish and Russian. A concession was made to another civilization—by recognizing the Chinese language.

A kind of bicameral legislature began to emerge—an upper house, which was the more powerful but less representative, called the Security Council—and a lower house which was less powerful but more representative called the General Assembly. This bicameral concept developed by practice rather than design and was in origin very Western. The upper house was the global "House of Lords"—war-lords! The conception was basically from western civilization and history.

One of the major functions of the UN was to help keep the peace according to the principles of international law. The Law of Nations was itself a child of European diplomatic history and statecraft. It once used to be:

The Law of Christian Nations, and then became,
The Law of Civilized Nations, and then became,
The Law of Developed Nations[10]

That old International Law used to legitimize the colonization of other countries by Western countries. Intellectual ancestors of Western political thought were marked by an arrogant Eurocentrism. J.S. Mill distinguished between "barbarians and societies worthy of the Law of Nations." What was even more appalling was the approbation of colonialism by early socialists; Karl Marx applauded Britain's colonization of India.[11] Friedrich Engels applauded France's colonization of Algeria.[12] All these were civilizational criteria, accepted by almost the whole white world.

And then the UN began to admit not only more countries but also more cultures. These included the admission of Pakistan in 1947, Myanmar (Burma) and Sri Lanka (Ceylon) in 1948 and later Malaysia and Singapore. From the Arab world there later followed some additional countries: Morocco, Tunisia, Sudan, Algeria (Egypt was already a member), and subsequently newly-independent Black African countries, beginning with Ghana in 1957. New values were trying to express themselves through a Eurocentric infrastructure.

Later, the UN became the channel through which other countries and cultures began to insist on changes in International Law. When India occupied Goa, thus liberating it from Portuguese rule, Krishna Menon enunciated the principle that "colonialism was permanent aggression"—thus delegitimizing colonialism.[13]

African struggles against apartheid led to the shrinkage of the principle of domestic jurisdiction as applied to South Africa's policy of apartheid. Eventually apartheid was regarded as a matter of relevance to international security and as virtually a "crime against humanity." The United Nations began to take a more active role in combating apartheid.[14]

In the post-Cold War era, is the UN likely to be used by the dominant civilization (the West) against other civilizations? Is that what happened during the Gulf War? Was the UN hijacked by the West to legitimize massacres in defense of its oil interests? In Bosnia, was the UN being used by the West to make sure there is no viable Muslim state in the middle of Europe?

The UN has sometimes been guilty of sins of omission. Such sins of omission include:

1. Standing by while Patrice Lumumba was literally dragged to his death in 1961 in the Congo (now Zaire).[15]
2. Standing by while thousands of people were massacred in the bombing of Iraq—euphemistically termed "collateral damage"—during the Gulf War, and in the aftermath, continuing to ignore the privations of Iraqi individuals due to sanctions.
3. Standing by while hundreds of thousands of Bosnians are maimed, murdered, mutilated, or raped in the 1990s. Is this a clash of civilizations?

In an earlier work, we had raised the issue of the West, particularly the United States, becoming the defender of the holy places in Islam—Mecca and Medina—during the Gulf War.[16] At the time of writing this particular piece (December 1995) the United States had emerged as the peacemaker acceptable to all parties in the Bosnian imbroglio—including Bosnian Muslims. Part of the peace plan envisaged reducing Serbian and Croatian armaments, while increasing Bosnian Muslim arms. The peacekeeping forces were not directly involved with this exercise, but the United States was apparently trying to get third parties to undertake the task of arming the Bosnian forces so that they would be able to repel any future challenge.[17]

It is striking to note that while the United Nations and the European allies, along with the Clinton administration, were reluctant to lift the arms embargo so as to allow the Bosnian Muslims to arm itself, conservative Republicans (like Senator Bob Dole) long called for allowing Bosnia to arm itself.[18] As in the case of the Gulf War, where conservative George Bush was ready to defend the holy places of Islam, would a conservative Bob Dole as President have been more supportive of Bosnian Muslims arming themselves? Unfortunately, the world of Islam was out in front to enable the poorly armed Bosnians to defend themselves. Huntington was concerned about an alliance between the world of Islam and the countries of the Confucian legacy. In our terms would this be a new *Dār al-Ḥarb* (Abode of War) for the West?

In the UN the temporary omen was in the 1970s. There was in 1971 the euphoric recognition of the People's Republic of China (PRC) by the United Nations.[19] There was also Yasser Arafat's address to the General Assembly in plenary session virtually as Head of State in the Fall of 1974.[20] Third was Algeria's launching of the campaign for a New International Economic Order (NIEO) also in 1974.[21] Fourth was the subsequent recognition of Arabic alongside Chinese as the only non-European languages accepted as official idioms of the world body for some occasions. Did these events portend a Muslim-Confucian coalition?

All these are modest even if significant achievements. On the whole the UN system, along with the Bretton Woods institutions (World Bank and the IMF), continue to be major disseminators of Western ideas, concepts and values. In conception, and in much of their operations, the institutions are rooted in the Western worldview *(weltanschauung)*. Future Directors-General of UNESCO are unlikely to be as assertive as Amadou-Mahtar M'Bow.[22] And most developing countries have in any case been forced to toe the Western party line since the disintegration of the Soviet Union.

At the moment the UN Security Council is still primarily a "White Man's Club" with non-white visitors. Four of the five permanent members are essentially white countries rooted in a Euro-Christian legacy (U.S.A., France, Britain, and Russia). Has the United Nations inevitably become a future arena for a clash of civilizations?

THE BLEEDING FACE OF ISLAM

The different conflicts in the Muslim world dictate an agonizing reappraisal. The majority of the victims are Muslims, but there are conflicts where Muslims are the villains.

Has the ancient *Dār al-Islām* (the Abode of Islam) now become the modern *Dār al-Ḥarb* (the Abode of War)? In traditional Islamic international law, *Dār al-Islām* were the lands where Muslims were free and secure. But now Muslims are caught up in conflict in different lands.

In this regard we have three main categories of societies. First, those societies where Muslims are the victims of the violence of others. This has included the wars in Bosnia, Chechnya, Kashmir, southern Lebanon, and occupied Palestine. It once included Afghanistan under Soviet occupation.

Second is the category where Muslims are at war with each other. This includes Afghanistan, Algeria, the city of Karachi in Pakistan, and to some extent Egypt.

Third is the category where Muslims are more culprits than victims—where Muslims victimize others. Although the war in Sudan is not primarily a religious war, its net effect casts Muslims as the greater culprits in the conflict. What about the November 1995 terrorist act in Riyadh, Saudi Arabia against Americans?[23] Is that a case of Muslims against foreigners? Or is it the beginning of something comparable to Algeria and Egypt?

Within the ancient Abode of Islam, where conflict was not supposed to be the order of the day, we now have anguish and discord. The universalism of faith has yet to find a universality of peace.

The United Nations is involved in some of these conflicts affecting Muslims, but not in others. There are UN resolutions about Kashmir, and many more UN resolutions about Palestine. The UN sometimes attempted to help in the civil war in Afghanistan. The UN kept out of the war in Chechnya. What is heartrending for the Muslim world is how much fratricide, as well as victimization, there is.

While Muslims have failed in maintaining peace towards each other, Westerners have found it among themselves. A whole new body of literature is emerging based on the premise that "democracies do not go to war against each other."[24] The literature is not based on moral wishful thinking, but on what is presented as systemic and scientific analysis of the nature of the democratic process, especially in the liberal West. There is nothing in the democratic process to stop the United States from invading Panama, or to stop Britain and Spain joining a military coalition against Iraq. But the new school of thought asserts that these democratic countries are systemically unlikely to go to war against each other. In Huntington's phrase, "Military conflict among Western states is unthinkable."[25] But how much of this peace is due to the presence of economic prosperity and nuclear weapons?

Instead of a situation in which Muslims do not go to war with each other (as the ancient doctrine expected), we have a situation in which Westerners do not go to war with each other (as the new political science asserts). Instead of *Dār al-Islām* triumphant (the Abode of Islam in victory), we have *Dār al-Maghrib* victorious (the Abode of the West in triumph).

And the West controls the United Nations. Islam's universalism of faith has foundered because of the weakness of the Muslims. The United Nations' universalism of states has triumphed because of the power of the West.

Perhaps nowhere in the world was there such a stark confrontation between the universalism of faith and the universalism of nation-states as in Bosnia. The state called Yugoslavia disintegrated— and out of the fragments emerged several states including a country called Bosnia-Herzogovina with a plurality of Muslims. The idea of a Muslim-led government in the middle of Europe, however democratic, raised disturbing specters in some circles. Muslim Turkey was a Middle Eastern country trying to be recognized as European. Muslim Albania was technologically the most backward country in Europe. But relatively advanced Bosnia in the middle of Christian Europe was a disconcerting prospect in a world where influential professors from Harvard University expected "a clash of civilizations."

Let us therefore look at Bosnia-Herzegovina as a case study involving the confluence of a number of factors. Bosnia is an intriguing case-study pitting the universalism of faith against the universalism of statehood. It is a case-study of the United Nations in opposition to the aspirations of most of the Muslim world. It is a case-study of a clash of civilizations as Bosnia was gradually led towards de facto partition.

Bosnia-Herzegovina was originally invaded partly by troops from Serbia and partly by Bosnian Serbs armed by Serbia. The UN imposed an arms embargo on both sides. And yet the UN was wrong to impose the embargo on the Bosnian government. It was wrong for two main reasons:

1.   Because Bosnia had the right of self-defense under Article 51 of the UN charter;
2.   Because the Serbian side had inherited the bulk of the armory of the former Socialist Republic of Yugoslavia and thus came to acquire undue advantage.

If the Muslims are humiliated and totally defeated, not only in Bosnia but also in Kosovo and Macedonia, there may later emerge new forms of Muslim guerrilla movements in the heart of Europe in the decades ahead. Humiliated Muslims have been known to haunt their tormentors for generations afterwards. A Bosnian equivalent of the Palestine Liberation Organization and a Bosnian equivalent of the Irish Republic Army might be unnecessarily created tomorrow by the humiliation of the Bosnian Muslims of today.

The irony is that just when the Muslim world is, in spite of the Hebron mosque massacre perpetrated by a Jewish militant, learning to accept a Jewish state in the midst of a Muslim Middle East, Europeans are reluctant to countenance a Muslim state in a Christian Europe. Bosnia could be a kind of Muslim Israel in the middle of Christian Europe. Has Europe the will to help it survive? Or is Europe behaving like Baruch Goldstein, shooting Muslims in prayer? Has the UN provided universalist legitimation?

In Afghanistan in the 1980s, the West armed the liberation of a Muslim society in order to frustrate Moscow. In Bosnia in the 1990s, the West through the UN disarmed a Muslim society, partly in order not to offend Moscow. In Afghanistan the West helped the *Mujāhidīn* throw out their Soviet invaders. In Bosnia the West and the UN in the 1990s, were not ready even to defend some of the UN protected zones like Srebrenica, Zepa, and Gorazde. In any case, NATO's protection of Sarajevo may have frozen Serbian territorial gains. In Afghanistan under Soviets, the West did the right thing for the wrong reasons—it helped Muslims in order to check-mate the Soviets. In Bosnia the West has so far done the wrong thing for the wrong reasons—appease the Serbian invaders partly because of sectarian indifference. Is it not about time that the international community did the right thing for the right reasons—help Bosnia survive as a united pluralistic independent country because weak countries deserve the support of the world community?

The shadow of cultural prejudice persists. Would the West and the UN in the 1990s have been slow to react in Bosnia if it was a case of Muslims slaughtering and raping Christians instead of the other way round? Would the U.S. administration and the Senate have been slow if the Serbian concentration camps were for Bosnian Jews rather than for Bosnian Muslims? Would the UN not have been forced to respond more robustly and energetically if Jewish women were being raped by Muslim men as an instrument of war, instead of Muslim women being raped by Orthodox Christian Serbs?

Indeed, there is reason to believe that if it was Jews who were being subjected to such unspeakable humiliation, Israel would not have waited for either the UN Security Council or the U.S. Senate.[26] Israel would have staged a major international spectacular event to grab the world's attention—even if it meant bombing Belgrade. And Israel would certainly have got the world's attention. Fifty Muslim governments, on the other hand, were content to timidly obey the demands of the Security Council, refrain from arming the Bosnian Muslims or even evacuate refugees. The conclusion to be drawn from all this is that the universalism of states ostensibly achieved by the United Nations is still seriously flawed. The United Nations is still a creature of the Western World—and the West still views the world through the tripartite lenses of medieval Islam duly adapted (by the West).

What to medieval Muslim jurists was *Dār al-Islām* (Abode of

Islam) has now become *Dār al-Maghrib* or *Dār al-Gharb*, the Abode of the West. Westerners are the pre-eminent pioneer. Until the 1990s the Abode of War to Westerners were the lands of communism. Has the Abode of War now become the Muslim world in all its complexity? To some medieval Islamists there was the Abode of *'Ahd* and/or *Ṣulḥ*—the home of contractual co-existence in exchange for tribute. Tribute is what the Western world has been receiving from most of the Third world in profits, interest on the debt burden, and the returns on other forms of exploitation. And the United Nations has sometimes unwittingly provided an umbrella for this tripartite division of the world.

THE UN AND ISLAM: ALLIES OR ADVERSARIES?

But when all is said and done, under what circumstances is the United Nations ever an ally of the Muslim world? First, the UN is an ally in the humanitarian role of the world body and its agencies—such as crises of refugees or international responses to famine, draught and other catastrophes. In such roles it does not matter whether the immediate beneficiaries are Muslims, as in Somalia and Bangladesh, or non-Muslims, as in Rwanda. The UN is supportive of all such efforts.

Second, the United Nations is an ally when it provides an umbrella for mediation for some of the quarrels between Muslims—as in the effort to resolve the destiny of Western Sahara. The UN in such instances helps the *Ummah* more directly. The UN helped in the quest for peace between Iran and Iraq in their conflict in the 1980s.[27]

Third, the United Nations is an ally to Muslims when the world body provides peacekeeping troops and peacekeeping auspices in conflicts between Muslims and non-Muslims. Over the years United Nations troops have often been involved in the often thankless task of trying to keep the peace between the Arabs and the Israelis especially prior to the Oslo peace process. The UN's long-drawn role in Cyprus is another example of attempted mediation between Muslims and non-Muslims.

Fourth, the United Nations is allied to Muslims—when the Western world has been divided! The Muslim world has sometimes had the UN move decisively as an ally in such a situation—as during the Suez war of 1956 when, in spite of the veto by Britain and France in the Security Council, the mood of the world body was opposed to the invasion of Egypt by Britain, France and Israel. When the Western world was divided, the United Nations was also able to play a major decolonizing role. This is the fifth positive role of the UN. The United States was historically opposed to some of the older varieties of European imperialism. By the second half of the twentieth century the United States was often on the same side as the Soviet Union among the critics of old-style European colonialism. Under these conditions it was indeed easier for the United Nations to become increasingly one of the great arenas for the anti-colonial struggle waged by the peoples of Asia, Africa and the scattered islands of the seas. The anti-colonial role of the United Nations encompassed not only the Trusteeship Council but also the General Assembly, especially from the late 1950s onwards. This anti-colonial role was often a great service to the Muslim world.

Sixth, the United Nations can be an ally of the Muslim world when it takes seriously the idea of prosecuting war criminals and those who have committed crimes against humanity. Especially relevant for the Muslim world would be the prosecution of war criminals in Bosnia and some Serbs in Serbia and many Serbs in Bosnia who have committed crimes against humanity as in the current proceedings at the Hague involving war crimes committed in Bosnia in the 1990s. The United Nations has done well to appoint the relevant tribunal for the task, but has fallen far short of providing the resources for this complicated task.

Seventh, the United Nations has been an ally when the Muslim world was united. It has at times been possible to pass through the General Assembly highly contentious points of principle. The state of Israel is based on an ideology which says that a Russian who claims to be descended from Jews, and whose family has had no connection with the Middle East for the last two thousand years, has more right to go and settle in Israel than a Palestinian who ran away from Israel during the 1948 war. Was such discrimination racist? When Muslims were united in 1975, they managed to persuade the UN General Assembly to pass a resolution affirming that Zionism was a form of racism. But when Muslims were divided in 1991, that resolution was repealed by an overwhelming majority.[28] When the Muslims were united they could persuade the General Assembly not only to defy the United States but move the Assembly itself out of New York in further defiance. Thus when in 1988 the United States refused to grant a visa to Yasser Arafat, thereby preventing him from coming to New York to address the UN General Assembly on his declaration of an independent Palestinian state, the General Assembly denounced Washington's action as a violation of the host country's legal obligations under the 1947 Headquarters Agreement. The General Assembly then shifted this December 13-15 session to Geneva, Switzerland, to make it possible to listen to Chairman Arafat. It was the first and only such move in the history of the United Nations. The unity of the Muslim members of the UN helped to persuade others to join their ranks.[29]

Finally, is the UN an ally or an adversary of Islamic values when the UN promotes such mega-conferences as the one in Beijing, China, in 1995 on the issue of women; the one in Copenhagen on the issues of poverty and development in 1994 and the one in Cairo, Egypt, in 1994 on the issue of population?

Muslims themselves are divided as to whether these UN mega-conferences lead on to the erosion of Islamic values or help Islamic values find a new historic setting in the 20th and 21st centuries. For example, are Muslim women being helped by new global standards of gender equity that are promoted at these conferences? These mega-conferences have of course been global and have been part of the United Nations' universalism of nation-states. Some tension has at times been created with Islam's universalism of faith. However, it is a tension that can itself be creative; it is a dialectic which can have a human face. At the very minimum, Islam and the UN have one paramount interest in common—to ensure that *Dār al-Ḥarb*, the Abode of War, shrinks further and further into the oblivion of history, and Planet Earth becomes a House of Peace at long last.

NOTES

1. This chapter is a revised version of "Evan Luard Lecture" to mark the 50th anniversary of the United Nations, sponsored by the United Nations Association at Oxford and the Oxford Centre for Islamic Studies, given at Oxford University on November 14, 1995. Earlier version of this chapter appeared as "The United Nations and the Muslim World: Allies or Adversaries," in Tareq Y. Ismael (ed.), *The International Relations of the Middle East in the 21st Century: Patterns of Continuity and Change* (Aldershot: Ashgate, 2000), pp. 360-379.

2. Arthur S. Banks, (ed.), *Political Handbook of the World, 1994-1995* (Binghamton, NY: CSA Publications, 1995), p. 1107, reports 184 members; the updated figure is drawn from the Internet at http://www.un.org/overviews/unmember.html. This source also provides details on membership accession dates and other relevant details.

3. On population distribution and trends among Muslims, consult John Weeks, "The Demography of Islamic Nations," *Population Bulletin*, vol. 43, no. 4 (1988), especially pp. 5-9.

4. The Secretaries-General of the United Nations have been Trygve Lie (of Norway), Dag Hammarskjold (of Sweden), U Thant (of Burma (Myanmar), Kurt Waldheim (of Austria), Javier Perez de Cuellar (from Peru), Boutros Boutros-Ghali (from Egypt), and Kofi Annan.

5. See Evan Luard, *The United Nations: How It Works and What It Does* (New York: St. Martin's Press, 1994) pp. 102-125.

6. Brian Urquhart, "Selecting the World's CEO," *Foreign Affairs*, vol. 74, no. 3 (May/June 1995), pp. 21-6.

7. See John Bulloch and Harvey Morris, *The Gulf War: Its Origins, History and Consequences* (London: Methuen, 1989), pp. 117 and 119.

8. On the peace plan and ECOMOG's role, see the following news reports: "Peace Plan is Accepted by Liberians," *The New York*

Times, (August 20, 1995), Section A, p. 17 and "8-Nation African force is Peacekeeping Model in War-torn Liberia," *The Washington Post* (April 1, 1994), Section A, p. 26.

9. For samples of attacks on M'bow in the Western Press, see *The Economist*, (October 3, 1987) p. 48, and *Nature* (October 8, 1987), p. 472.

10. See, for example, Adam Watson, "European International Society and Its Expansion," in Hedley Bull and Adam Watson (eds.), *The Expansion of International Society* (Oxford: Clarendon Press, 1985) pp. 13-32 and Ian Brownlie "The Expansion of International Society: The Consequences for the Law of Nations," in Hedley Bull and Adam Watson (eds.), *The Expansion of International Society,* pp. 357-369.

11. Consult, for example, Karl Marx, *On Colonialism: Articles from the New York Tribune and other Writings, by Karl Marx and Friedrich Engels* (New York: International Publishers, 1972), pp. 81-87.

12. See Karl Marx and Friedrich Engels, *Collected Works*, vol. 6, (New York: International Publishers, 1976, p. 471.

13. For a description of Menon's view of the Goa affair and Western reactions to the Indian action, see Michael Brecher, *India and World Politics: Krishna Menon's View of the World* (New York: Praeger, 1968), pp. 121-136.

14. Guides to the UN's role in combating apartheid may be found in "The UN and Apartheid: A Chronology," *UN Chronicle*, vol. 31 (September 1994), pp. 9-14; Newell M. Stultz, "Evolution of the United Nations Anti-apartheid Regime," *Human Rights Quarterly*, vol. 13 (February 1991), pp. 1-23; and Ozdemir A. Ozgur, *Apartheid, the United Nations, & Peaceful Change in South Africa* (Dobbs Ferry, NY: Transnational Publishers, 1982).

15. See, for example, Michael G. Schatzberg, *Mobutu or Chaos?: The United States and Zaire, 1960-1990* (Lanham, MD: University Presses of America/Foreign Policy Institute, 1991).

16. See Ali A. Mazrui, "The Resurgence of Islam and the Decline of Communism," *Futures: The Journal of Forecasting and Planning*, vol. 23 (April 1991), pp. 283-285.

17. As stated by Vice-President Al Gore on *Nightline*, December 1, 1995. Also see *The New York Times* (December 5, 1995), Sec-

tion A, p. 7.

18. See, for example, Carroll J. Doherty, "Dole Takes a Political Risk in Crusade to Aid Bosnia," *Congressional Quarterly Weekly Report*, volume 53 (March 11, 1995), pp. 761-763.

19. See, Samuel S. Kim, *China, The United Nations, and World Order* (Princeton, NJ: Princeton University Press, 1979).

20. UN, *Yearbook of the United Nations, 1974* (New York: UN, 1977) pp. 189-251.

21. On the NIEO, consult, for example, Pradip K. Ghosh, (ed.), *New International Economic Order: A Third World Perspective* (Westport, CT: Greenwood Press, 1984).

22. See Lawrence S. Finkelstein, "The Political Role of the Director-General of UNESCO," in Finkelstein (ed.) *Politics in the United Nations System*, pp. 385-423.

23. On the bombing, see *The New York Times* (Tuesday, November 14, 1995), Section A, p. 1.

24. A recent evaluation of the literature may be found in James Lee Ray, *Democracy and International Conflict: An Evaluation of the Democratic Peace Proposition* (Columbia, SC: University of South Carolina Press, 1995). Also, several leading scholars on this subject, such as Bruce Russett, Christopher Layne, David Shapiro, and Michael W. Doyle, assess the state of the field in their contributions to the *International Security*, vol. 19 (Spring 1995) issue on this topic.

25. Huntington, "The Clash of Civilizations?," p. 39.

26. Witness the airlift of the "Falasha Jews" from Ethiopia, detailed in Ruth Gruber, *Rescue: The Exodus of the Ethiopian Jews* (New York: Athenuem, 1987).

27. For a critical account of the mediation, see Mohammed H. Malek and Mark F. Imber, "The Security Council and the Gulf War: A Case of Double Standard," Chapter 4 in Mohammed H. Malek (ed.), *International Mediation and the Gulf War* (Glasgow, Scotland: Royston, 1991).

28. On the change, see "Zionism No Longer Equated With Racism," *UN Chronicle*, vol. 29 (March 1992), p. 67.

29. For a report on this incident, see *The New York Times* (December 3, 1988), Section A, p. 1.

CHAPTER EIGHTEEN

A CULTURAL BETROTHAL?:
EURO-AMERICAN NORMS AND ISLAMIC VALUES[1]

W

e can identify three different phases of relations between America and the Muslim *ummah* both normatively and politically:

Phase 1

A. Relationships between Euro-American values and traditional Islamic values were close in the first half of the twentieth century.

B. Relationships between Euro-American people and Muslim people as an *ummah* were distant in the first half of that century.

Phase 2

A. In the second half of the twentieth century, relationships be-

tween Euro-American values and traditional Islamic values di-
verged—as America became more ethically and sexually libertarian. Sex, alcohol and drugs were ascending in America.

B.   Also in the second half of the twentieth century, relations between the Euro-American people and Muslim people converged—as America became more liberal and the world became
more internationalist.

Phase 3

A.   In this new twenty-first century, the relationship between American values and traditional Islamic values has continued to di-
verge as America has become even more socially libertarian.
America is now flirting with the idea of same-sex marriages—
or at least same sex civil unions, truly un-Islamic.

B.   Since September 11 the trend of tolerant convergence between
American people and Muslim people has either been interrupted
or is being reversed. Most Americans and Muslims (both in the
United States and worldwide) are regrettably in the process of
being pulled apart.

The fourth phase is a deeper democratization of America and
the rolling back of the excesses of American social libertarianism.
This is not to be confused with the political libertarian movement in
the United States that is concerned more with minimizing the power
of government than minimizing the restraints of a personal moral
code. This fourth phase of relations between Euro-America and Islam is really a scenario about the future rather than a report of what is
already happening. In that sense this fourth phase is for the time
being speculative.

CONVERGING FAMILY VALUES, DIVERGING EMPATHY

In the years between the two World Wars, the social and sexual
mores of the United States (including family values) were much closer
to those of a Muslim society than they are today. But the United
States at that time was less tolerant of other religions and less cultur-

ally accommodating than it later became. Normatively, America had more in common with Islam in that period, but America was less tolerant of Muslims at the same time.

The gap in cultural rules of the game between America and the Muslim world has been widening. But the standards of tolerance in the United States were rising until 2001. In behavior, mainstream America became more and more un-Islamic, but less and less anti-Islamic. In attitude mainstream America became more and more Islam-friendly.

On the single pervasive issue of racism and race-relations, the United States has been much worse than the Muslim world both in the years between the two World Wars and in today's world after the Cold War. But the U.S. itself was much more racist in the 1920s than it is today. That American racism of the 1920s contributed to the American lack of tolerance towards Muslims. Muslims were profiled as a different race. On the other hand, the decline of racism in America has also contributed to greater tolerance of Islam.

Personal mores and family values have changed rapidly in America since the two world wars. The norms and mores have become less and less akin to Islamic values. Premarital sex, for example, was strongly disapproved of in America in the 1920s. There were even laws against sex outside marriage in some states, some of which may still be on the books but hardly ever enforced. There were also laws forbidding sex and marriage across the racial divide. Today sex before marriage, with parental consent, is common. This is more distant from Islamic values. Some Arab societies even have "honor killings" for daughters who stray sexually, though this practice is un-Islamic.

Homosexual acts, especially between males, were a crime in most of the Western world as a whole in the first half of the twentieth century. Now such acts between consenting adults, male or female, are legal in America and Western Europe, though they remain illegal throughout most of the Muslim world. Indeed, a majority of Americans and Europeans would say today that laws against homosexual sexuality are a violation of the rights of gays and lesbians. Indeed,

293

North America may be edging towards same-sex marriages within a decade or two.

In the inter-war years the family in America was still as sacro-sanct as it is in much of the Muslim world. Unmarried couples living together were few and far between. Babies born out of wedlock were truly an exception. And the very idea of same-sex marriages had not even been conceived. Families in America in the interwar years still believed in having a head of the family with authority—usually the father or husband. Unfortunately both in America and the Muslim world women were still subordinate. Women in the United States did not have the vote until after a Constitutional Amendment in 1920. The coming of the franchise for women was sometimes as slow in coming to the Western world as it was in the Muslim world. In national elections in Switzerland women did not get the vote until 1971.

What is at stake here is that on the issue of women's liberation, the United States and the Muslim world were on the same stage of relative sexism early in the twentieth century. But since then American culture on gender has become more and more different from Muslim culture on gender. On the positive side, American women are more active in the economy and in the political process and have made enormous progress in the quest for equality.

On the negative side sexuality has been cheapened in America and female bodies are exploited in a wider range of ways than ever—from blue movies on television to techniques in advertising, from high-class prostitution to the legacy of mini-skirts and tight pants.

While American culture does give greater freedom to women than does Muslim culture, American culture extends less dignity to women than does Muslim culture. Sons in America respect their mothers less than sons in the Muslim world; husbands in America respect their wives more than husbands in the Muslim world.

By the measurement of women's liberation America now has outstripped the Muslim world; but by the yardstick of the empowerment of women, has the Muslim world outstripped America? The United States has never had a female president. Yet two of the most populous Muslim countries—Pakistan and Bangladesh—have had women prime ministers. Benazir Bhutto headed two governments in Pakistan, and Khalida Zia and Hassina Wajid have served consecutively in Bangladesh. Turkey too had a woman Prime Minister, Tansu Ciller. And Indonesia, the most populous Muslim country of them all, now has a woman Head of State, President Megawati Sukarnoputri. Muslim countries seem to be ahead in female empowerment, though still behind in female liberation. Four Muslim countries have experienced highest female political leadership long before the United States, France, Italy and Russia have had a female President, and long before Germany has had a female Chancellor.

CONVERGENCE AGAINST ALCOHOL

A less enduring normative convergence was the ban on alcoholic drinks in the history of the United States. This value was truly neo-Islamic. Initially, prohibition of alcohol was by individual states. The first state law against alcohol was passed in Maine in 1846, and was soon followed by a wave of comparable legislation in other states—rising up to 33 states affecting 63 percent of the population by the end of Ward War I. Orthodox Muslims around the world probably cheered when they heard about this trend against alcohol in America.

Meanwhile, a campaign for alcoholic prohibition at the Federal level had been gathering momentum. A constitutional amendment against alcohol needed a two-thirds majority in Congress and approval by three quarters of the states. Such a constitutional change was ratified on January 29, 1919, and went into effect on January 29, 1920, as the Eighteenth Amendment of the United States' constitution. On the issue of alcohol, the United States became almost Islamic.

Just as the *Sharī'ah* in Nigeria or Iran can only work where there is popular support for it, the Eighteenth Amendment of the United States only worked where public opinion was genuinely for temperance and against alcohol. Prohibition at the federal level created resentment among those states that were not against alcoholic drinks, and in large cities in the United States where alcohol had long become a way of life.

Bootlegging emerged as a new kind of crime—the most dramatic embodiment of which was Al Capone and his bootlegging gang (illicit alcohol underground) operating from Chicago. Prohibition at the federal level created more problems than it solved. In less than fifteen years the United States was ready to repeal the Eighteenth Amendment. In February 1933 Congress adopted a resolution proposing a new constitutional amendment to that effect. On December 5, 1933, Utah cast the 36th ratifying vote in favor of the Twenty-first Amendment. At the federal level alcohol was legal again—breaking the link with Islamic culture.

A few states in the Union continued to be "dry states," and chose to maintain a state-wide ban. But the disenchantment which the Federal-level prohibition had created adversely affected attitudes to temperance even in those states which had once led the way in favor of prohibition. It is arguable that prohibition at the state-level might have lasted much longer if the original asymmetry (some states for and some states against) had been respected and allowed to continue. The Eighteenth Constitutional Amendment was a pursuit of national symmetry in American attitudes to alcohol. The Eighteenth Amendment sought a premature national moral consensus on alcohol—and thereby hurt the cause of temperance in the country as a whole. By 1966 virtually all the fifty states of the Union had legalized alcoholic drinks—though some preferred that drinking be restricted to homes and private clubs rather than be served in public bars and saloons.

CONVERGENCE ON THE DEATH PENALTY

Another area of convergence between Islamic values and American values has been in the acceptance of capital punishment as one of the answers to human depravity. The most controversial elements of the *Sharī'ah* are the *ḥudūd* (Islamic physical punishments for criminal offenders). Saudi Arabia has been known to put to death even a

Princess on charges of adultery. One of the principles the American judicial system continues to share with majority opinion in the Muslim world is the acceptance of the death penalty. The most controversial of Islamic applications of the death penalty relates to the sexual offense of adultery. The most controversial of American applications of the death penalty relates to killing the mentally retarded and to the execution of juvenile offenders. Can the death penalty be applied to mentally retarded offenders? Can it be carried out on young offenders whose crimes were committed when they were still minors? Some states have said "Yes" to both questions—"kill them!" Surprising as it may seem, the U.S. Supreme Court ruled in 1989 that it was perfectly constitutional to execute the mentally retarded or young offenders whose offenses were committed when they were minors.

Twelve years later, in the year 2001, the issue of executing the mentally retarded was back before the U.S. Supreme Court with the case of a convicted killer whose mental capacity was that of a seven year old. The U.S. Supreme Court had previously said it was constitutional to execute this very offender, but new considerations had brought the case back to the Court. The Supreme Court was on the verge of a major shift in opinion.

America had been executing the mentally retarded and juveniles who committed crimes as minors. The *Sharī'ah* in Nigeria has decided not to execute Amina Lawal on the charge of adultery. But are the *ḥudūd* generally as unacceptable in the twenty-first century as executing juveniles and the mentally retarded should be in America? Behind it all is an America still divided on the death penalty with some states upholding it and others rejecting it as "cruel and unusual punishment." It seems almost certain that the United States will abolish the death penalty long before the Muslim world as a whole is similarly converted to the proposition that the death penalty in the 21st century is not the best solution to human depravity.

DIVERGENCE ON THE SECULAR STATE

Another paradox is that while American secularism is good news for most Muslims (separating church from state), American social libertarianism is bad news for Islam (such as the latest American debate as to whether same-sex marriages should be legally recognized nationwide as they already are in Hawaii).

The Democratic Party in the United States is more insistent on separating church from state, including its opposition to prayer in schools. This draws African American Muslim parents even more towards the Democrats, since the Muslim parents do not want their kids to be under peer pressure to attend Christian prayers. More recent immigrant Muslims from the Middle East or of Asian descent regard prayer in school as potentially more Islamic. These latter Muslims may be drawn to the Republicans. On the other hand, the Republicans are stronger on traditional family values and are more opposed to sexual libertarianism. This draws many Muslims (especially immigrant Asians) to the Republican Party. Most Muslims share Republican concerns about abortion and gay rights.

In the United States Western secularism has protected minority religious groups by insisting on separation of church and state. That is a major reason why the Jews in the United States have been among the greatest defenders of the separation of church and state. Any breach of that principle could lead to the imposition of some practices of the religious majority—like forcing Jewish children to participate in Christian prayers at school.

In discussing the role of American Muslims *qua* Muslims (heirs of the *Hijrah),* we have to look more closely at their moral concerns in relation to American culture. Curiously enough, and in spite of Muslim opinion, American secularism is indeed good news for Muslims in America. The bad news is the expanding arena of American socio-sexual libertarianism, which has resulted in greater divergence in values. Secularism in the political process does indeed help to protect minority religions from the potential intrusive power of the Christian Right. On the other hand, expanding American socio-cultural libertarianism in such fields as sexual mores alarms both the Christian Right and Muslim traditionalists in the United States. Social libertarianism is what has eroded what American values have in common with Islamic values.

These moral concerns in turn have consequences on how American Muslims relate to the wider political divide between Republicans and Democrats in both foreign and domestic policies. From the 1990s onwards more and more American Muslims have apparently been registering to vote and seeking to influence candidates in elections. On such social issues as family values and sexual mores, Muslims often find themselves more in tune with Republican rhetoric and concerns. On the need for a more strict separation of church and state, which helps to protect religious minorities, it is the more liberal Democrats who offer a better protection to Muslims. Let us look at these contradictions more closely.

The First Amendment permits religious minorities to practice their religions in relative peace. Of course, like all doctrines, secularism has its fanatics who sometimes want to degrade the sacred rather than permitting it. But at its best a secular state is a refuge of safety for minority religions. It is in that sense that American secularism is a friend of Muslims living in the United States.

While secularism is a divorce from formal religion, Muslims see socio-sexual libertarianism as a dilution of spirituality. Socio-sexual libertarianism makes America less and less Islamic. One can be without a formal religion and still be deeply spiritual in a humanistic sense. John Stuart Mill and Bertrand Russell were without formal religion, yet each had deeply spiritual values. Albert Schweitzer, the Nobel Laureate for Peace, was at times an agnostic, but he was deeply committed to the principle of reverence for life—even protecting the lives of insects in Africa.

Religion has been declining in influence in the West since the days of the Renaissance and the Enlightenment. But it is mainly in the 20th century that spirituality in the West has taken a nose-dive. From an Islamic perspective, America has become not only less religious, but dangerously less spiritual. America has become not only more secular but dangerously more socially libertarian. Again we use the term libertarianism not in the sense of minimum ethical restraint and more in the sense of minimum political control.

It is such social libertarianism that is regarded as a danger to Muslims living in the Western hemisphere. There is the libertarian materialism of excessive acquisitiveness (greed), libertarian consumption (consumerism), the materialism of the flesh (excessive sexuality), the materialism of excessive self-indulgence (from alcoholism to drugs). These four forms of libertarianism could result in a hedonistic way of life, a pleasure-seeking career.

What is more, Muslim parents fear that American socio-cultural libertarianism is likely to influence the socialization and upbringing of the next generation of Muslim children—excessive levels of acquisitiveness, consumerism and diverse forms of sexuality.[2] It is because of all these considerations that Islam within the United States feels threatened less by American secularism than by American socio-sexual libertarianism. And American socio-sexual libertarianism is what has made United States mores more and more un-Islamic— while American domestic policies have fluctuated between Islam-friendly and terrorist-paranoid.

Normative divergence once coincided with a convergence of tolerance. Should American Muslims help to reverse this divergence in values without triggering off the return of those darker forces of racism and intolerance of those yesteryears? Can American Muslims help to remind America of what was best in its own quality of life once upon a time—without completely negating the pre-September 11 trends in tolerance, which America had once achieved? If such is the destiny that awaits American Muslims, theirs will be a marriage of the heritage of the *Hijrah* with the legacy of the Mayflower.

DIVERGENCE: ISLAM IN PAIN

Are we now entering a phase of world history when Muslims are suffering as Muslims rather than as citizens of particular countries? Are we beginning to experience the kind of targeted suffering which in the long run helped to unify the Jews? Is this the third phase of Islam's relations with the Euro-American legacy?

Muslims under direct military occupation include Iraq, Palestine and Afghanistan. Muslims militarily struggling for self-determination include Chechnya and Kashmir. Muslims on the radar screen for possible military intervention by Western powers include Iran, Syria, and Somalia. Muslims being harassed under new anti-terrorist legislation already include Tanzania, Kenya, potentially South Africa and a host of other countries under pressure from the Bush administration. Muslims under other methods of oppression include the appalling suffering of the Muslims of Gujarat in India.

Muslims harassed at American and international airports are beginning to multiply. On August 3, 2003, on arrival from overseas, I was detained at Miami airport for seven hours under repeated interrogation. I was interrogated by (a) immigration (b) customs (c) Homeland Security and the Joint Terrorism Task Force in that order. Paradoxically, the last interrogators were the most apologetic and the most courteous. But they still questioned me behind closed doors. Of course, I was truthful about all the Muslim organizations I belonged to, including the Muslim American Congress, the old American Muslim Council and the Center for the Study of Islam and Democracy (CSID).

In fairness to the Anti-Terrorism Task Force, they subsequently booked me a hotel room for the night in Miami and paid for it. They arranged for me to be taken to the airport hotel. And they paid for my dinner that night (giving me $25 for it). The Homeland Security interrogators were the most friendly. Yet I felt that I would not have been kept for so long if they had not been interested in interrogating me personally. I was kept waiting until they arrived.

After living in the United States for more than a quarter of a century, did I arouse suspicion on August 3, 2003 because of where I was coming from? Was I coming back from Afghanistan? Had I visited Baghdad? Perhaps I was coming back from Indonesia? Negative to all of those!! I was coming back from Trinidad and Tobago in the Caribbean. My mission in Trinidad had almost nothing to do with

Islam.

The questions I was asked included whether I believed in *jihād* and what did I understand by *jihād?* What denomination of Islam did I belong to? Since I was a *Sunnī*, why was I not a *Shī'ah?* And since I was coming from Trinidad and Tobago, had I seen Yaseen Abubaker, the Islamic militant who had held the whole cabinet of Trinidad hostage in the parliament building nearly fifteen years earlier? I replied at Miami Airport that I had not met Abubaker, but I had tried to see him. After all, I was teaching a course at Cornell on "Islam in the Black Experience." Was that a risk in the new American democracy?

We must not forget that if America's own democracy decays, it makes it easier for the Third World's own dictators (Muslim and non-Muslim) to justify their own tyranny.[3] Indeed, the aftermath of September 11 has already been compromising some civil liberties in the United States to ominous proportions, as discussed in a chapter in this book entitled "The Global Hostage Crisis."

RESTRAINING AMERICA: EMPOWERING ISLAM

This fourth phase is a scenario for the future rather than a report of historical trends. The United States needs greater political democratization and reduced social libertarianism. The Muslim world needs greater doctrinal liberalization and deeper intellectual modernization. Rolling back American socio-sexual libertarianism would require new disciplines in the areas of:

1. greed, corporate and personal;
2. consumerism and depletion of the world's resources;
3. the rules of sexuality;
4. hedonistic inebriation (alcoholism and drugs).

As for the greater democratization of America, it is tied up with America as Empire. The United States as an Empire can only be checked by the United States as a democracy. African Americans, Latinos and Muslim Americans have a lot to learn from Jews about how to be empowered Americans. So indeed do women of America of all races. American women are substantially liberated, but they have yet to penetrate the citadels of power. Jews have been staggeringly successful not only politically in America, but also economically, educationally and culturally. Jews are the supreme example and ideal model of an American minority that has successfully used the American system to its full advantage. Jews have also exploited the American system for the benefit of Israel.

A new global clash of civilizations has indeed begun, with the United States at the center of it. But the seeds of redemption may also lie in America. Those seeds are carried by emerging populations potentially more responsive to other cultures and civilizations than the contemporary U.S. power-elites seem to be. The imperial tunnel is still dark—but the light of a more inclusive American democracy can be seen at the end of this tunnel.

A particularly important issue is whether Muslims can use their present pain and anguish as a basis of a new sense of unity. The unity needs to be constructive rather than destructive, benevolent rather than malevolent, determined to protect Muslims rather than harm others. Who knows? Perhaps out of such unity of anguish there will subsequently emerge the unity of achievement, a triumphant American Muslim identity at long last, combining faith in Islam with what is best about America.

As for a future Islamic Renaissance and liberalization, this may one day have to be led by Muslims receptive to other cultures, like those in the West. For our purposes in this dialogue, we may distinguish among three schools of Islam—Orthodox, modernist and liberal.

Orthodox Islam is literalist in its interpretation of the Qur'ān and the *Sunnah*, ritualistic in its observances, traditionalist in gender relations, with an emphasis on a God of Justice. On the whole, such Orthodox Muslims are far less receptive to other cultures.

Modernist Islam seeks to bring Islamic beliefs closer to modern science, technology and the expansion of human knowledge. Modernist Muslims put less emphasis on Islamic rituals and more emphasis on Islamic rationalism. The modernist Allah is a God of Enlightenment. Beliefs about Satan, jinn, devils and spirits are interpreted metaphorically rather than literally. Even angels are seen as figurative manifestations of God. Perhaps Abdolkarim Soroush of Iran is a modernist Muslim. Modernist Muslims also include most theorists of the Islamization of knowledge.

Liberal Islam is less concerned with updating Islam scientifically and more concerned with updating Islam ethically. The Liberal Muslim is less worried about whether *Iblīs* exists physically or only figuratively. Islamic liberalism is anxious that Muslim women be treated as equals; that slavery be declared *ḥarām* under any circumstances; that the amputation of hands of thieves be relegated totally to history; and that the death penalty be either abolished completely or be limited to such egregious offenses as first-degree murder (and never be imposed on adulterers). To liberal Muslims, Allah is a God of Compassion. Perhaps Fatima Mernissi of Morocco is a liberal Muslim.

The modernization of Catholicism has been relatively easy because the Roman Catholic Church has a spiritual head who enjoys some "divine infallibility" in some of his interpretations of the faith. The modernization of other branches of Christianity had to ride on the immense cultural revolution of the Protestant Reformation. The modernization of Judaism occurred mainly in the Jewish Diaspora as the Jews engaged in brilliant cultural synthesis.

IN SEARCH OF ISLAMIC CONSTITUTIONALISM

How can Muslims either modernize or liberalize Islam without having a Muslim Pope, or a Muslim Protestant Revolution or a new Muslim cultural synthesis? First and foremost, Muslim liberal thinkers and modernist theologians need to be assured greater intellectual freedom, without the fear of harassment or the risk of violent bigotry. Secondly, the liberal thinkers and modernist theologians need to invoke *ijtihād* more systematically in order to address the contradictions between ancient doctrine and modern realities. Thirdly, these new ideas should be made more accessible to the wider Muslim *ummah,* taking advantage of the new "information superhighway" and the computer revolution.

The three schools of Islam (Orthodox, Modernist and Liberal) are not to be conceived as *madhāhib.* They can be reformulations of some of the existing *madhāhib.* It is possible to modernize Sunnī Islam and liberalize Shī'ī Islam.

Let us agree that a good Muslim cannot deny, disobey, contradict or neglect Allah's commands. But the whole point of this debate is whether a good Muslim can re-interpret God's command in the light of new evidence or changed circumstances. Of course the word of God is infallible, but those who interpret it are not. Unlike Christians, Muslims do not believe that God walked among men and conversed with human beings directly (Jesus as "the word of God made flesh"). But even for Christians, God is not personally available on earth today to give lessons on how to interpret their scripture.

The Qur'ān is infallible, but those who have interpreted it are fallible human beings. The United States' constitution was drafted by Founding Fathers who were not themselves necessarily lawyers. However, those who interpret the Constitution today are judges who live in the twenty-first century. Since the adoption of the U.S. Constitution in the eighteenth century, slavery has been declared unconstitutional, segregated schools declared illegal, women and Blacks have been given the vote, and the right to privacy has been read into the Constitution through judicial review. The fundamental law of the country has been repeatedly re-interpreted by its judges without abandoning the sanctity and dignity of the Constitution.

There is a debate about the U.S. Constitution comparable to our own debate about how to interpret the Qur'ān. There are conservative jurists even on the Supreme Court itself who insist that the text of the Constitution should be interpreted as closely as possible to the original intent of the founders. There are others who believe that the U.S. Constitution is a living guide to the nation and is therefore subject to reinterpretation according to changing social and political realities.

Minorities like Black people and Muslims in the United States have benefited far more from the second juridical school (historically relative) than by the first (constructionist and orthodox). The gains of the Civil Rights Movement were mainly under the Warren Supreme Court, which was historically relative and reformist. Since then the U.S. Supreme court has been moving back to rightwing orthodoxy.

We need to distinguish between rules of evidence and fairness of punishment. Even if one of our loved ones had adversely satisfied the rules of evidence on adultery, would we still be comfortable with their being executed for adultery? We must remember that such sins as adultery or homosexuality in *Dār al-Islām* might have been committed by one's cousin or one's brother, or even by one's father. Even if the rules of evidence were satisfied, would one still regard such punishments as fair in the twentieth or twenty-first century? Individual Muslims must reflect carefully and be honest with themselves before they answer. Would they be prepared to kill one of their brothers for adultery if four witnesses had witnessed his sin physically? Islamic modernism and Islamic liberalism would not seek to end a human life for a sexual offense, however revolting.

The Qur'ān and the *Sunnah* are the sources of the Islamic Constitutional Order. The Qur'ān is older than the U.S. Constitution by more than a thousand years. If things in the world have changed a lot since the days of Thomas Jefferson, how much more have they changed since the days of the Prophet Muhammad (pbuh)? If American jurisprudence is allowing itself to learn from the lessons of the two hundred years of history, why cannot Islamic jurisprudence learn from fourteen centuries of historical change? Muslims must always remember once again that while the word of God is infallible and immutable, the human interpreters of the word of God are not. New Muslim intellects should review the doctrines once again.

Is Religion in Conflict with Science?

Narrow orthodoxy is precisely what has left Muslims behind and made Muslims vulnerable to being humiliated and brutalized by others. Nor must we forget that Black people have also been under-achievers and that women have been left below the commanding heights of science and philosophy.

However, there has never been a time when women were at the pinnacle of global power, or when Black people were at the center of the global equation. But there was a time in history when Muslims were globally triumphant. Why did Muslims decline so disastrously? And why have they continued to be marginalized? Is it possible that Muslim refusal to let the message of Islam be re-interpreted is at the core of the retardation of the Muslim world? Is orthodoxy a disservice to Islam?

During the one hundred years of the existence of the Nobel Prize, Muslim winners of the Nobel Prize in the Sciences (chemistry, physics and medicine) can be counted with the fingers of one hand. Jewish winners are in their dozens. Christian winners are probably in their hundreds. The few Muslim winners of the scientific Nobel Prizes are not products or alumni of Islamic universities. They are almost always products of Western education.

A publication of the Third World Academy of Sciences has estimated that less than one percent of world scientific publications are published in the Arab world, in spite of oil wealth. Even rich Arab states spend one seventh of the global average spent by other nations on research and development.

There are indeed two ways for Muslims to judge themselves. One is to look at those who have outperformed us – such as Jews and Euro-Christians. The other is to look at those who have performed worse than ourselves in the sciences, such as Black people, women and perhaps the Chinese. Are Muslims sure that they would like Islam to be judged on the basis of below-average performance? Women and Black people have a more solid excuse for under-performance than Muslims have. The Chinese may be facing the same dilemmas

307

as the Muslim *ummah*. Why has China been outperformed by the much smaller Japan? The Muslim world has also been outperformed by a Japan which is less than a tenth of the Muslim population of the world. Muslims need to address the issue of why we are so far behind. Liberal Muslims believe that the *ummah* has refused to change in the light of expanding knowledge and changing circumstances. What do Orthodox Muslims believe are the causes of our retardation?

My late father of blessed memory used to argue that Muslims were left behind when they stopped observing the tenets of their religion. But Jews and Christians observe the tenets of Islam even less. Why have Jews and Christians forged ahead in science and technology in spite of their not being Muslims at all? Modernist Muslims are urging a review of our dogmas.

Muslim doctrines which have hurt our progress have included the concept of *bid'ah*. Originally intended to protect the young religion from premature reform and distortion, *bid'ah* became a symbol of Muslim distrust of all kinds of innovations and inventions. While the word innovation has positive connotations in the English language, the word *bid'ah* in Islamic discourse carries negative and sinful implications. The concept of *bid'ah* came to symbolize a fundamental Muslim resistance to change. Orthodoxy defended itself against innovation. On the other hand, the highly progressive Muslim principle of *ijtihād* has been grossly under-utilized. Indeed, among Sunni Muslims, the doors of *ijtihād* have been closed in reality, though not necessarily in theory. Had the doors been open, there would have been more than four Sunni denominations in Islam by now.

Sudan's Mahmoud Muhammad Taha should be counted among Muslim *'ulamā'* who invoked *ijtihād* in a bid to reinterpret Islam. Taha paid with his life in 1985 under Ja'far Numeiri's version of the *ḥudūd*.

The future of the human race may depend upon the gradual restraint of the United States, on one side, and the gradual empowerment of the Muslim world on the other. But the Muslim world will never be empowered until it understands the dynamics of human knowledge.

The origins of Islam rest on the miracle of wisdom without formal qualifications. Islam is the religion of a man who could not read or write and yet helped to produce the most influential book in its original language in human history. This is similar to the Bible as the most influential book in translation. Islam is a religion of a man who, when commanded by an angel to read *(Iqra')*, confessed meekly that he could not read. That exchange between Gabriel and Muhammad broke the link between inspiration and instruction forever. Illiteracy can be the mother of supreme wisdom. I affirm that in spite of my being a professor with multiple degrees and author of more than twenty books.

However, the future of Islam needs to narrow the gap between religious ritual and intellectual rationalism, and bridge the gap between faith and reason. Only then will Muslims be able to defend Islam not just with word of mouth but also with the power of knowledge. Only then will Muslims be able to fight for Islam not by terrorizing the enemy but by educating the adversary.

CONCLUSION

We have tried to identify in this essay four phases in the history of relationships between Islam and the Western world, with particular reference to the Americo-Islamic interaction. The paradox of the first half of the twentieth century was a convergence in values between Islam and Euro-America, but a divergence of empathy between Muslims and Westerners.

The sanctity of the family, the distrust of extra-marital sex, the rejection of homosexuality, the emphasis on modesty and chastity, were all values shared by Islam and the Euro-American experience. The United States even went to the extent of prohibiting alcohol through a constitutional amendment in the years between the two world wars—a major convergence with Islam as a profoundly anti-alcohol culture.

Yet those years of Americo-Islamic convergence in values were also the years when Americans regarded Islam as the equivalent of the anti-Christ. American racist culture dismissed Muslims among the darker and ominous races of humankind. Similarity of values coincided with hostility in relationships between the two peoples.

In the second half of the twentieth century, the paradox was reversed. Euro-American political values became more and more liberal, improving the relationship between Westerners and Muslims as human beings. On the other hand, the social, sexual and family values of Westerners (including Americans) became more permissive and open. In the West pre-marital sex, extra-marital fornication, homosexuality and lesbianism, alcoholism and marijuana moved closer to cultural acceptance. Dress culture for women became less modest as miniskirts, tight pants, and low necklines became the order of the day. A cultural divergence was occurring between the new Euro-American norms and the more conservative values of Islamic traditions.

On the other hand, the relationship between the American people and the Muslim people in the second half of the twentieth century became increasingly more positive. America seemed to be in the process of accepting Islam not as an alien intrusion but increasingly as part and parcel of the American mosaic. Islam was becoming "indigenous" to American pluralism.

Especially crucial were the years of the Presidency of Bill Clinton. In foreign policy his administration had been more pro-Israel than any other U.S. administration since Lyndon Johnson. But the same Clinton administration had domestically been more Muslim-friendly than any other U.S. administration in history. Those Clinton years were a measure of growing American acceptance of Islam in fits and starts—in spite of the differences in standards. President Clinton sent greetings to Muslims during the fast of Ramadān from 1996. We should also note how Hillary Clinton hosted a celebration of 'Id al-Fiṭr (the Festival of the End of Ramadān) in the White House in April 1996 and 1998. Vice President Al Gore visited a mosque in the fall of 1995. And the first Muslim chaplain to serve the 10,000 Muslims in the U.S. armed forces was sworn in under

Clinton's watch.[4]

President Clinton received in the White House a delegation of Arab Americans to discuss wide-ranging issues, domestic and international. We should refer to the National Security Advisor, Anthony Lake, receiving a delegation of Muslims (including Ali Mazrui) in 1996 to discuss the ramifications of the Bosnian crisis.

The Clinton gestures towards Muslims were sufficiently high profile that a hostile article in the *Wall Street Journal* in March 1996 raised the specter of "Friends of Hamas in the White House"—alleging that some of President Clinton's Muslim guests were friends of "Arab terrorists," and supporters of the Palestinian movement. The critic in the *Wall Street Journal* (Steve Emerson) had a long record of hostility towards U.S. Muslims. His television programme on PBS entitled *Jihad in America* (1994) alleged that almost all terrorist activities by Muslims worldwide were partially funded by U.S. Muslims. President Clinton's friendly gestures to Muslims probably infuriated this self-appointed crusader of Islamophobia.[5] Yet Clinton's Muslim-friendly strategy continued.

The third phase in America-Islamic relations is now unfolding since September 11, 2001. The new Bush administration would like to trade in the currency of fear in order to mobilize political support. This is a far cry from the anguish of Franklin D. Roosevelt after the Japanese attack on Pearl Harbor. Roosevelt proclaimed: "The only thing we have to fear is fear itself."

With George W. Bush's administration, it has become a different silent imperative—"The only thing we have to sell to the American people is fear itself." In spite of assurances that the war on terrorism is not a war on Islam, Muslims are paying a disproportionate price for this latest American campaign—from the war on Afghanistan and Iraq to the harassment of Muslim citizens of the United States.

The fourth phase of America-Islamic relations requires the taming of the imperial power of the new United States following the collapse of the Soviet Union and the end of the Cold War. America's own internal democracy needs to develop the skills of restraining

America as an empire. In the final analysis, only America as a democracy can effectively control America as an empire.

Yet one additional force is needed for restraining the United States. That other future force is the potential power of the Islamic civilization when its petro-wealth is combined with a truly emergent Islamic renaissance. Such an Islamic rejuvenation may be needed to help the global system realize the virtues of checks and balances once again.

NOTES

1. This chapter is based on the Keynote Address at the 32nd Annual Conference of the Association of Muslim Scientists (AMSS), entitled "A Marriage of Civilizations?: Euro-American Norms and Islamic Values" on the theme "East Meets West," co-sponsored by Indiana University, and held in Bloomington, Indiana, September 26-28, 2003.
2. See Cooper, *A Muslim in America,* p. 36.
3. A Human Rights Watch report pointed out that country leaders were taking advantage of the anti-terror campaign to suppress dissent and abuse human rights; see *The Washington Post* (January 18, 2001), p. 12.
4. Other groups and organizations established by Muslims in the United States to correct stereotypes and influence policy include the Council for American Islamic Relations, based in Washington, D.C. and the Muslim Public Affairs Council; see "Muslims Learn to Pull Political Ropes in U.S.," *Christian Science Monitor* (February 5, 1996), p. 10.
5. Emerson's article appeared in the *Wall Street Journal* (March 13, 1996), p. 14.

INDEX

autocolonization 6, 8, 9
Axis of Evil 218
Azerbaijan 230
Aziz, Tareq 85, 231

B

Ba'ath Party 99
Badr, Battle of 82
Balfour, Lord 193, 203
Barcelona 214
Batista 40
Begin, Menakken 49, 99, 140
Bejaouni, Mohammed 181
Belfour Declaration 233
Ben-Gurion, David 147
Bhutto, Benazir 90, 245, 295
Bhutto, Zulkifar Ali 154
Bible 85, 104, 113, 309
bigotry 304
Binghamton University 119
Blair, Tony 76
Bombay 247
Bosnia-Herzogovina 88, 91,
172, 278-9, 281-6, 290
Botswana 31, 51, 168
Boutros-Ghali, Boutros 62, 85,
214, 231, 251, 288
Brahmaputra 137
Brazil 159, 170
British Broadcasting Corporation
(BBC) xi, xiii, 127, 140, 174,
216
British colonial regime (British
colonial administration) 201
Brussels 117
Buddhism 83
Buddhist 83, 137, 252, 267, 276

Bull, Professor Hedley 23
Bunche, Ralph 62-3, 227
Burkina Faso 30
see also Upper Volta
Bush, George 60, 136, 279
Bush, George W. 37, 57-8, 60,
65, 75-7, 86, 93, 96, 131, 139,
180, 187, 208-9, 229, 311

C

Cairo 16, 42, 47, 74, 157, 255,
272, 287
Caliphate 16, 151
Cambridge 247, 272
Camel, Battle of 89, 90
Cameroon 56
Camp David Accords 45
Capetown 137
capitalism 24, 69, 165, 229,
230, 232, 237, 269, 273
Capitol 201, 236
Caribbean 60, 72, 137, 185,
188, 301
Carter, Jimmy 47, 51, 60, 134,
150
Castro, Fidel 40
Catholic 74, 85-6, 129, 213,
230-1, 244, 250-1, 304
Catholicism 19, 227, 304
Catholic Church 86, 244, 304
Center for the Study of Islam
and Democracy (CSID) xiv,
58, 301
Central America 72, 209
Central Intelligence Agency
(CIA) xiv, 26, 48, 147-8, 157,
240-1

118, 162, 179, 181, 188, 194,
204, 214, 231, 251, 264-5,
275-6, 277-2, 284-90
General Assembly 277, 280,
286
Security Council 10-1, 14, 21-2,
65, 108, 162, 179, 277, 280,
284, 286, 290
United Nations Educational,
Scientific and Cultural Organization (UNESCO) 6, 62-3,
181, 277, 280, 290
United States of America (USA)
x, xii, xiv, 3-6, 8, 10-1, 15, 21,
23, 25-9, 32-7, 42, 49-53, 57-
61, 63, 65, 69-74, 77, 85-6,
90, 92, 98, 100-1, 103, 105-9,
113-4, 117-8, 120-3, 128-31,
135, 140-3, 146-52, 155-8,
162-3, 166, 172, 177-1, 183-
90, 200, 202, 205, 206-7,
209-10, 215, 217-8, 229-30,
233, 235, 238-40, 244-7, 249-
50, 252, 256, 261, 263, 265-6,
268-9, 271, 277, 279, 282,
286-7, 289, 292-303, 305-6,
308-9, 311-2
Constitution of 106, 296,
305-6
Supreme Court 129, 135, 297
universal nuclear disarmament
173
universalism 10, 15, 83, 182,
275-6, 281-4, 287
University of California 20, 273
University of Manchester xi,
116
Usamahism 58

Usamahphilia 58
Usamahphobia 58, 61
Utah 296

V

Vietnam 13-4, 39-40, 60-1, 65,
132, 216, 226, 229, 239, 252
Vietnam War 39, 60, 65
violence xiii, 25-6, 35, 37, 39-
41, 48-51, 57, 73, 75-6, 79,
96, 99-100, 103, 106, 115-7,
121, 123, 127-8, 131, 136,
138-41, 160-1, 163, 166, 185,
201-2, 204, 207-8, 226-7,
229, 234, 252, 255, 257, 281,
304

W

Wakiso 33
Walachia 8
Wall Street Journal 250, 311,
312
war ix-xi, xiii, 4-6, 10, 12-4, 22,
26, 28, 34, 38-40, 50, 52, 55-
7, 59, 60-1, 64-5, 69-71, 75-6,
81-3, 88, 92-3, 97, 99, 101-3,
106, 108, 110-3, 116, 122-3,
126, 129, 132, 135-6, 148-9,
153, 155, 157, 159, 162, 164-
5, 168, 171, 173-4, 178, 180,
187-8, 194, 198, 200-1, 208-
10, 216-9, 223-5, 227, 229,
239-40, 255, 257, 263-4, 277,
280-2, 284-90, 294-5, 311
global 4, 57, 159
Warsaw Pact 13, 263

ABOUT THE AUTHOR AND EDITORS

AUTHOR:

Ali A. Mazrui is Albert Schweitzer Professor in the Humanities and the Director of the Institute of Global Cultural Studies at Binghamton University. He is the author of more than twenty-five books and has written extensively for refereed journals, magazines and newspapers all over the globe.

CO-EDITORS:

Shalahudin Kafrawi is Assistant Professor of Islamic Studies at Moravian College. He has written a number of articles in various journals and anthologies. He is the author of *The Methodology of Qur'ānic Exegesis: Fakhr al-Dīn al-Rāzī Philosophical Tafsīr* (2004) and the editor of *Light, Salvation and Divine Intimacy* (2004).

Alamin M. Mazrui is Associate Professor of Africana Studies at Ohio State University. He co-authored with Ali A. Mazrui *Swahili, Society, and the State* (1995) and *The Power of Babel: Language and Governance in the African Experience* (1998). He is also the author of *English in Africa: After the Cold War* (2004).

Ruzima Charles Sebuharara is a Lecturer in Economics and Africana Studies, and Assistant to the Albert Schweitzer Professor in the Humanities at Binghamton University.